THE PAINTER LE CORBUSIER

Eileen Gray's *Villa E 1027* and *Le Cabanon*

Tim Benton

THE PAINTER LE CORBUSIER

EILEEN GRAY'S *VILLA E 1027* AND *LE CABANON*

Photography by Manuel Bougot

BIRKHÄUSER

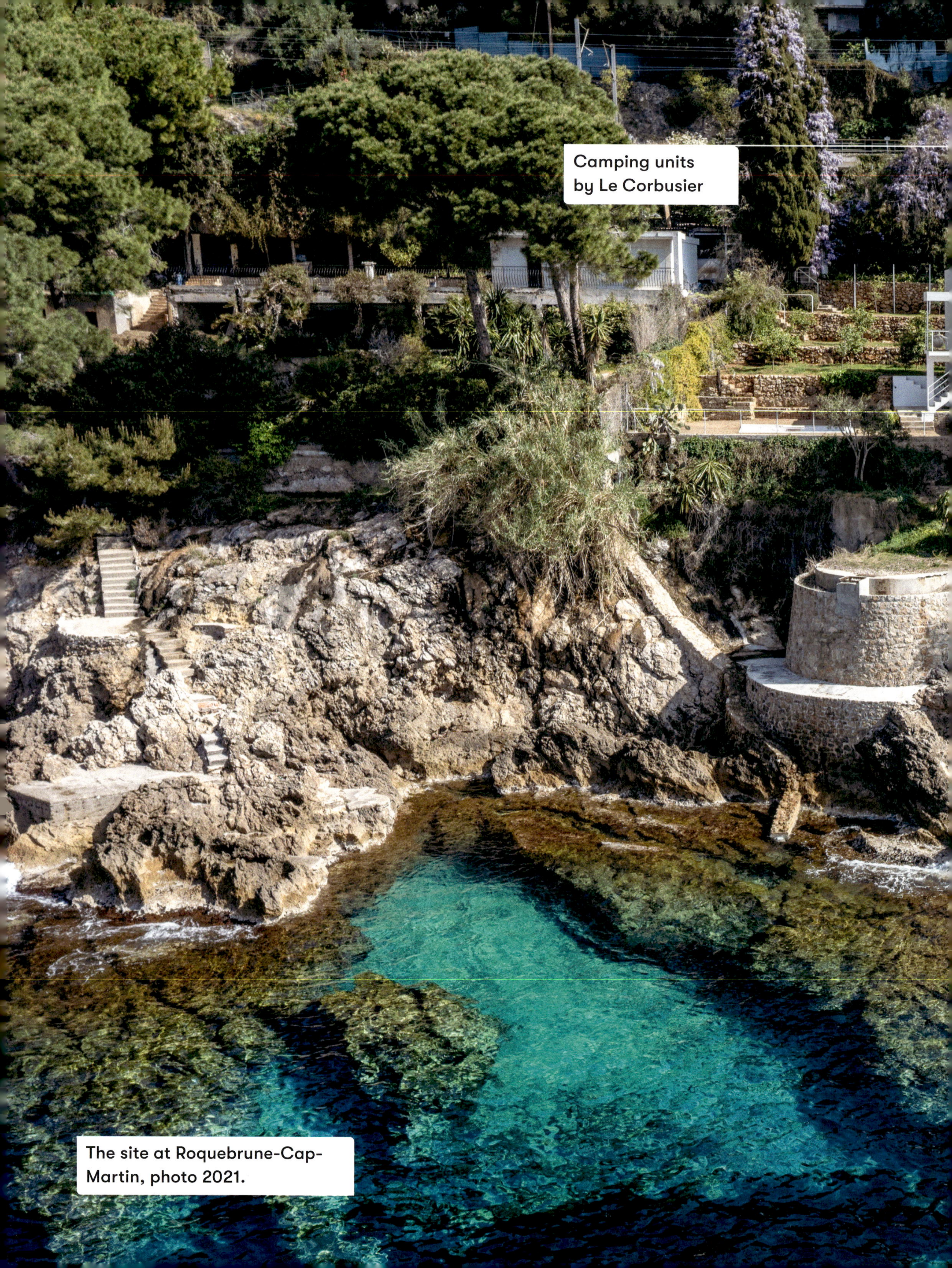

The site at Roquebrune-Cap-Martin, photo 2021.

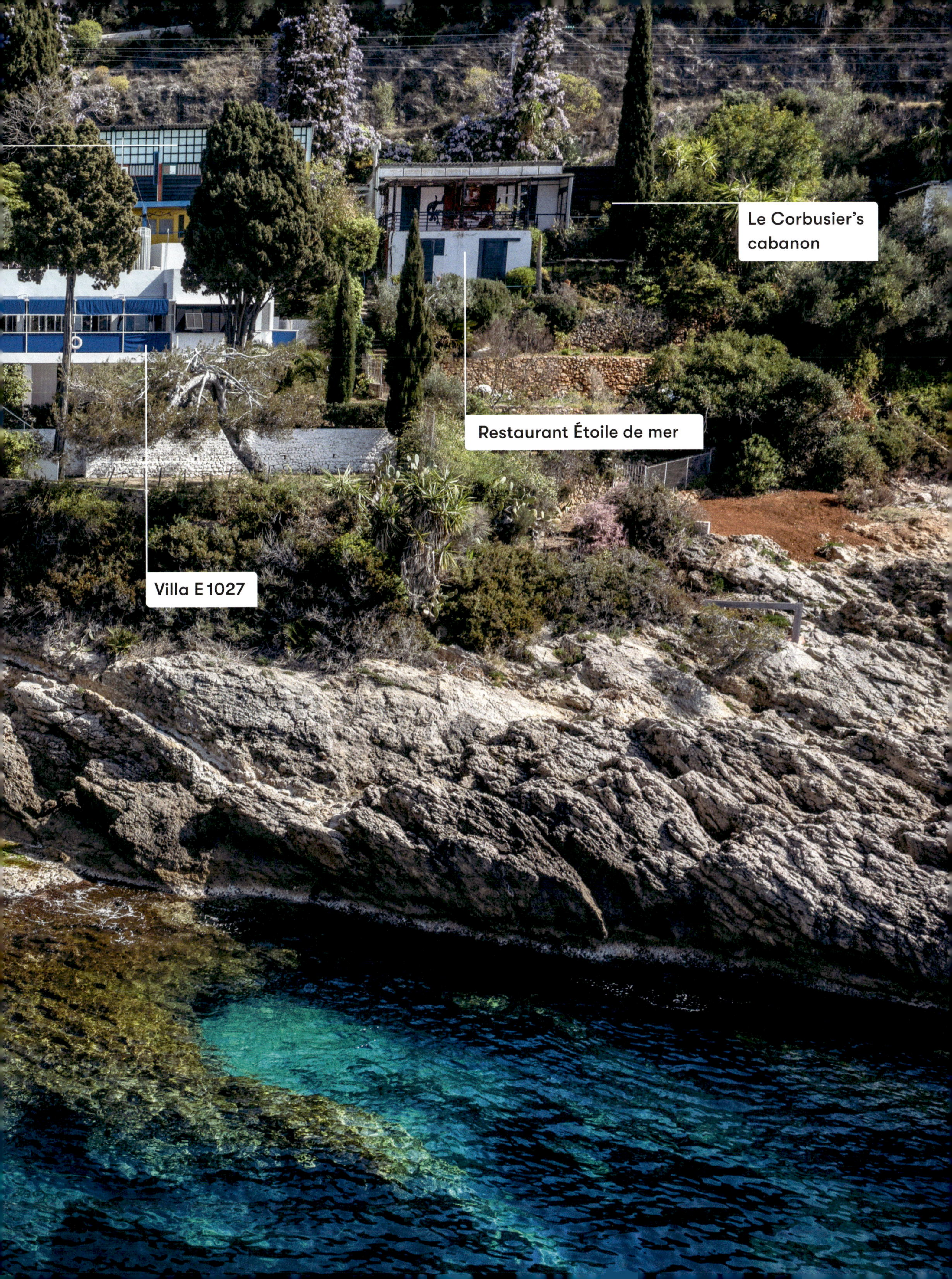
Le Corbusier's
cabanon
Restaurant Étoile de mer
Villa E 1027

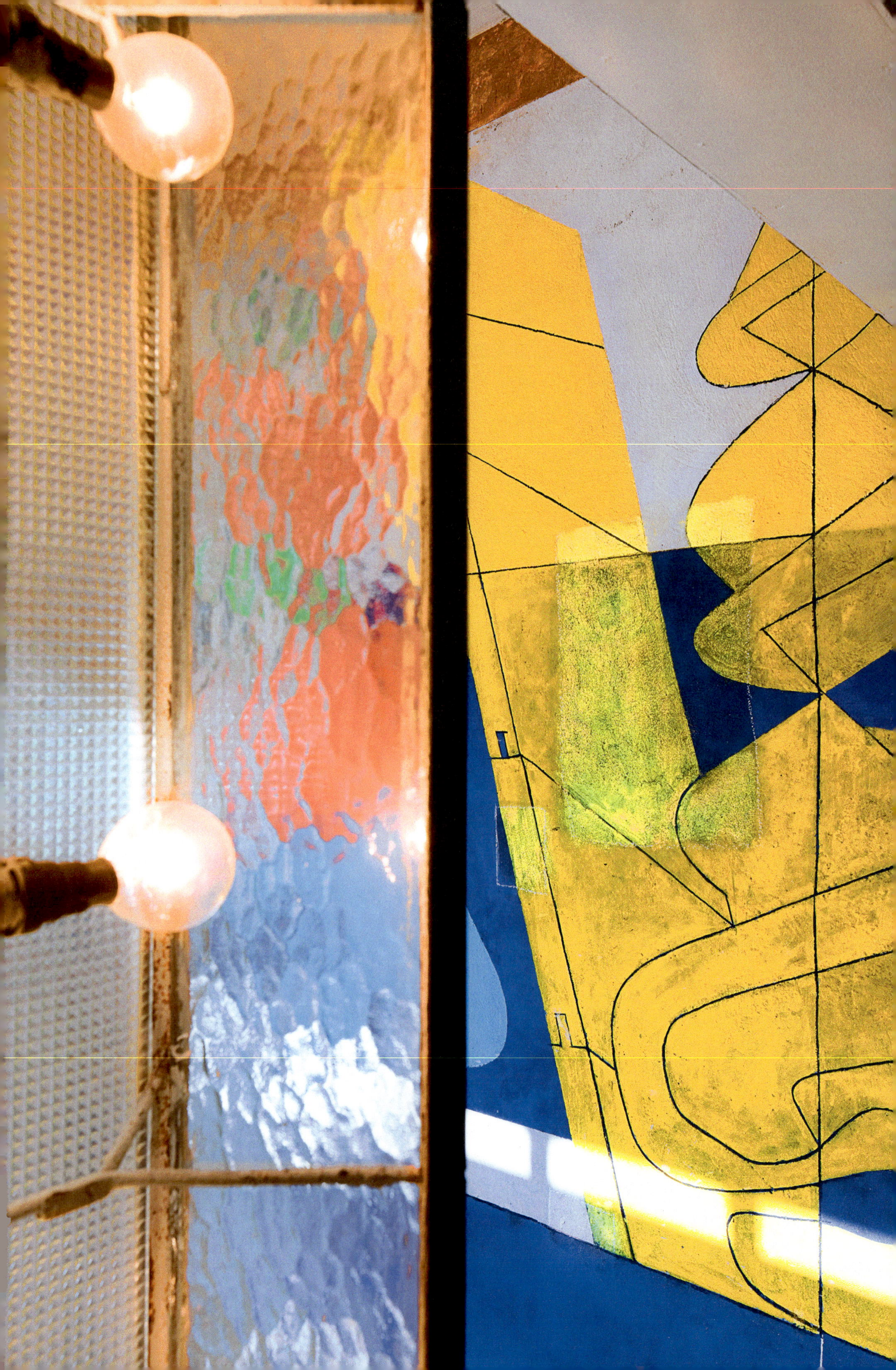

FOREWORD

ANTOINE PICON

Le Corbusier's drawings and paintings have received renewed attention in recent years, not least because of the close links they have to his architectural work. Their connection with the architecture explores in particular new and implicit spatial combinations; a role that they have played on many occasions for an architect whose sensibilities as a plastic artist is widely acknowledged.

From the end of the 1930s onwards, Le Corbusier also tested the possibilities of mural painting to enliven architectural space. Following a first project in Vézelay in 1936, the walls of the Villa E1027 designed by Eileen Gray provided him with the opportunity to experiment with an artistic practice that was still new to him. The Cap-Martin site would later host many other murals by the architect. It is this collection that is presented by this publication. Tim Benton provides clues to this œuvre in an analytical text that captures the complexity of Le Corbusier's approach.

Le Corbusier did not immediately adopt the principle of mural painting, far from it. It contradicted his famous definition of architecture as a pure play of light and volume. A whole series of factors combine to explain this conversion: The architect's pictorial evolution was struck by Picasso's vigorous compositions; the desire to explode space in some way while pursuing, paradoxically, a desire for a synthesis of the arts inspired by the great examples of the Renaissance. But the impact of personal circumstances should not be underestimated either. As Tim Benton shows, in the 1930s Le Corbusier was going through a deep crisis that influenced his ideas and his practice. The new relationship between wall and painting to which the frescoes of E1027 bear witness cannot be reduced to the mere 'rape' of Eileen Gray's work, as several Anglo-Saxon critics have insisted, even if there can be no question of minimising the symbolic violence of Le Corbusier's intrusion into a space he did not design.

By also presenting the other paintings produced at Roquebrune-Cap-Martin, from the restaurant Étoile de mer to Le Corbusier's cabin, the book also places this episode in the context of a much longer evolution. The Fondation Le Corbusier is delighted with the publication of a book that provides the reader with valuable information to better appreciate the Cap-Martin paintings, these major testimonies of Le Corbusier's indissociable plastic and architectural approach.

Paris, April 2023

Detail of Le Corbusier's mural in the bar of E1027, 1939.

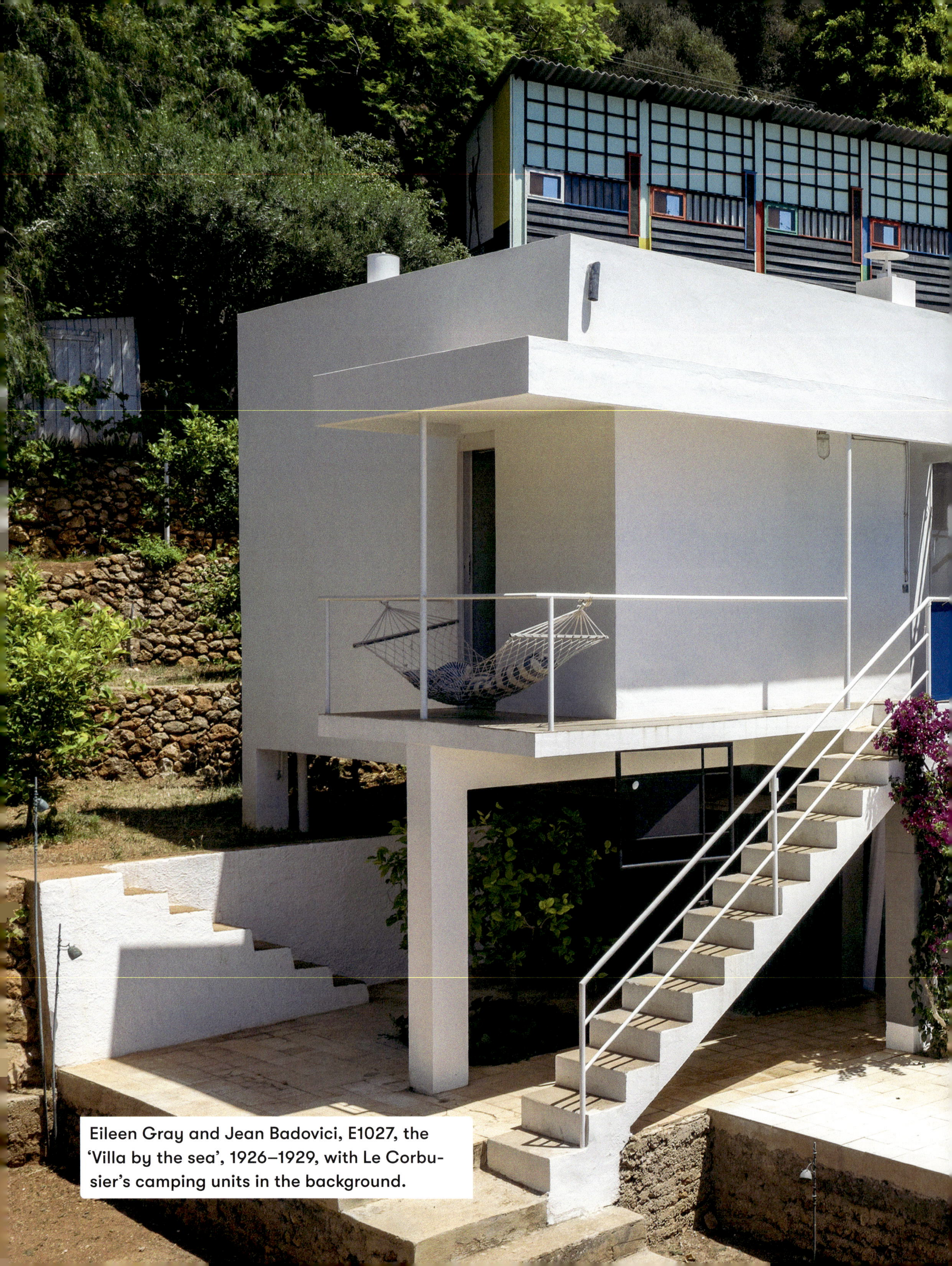

Eileen Gray and Jean Badovici, E1027, the 'Villa by the sea', 1926–1929, with Le Corbusier's camping units in the background.

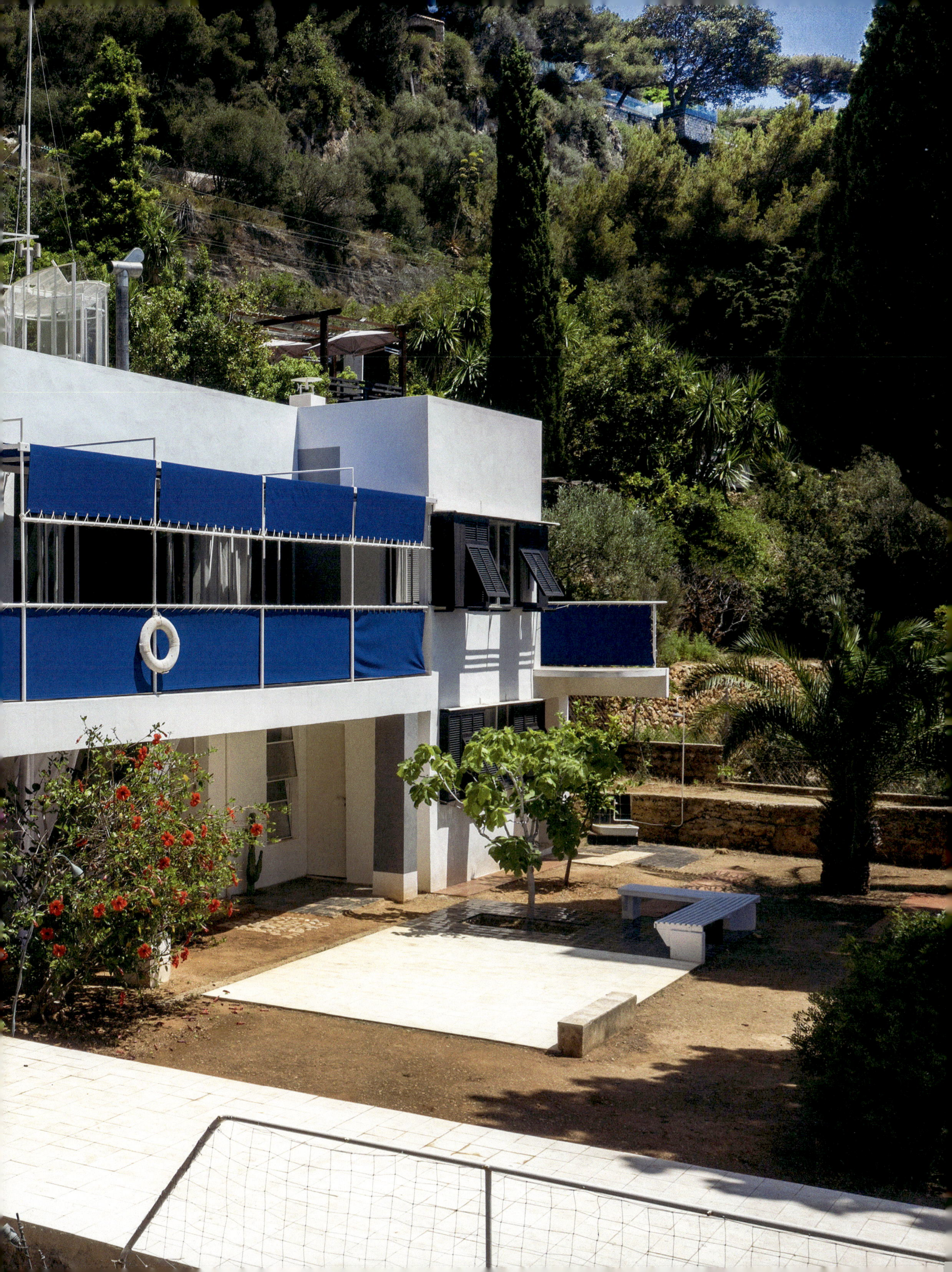

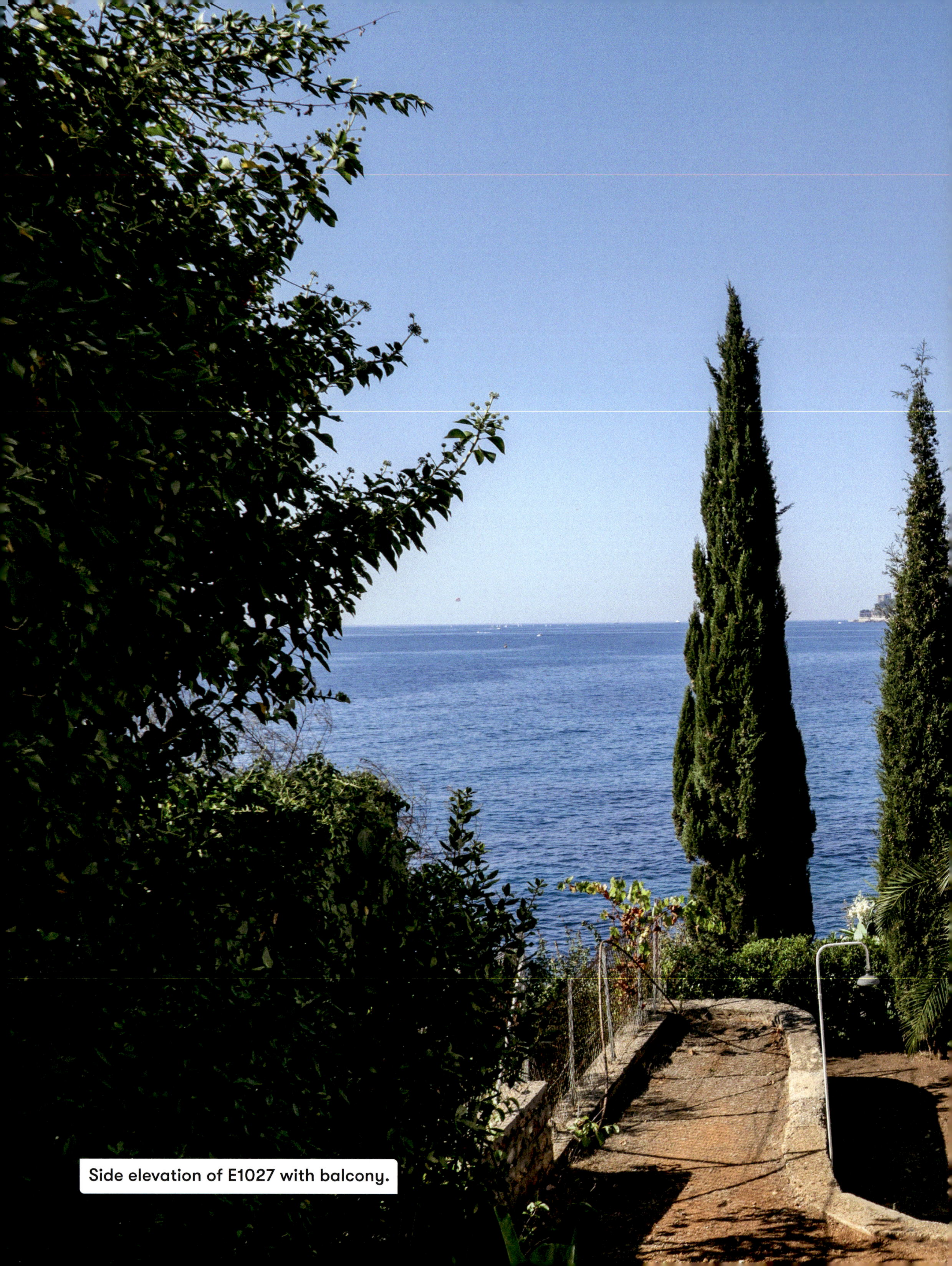

Side elevation of E1027 with balcony.

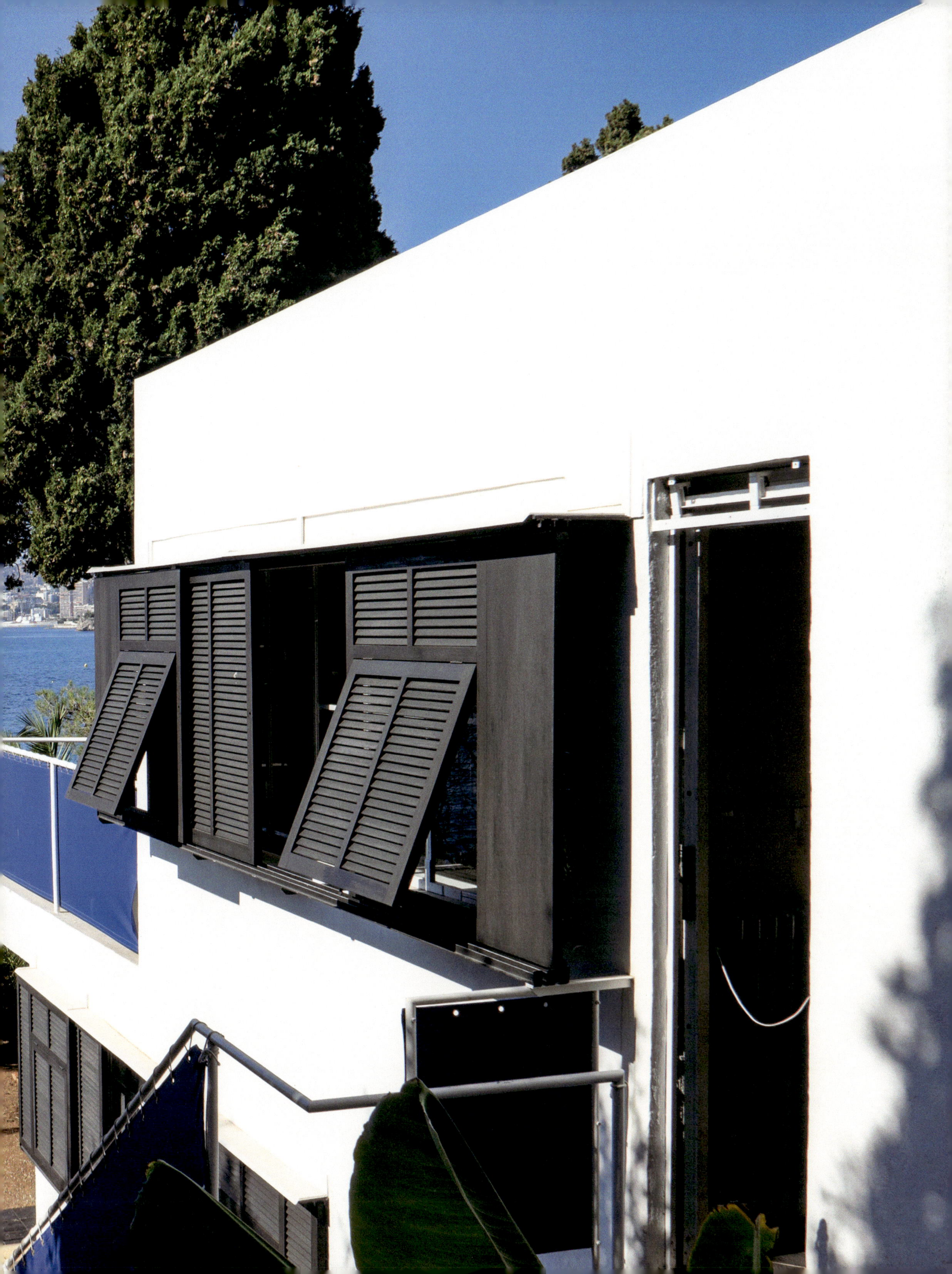

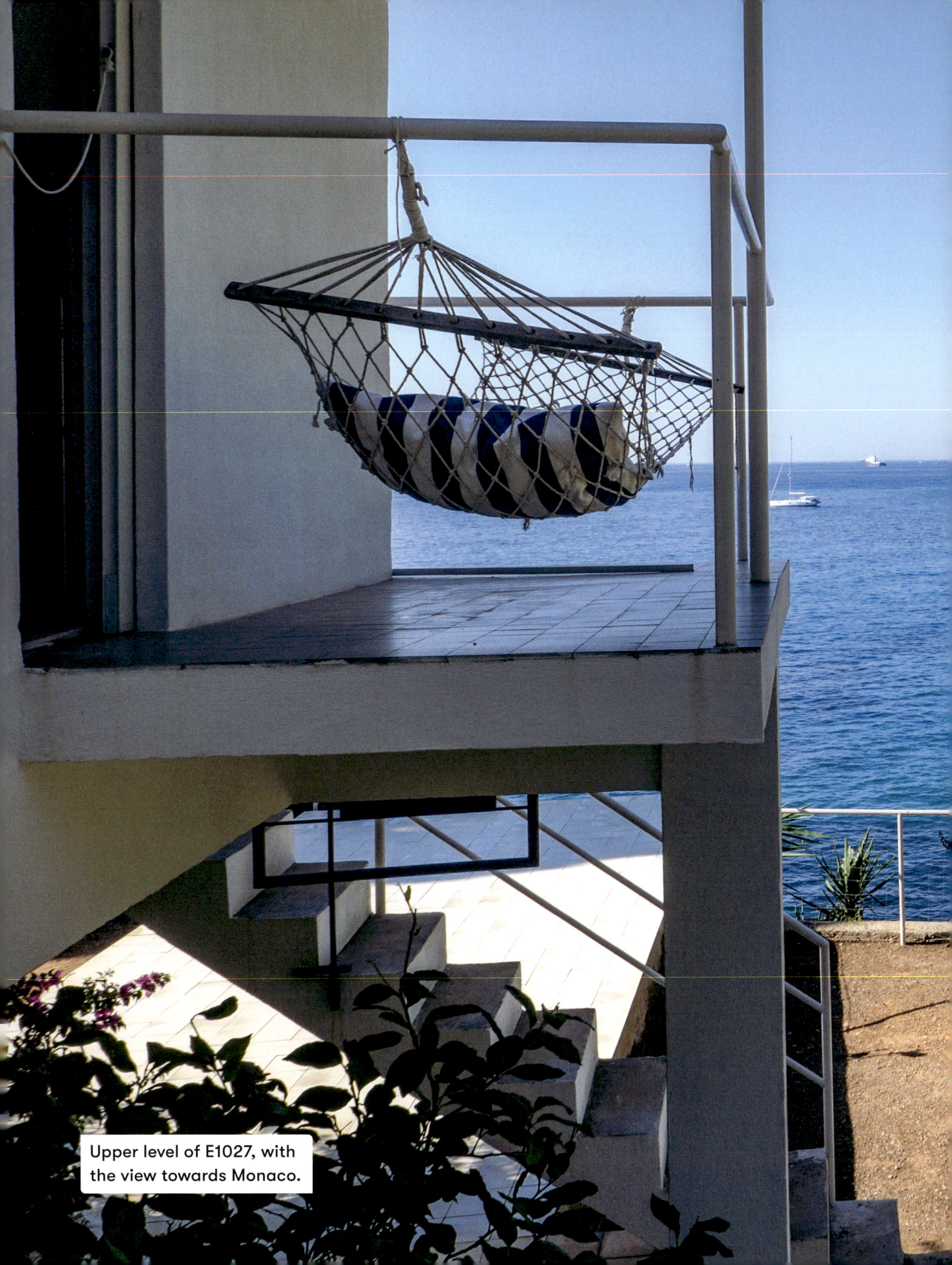

Upper level of E1027, with the view towards Monaco.

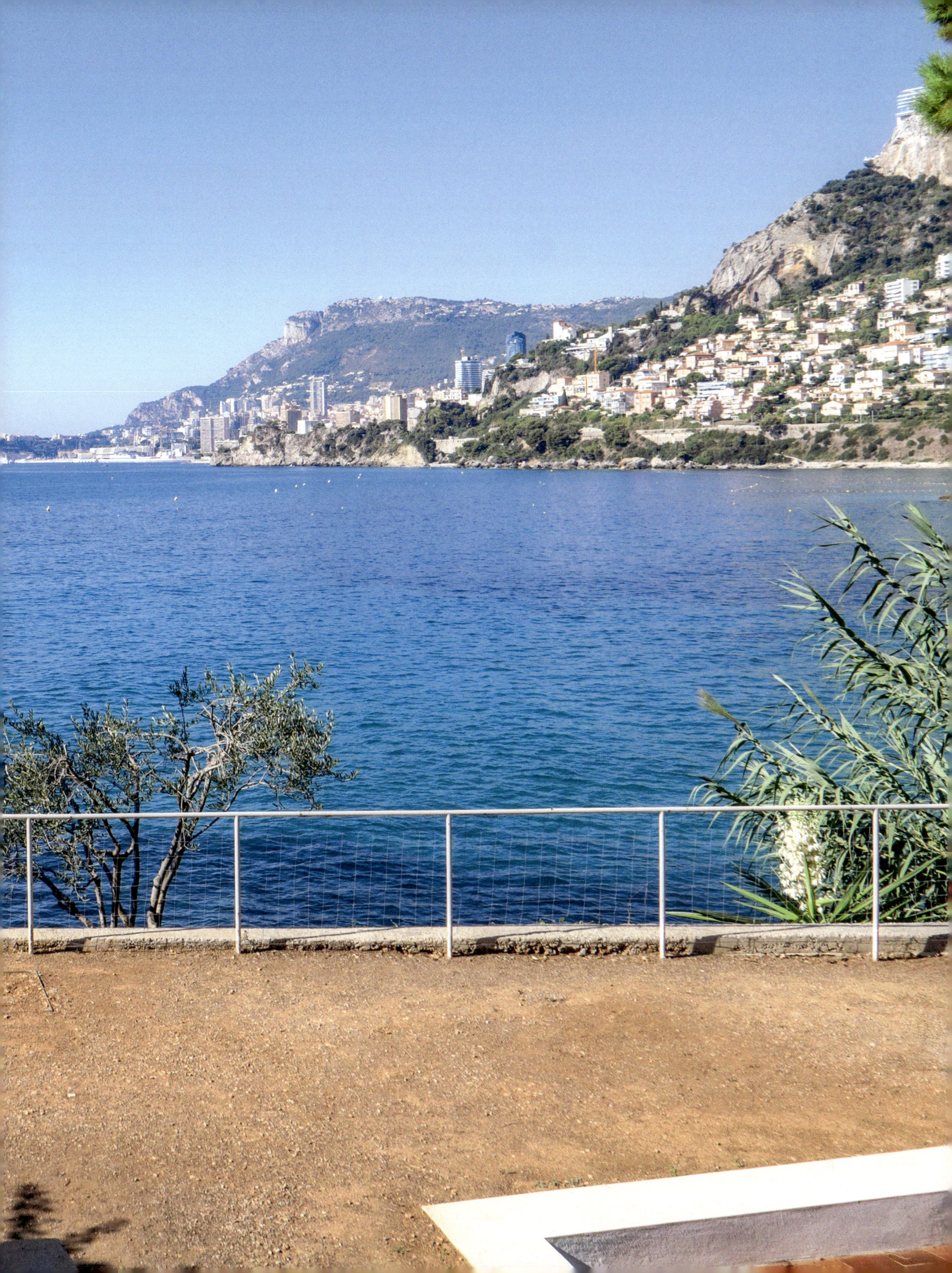

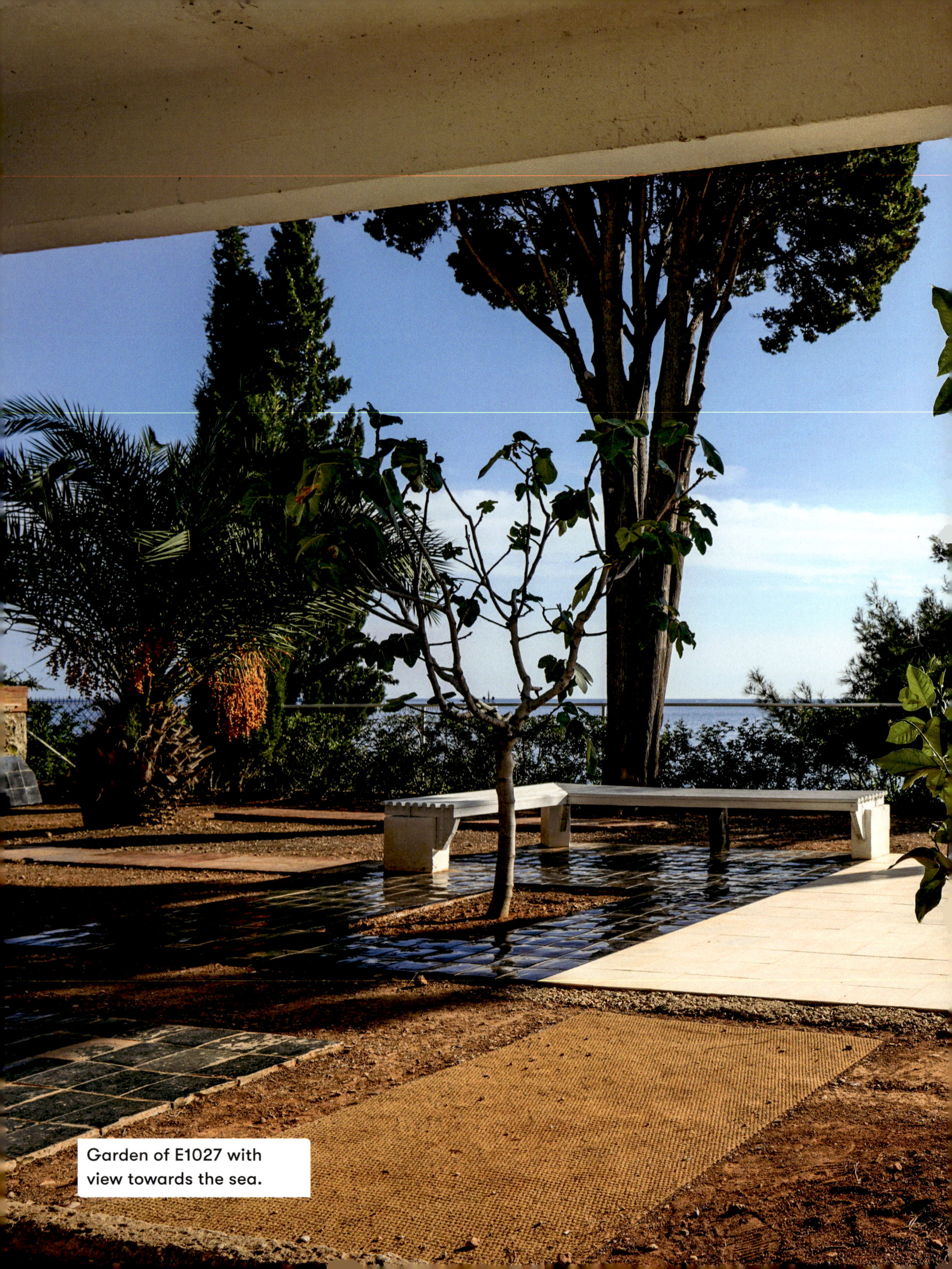

Garden of E1027 with view towards the sea.

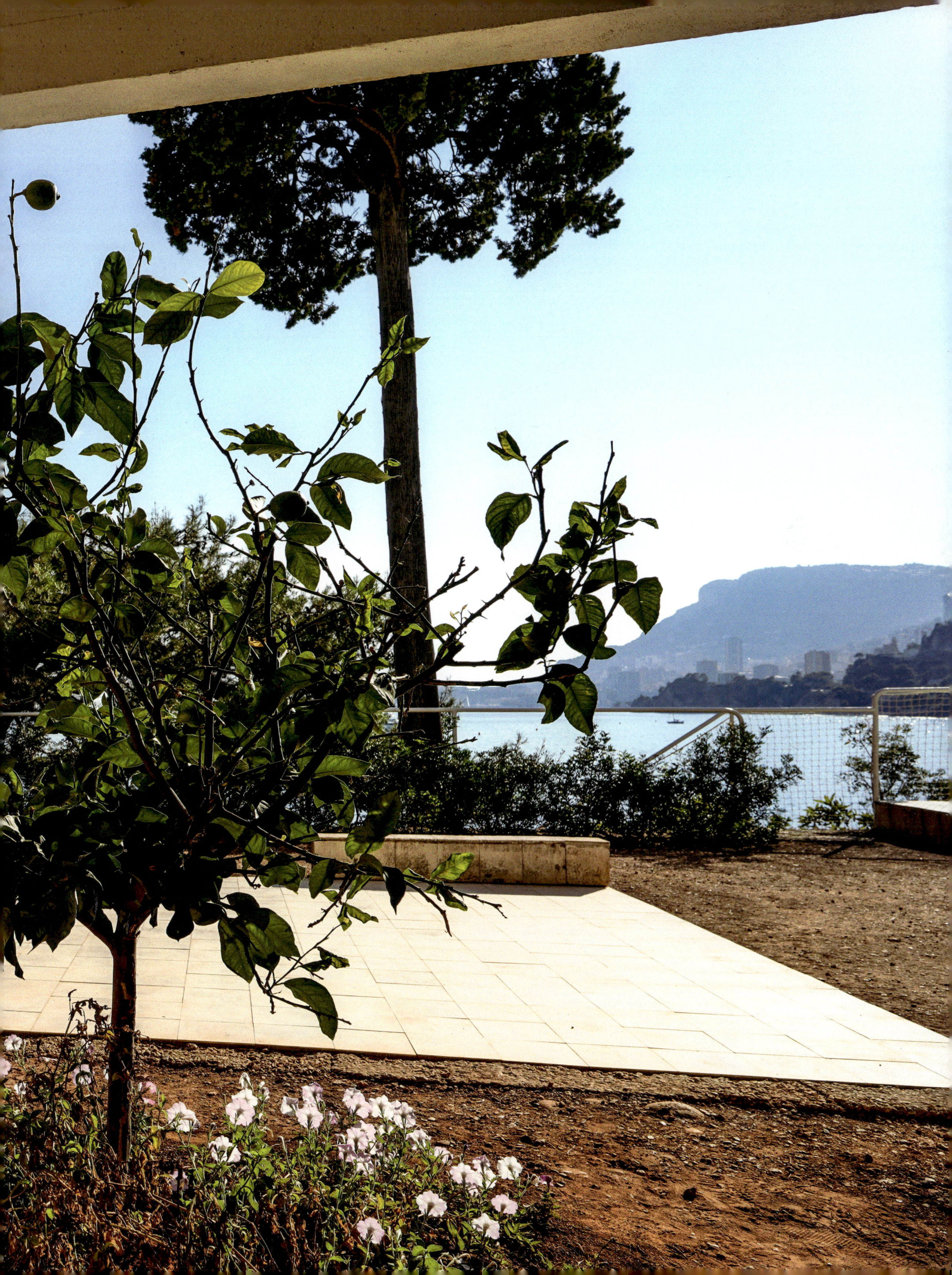

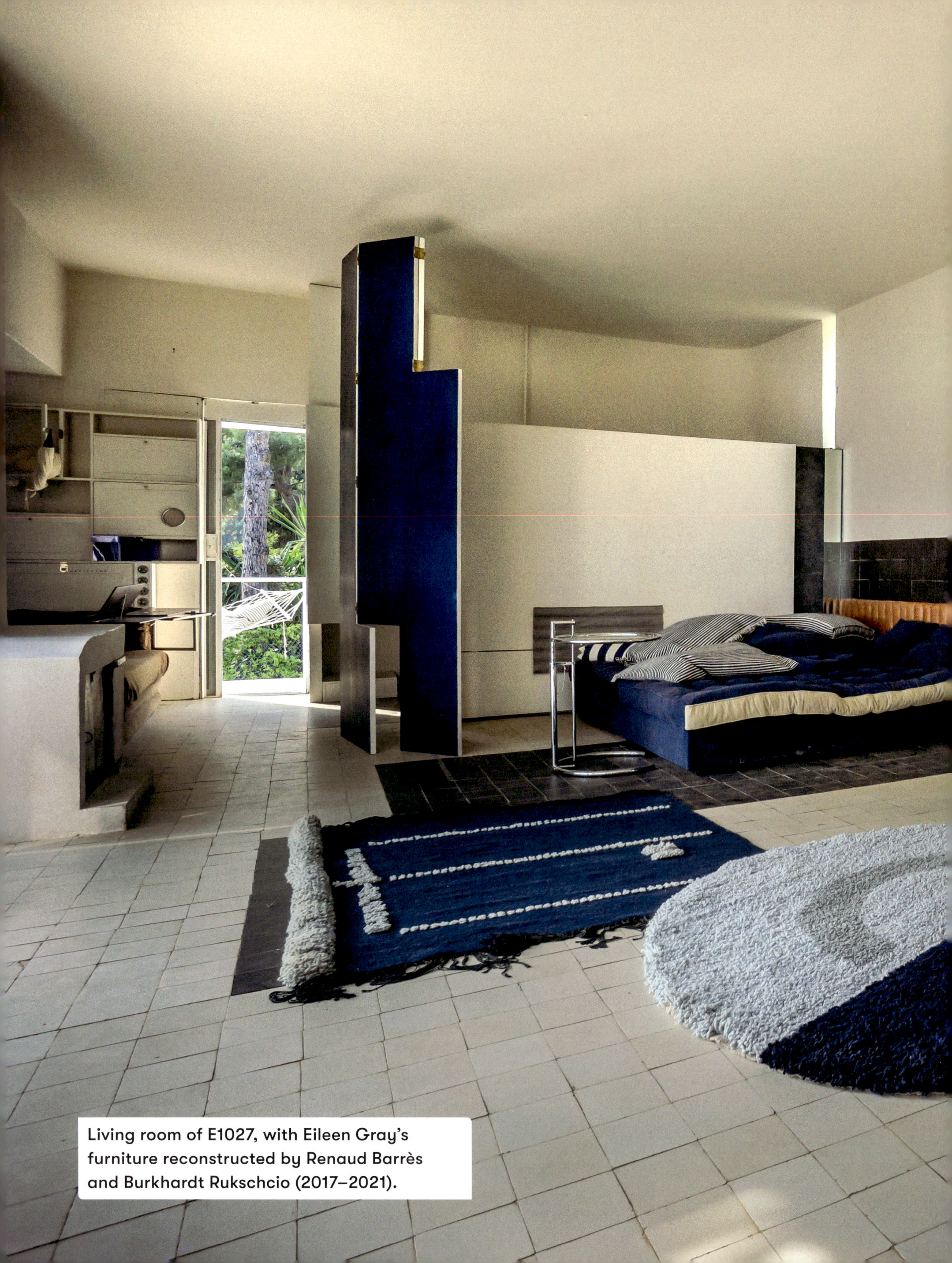

Living room of E1027, with Eileen Gray's furniture reconstructed by Renaud Barrès and Burkhardt Rukschcio (2017–2021).

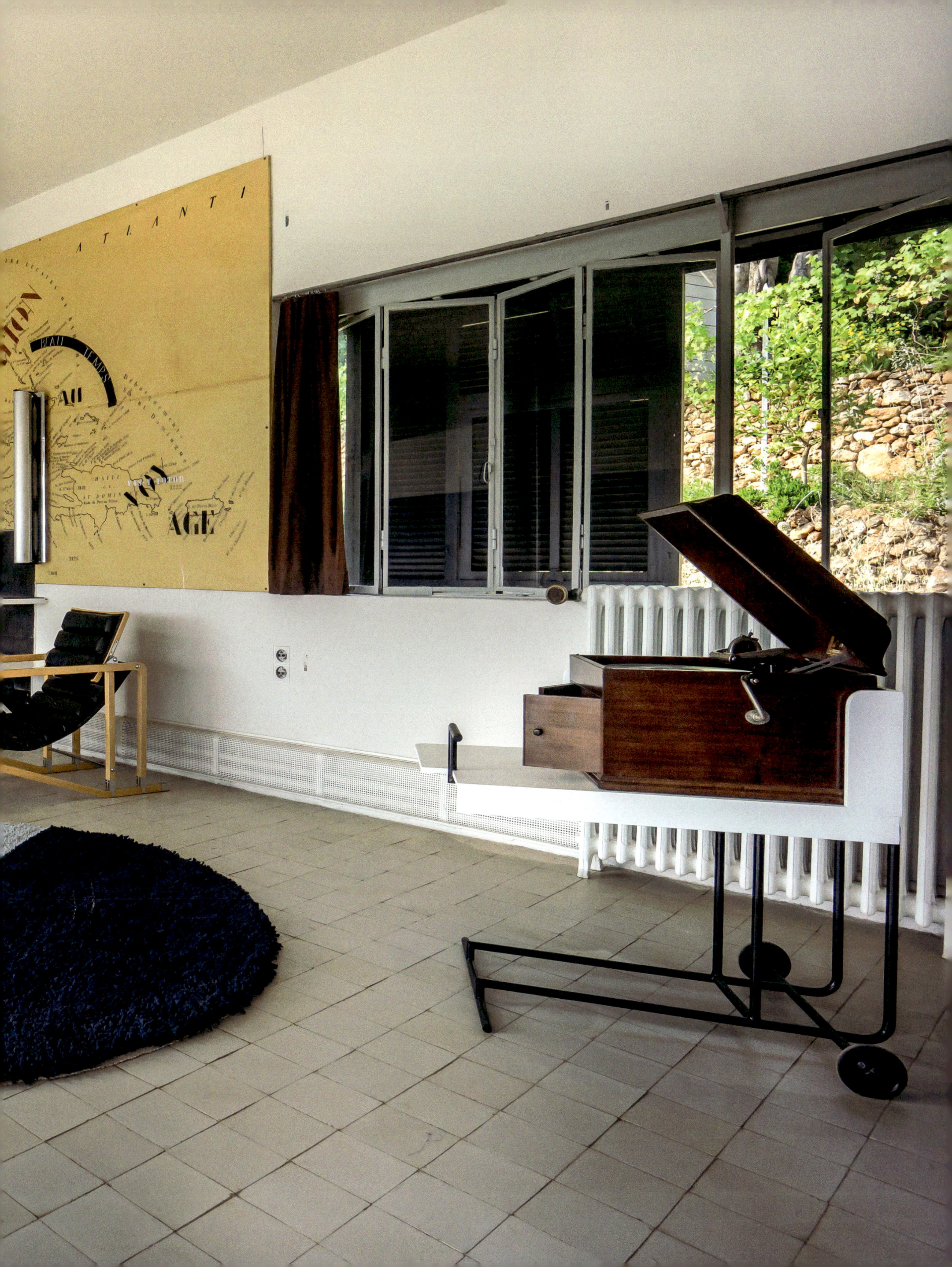
ATLANTI
BEAU TEMPS
AGE

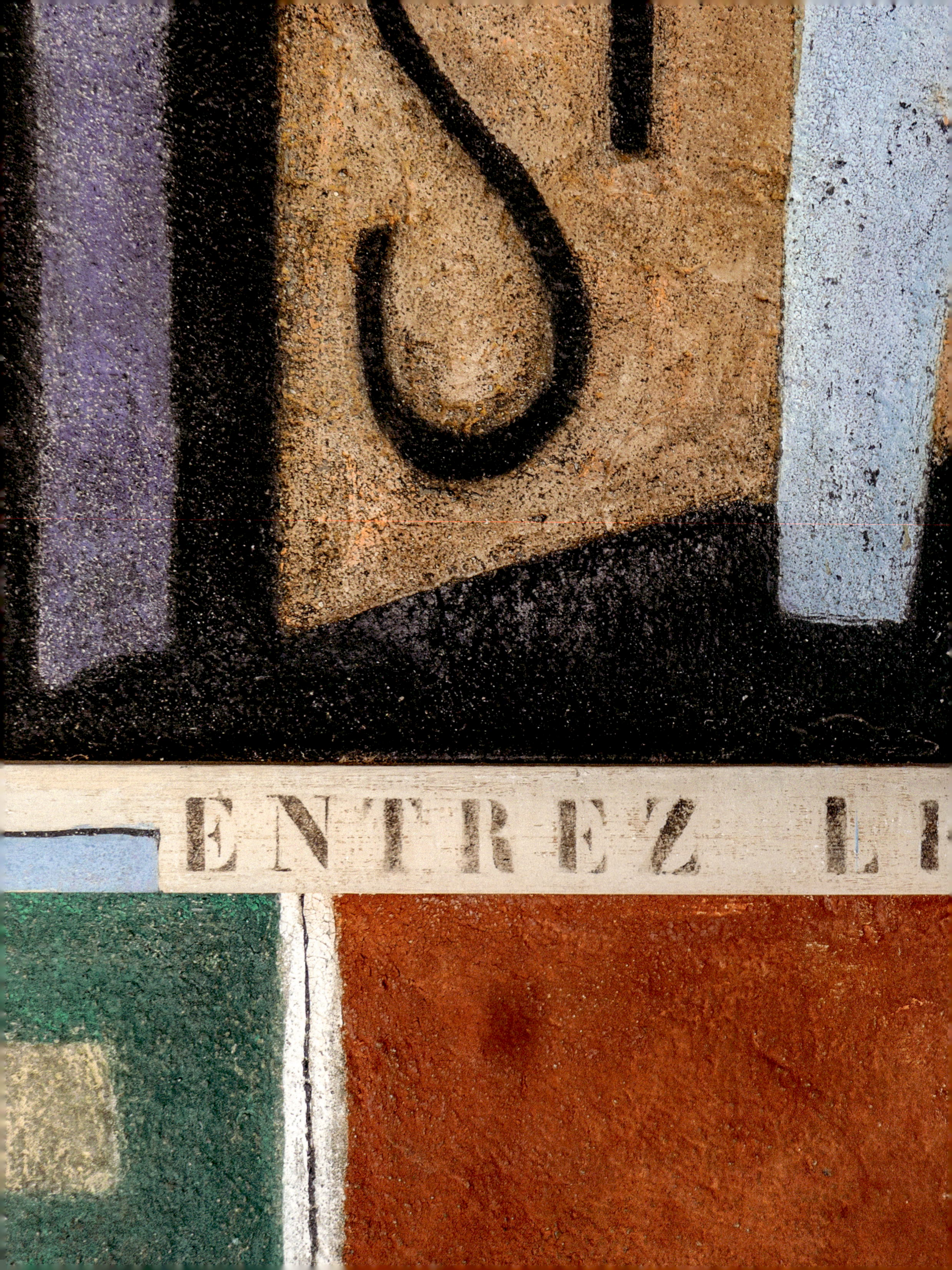
ENTREZ

LE CORBUSIER, ART AND THE WALL

Le Corbusier first visited E1027 at the end of March 1937.[1] The house in Roquebrune-Cap-Martin had been designed in large part by the brilliant Irish designer Eileen Gray and constructed between 1927 and 1929.[2] The name encodes the initials 'E' and 'G' (7th letter of the alphabet) enclosing 'J' and 'B' (tenth and second letters of the alphabet), standing for the initials of her own name and those of her friend and partner at the time, Jean Badovici. There is also a marine reference: local boats were identified by four figure numbers beginning with 'E'. In the autumn and winter 1929 edition of the journal that Badovici edited, *L'Architecture Vivante*, the house was given extensive coverage.[3] Between 16 June and 5 July 1926, Gray had already purchased another house and adjoining plots of land, on the hills above nearby Menton, not far from Roquebrune-Cap-Martin, and began restoring it.[4] She called this house near the village of Castellar 'Tempe a Pailla', the name drawing upon the Provencal proverb 'Avec le temps et la paille, les nèfles mûrissent'.[5] After breaking up with Badovici, she moved into this house around 1932 and apparently never revisited E1027, although she remained friendly with Badovici and collaborated with him on a number of projects. Badovici helped her with the builders during the construction of her villa Tempe a Pailla and again after the war when the villa had to be restored after vandalisation by German troops.

On or just after 25 April 1938, just off the boat after a trip to Algeria, Le Corbusier joined his wife Yvonne and his friend Jean Badovici in E1027. Before returning to Paris on 1 May 1938, he painted two mural paintings, one in the living room and one underneath the

1 Mentioned in a letter from Pierre Guéguen to Jean Badovici on 14 April 1937 (Getty Research Institute, Los Angeles, Badovici archive 880412, Box 6).

2 Badovici purchased the site on 27 March 1927 (Conservatoire des hypothèques de Nice, 2e bureau: deed 67, vol. 140, no. 86, first cited by R. Stella (2017). 'Where the Paper Trail Leads', in W. Wang (ed.), *E.1027 Eileen Gray*, Austin, University of Texas Press, pp. 92–99. A preliminary agreement for this purchase dated 8 March 1926 is in the Renaud Barrès and Mireille Rougeot archive. It is likely that Eileen Gray subsidised the purchase, but the house always belonged to Badovici.

3 For a facsimile edition of this volume: Jean Badovici, Eileen Gray et al. (2015). *E 1027 maison en bord de mer [textes liminaires par Jean-Paul Rayon, Jean-Lucien Bonillo, Pierre-Antoine Gatier]*, Marseille, Éditions Imbernon.

4 Stella, R. (2017). 'Where the Paper Trail Leads', op. cit., p. 92. Gray designed a new set of furniture for Tempe a Pailla. See P. Adam (2009). *Eileen Gray. Her Life and Work*, London, Thames & Hudson, pp. 119–126 and 218–243.

5 'With time and straw, the loquats ripen', a reference to the time it takes for ideas to mature. Caroline Constant (2020). 'Tempe a Pailla and Lou Pérou: The Architectural "Soul" of Eileen Gray', in Cloé Pitiot and Nina Stritzler-Levine (eds.), *Eileen Gray*, New York, Bard Graduate Center, p. 206.

Detail of Le Corbusier's mural at the entrance to E1027, with Eileen Gray's stencilled message *Entrez lentement* (Enter slowly).

house next to the guest bedroom.[6] In August 1939 he returned and painted five more. In 1949, he borrowed the villa in order to host a work session with Josep Lluís Sert, Paul Lester Wiener and some other architects, working on plans for Bogotá. On this occasion he made friends with a retired plumber, Thomas Rebutato, who had opened a small fish restaurant on the plot adjoining E1027, called Étoile de mer. He returned for his vacation in 1950, renting a room in the village, and, on the last day of 1951, sketched out a design for a small wooden cabin, adjoining the fish restaurant, which was built the following year.[7] In the course of the next few years, Le Corbusier decorated the wall of the restaurant, the bedroom of the Rebutatos' cabin and the entrance to his 'cabanon' with some more mural paintings. All these murals were first inscribed on the French supplementary list for protection on 29 October 1975 and classified as a historic monument, along with the house E1027, on 27 March 2000.[8] This book is about these paintings, why they were made and their place in French mural art.

Le Corbusier and the wall

There is a long list of reasons why Le Corbusier's decision to paint on walls is puzzling. Architecture, for Le Corbusier, was 'the masterly, correct and magnificent play of volumes assembled in light.'[9] Anything which might disrupt or confuse this magnificent play of volumes and light was to be criticised. As long ago as 1925 he had entered into an argument with his friend Amédée Ozenfant about the hang of Raoul La Roche's collection of Cubist and Purist paintings in the house he had just designed for him:

> *I insist categorically on keeping some parts of the architecture absolutely free of paintings, in order to create a double effect of pure architecture on the one hand, and pure art on the other.*[10]

Paintings challenged the authority of the walls as architecture – the poetry of the 'prisms' (as Raoul La Roche called them).[11] Le Corbusier's suggestion was that La Roche's paintings be stored out of sight

---

6 See B. Gandini (2008). *La Villa E1027 d'Eileen Gray, première étude de l'état de conservation des peintures murales de Le Corbusier, septembre 2009, maitrise d'ouvrage, Commune de Roquebrune-Cap-Martin.*

7 Chiambretto, B. (1987). *Le Corbusier à Cap-Martin*, Marseille, Éditions Parenthèses, pp. 33–59.

8 Goven, F. (2021). 'The State Steps In', in J.-L. Cohen (ed.), *E1027: Restoring a House by the Sea*, Paris, Éditions du Patrimoine, pp. 67–74.

9 Le Corbusier-Saugnier, 'Trois Rappels à MM les architectes: I le volume', *L'Esprit Nouveau*, 1 October 1920, p. 92, later reprinted in *Vers une Architecture*, October 1923.

10 Typescript letter from Le Corbusier to Amédée Ozenfant, 16 April 1925 (FLC P5(1)208). Unless noted otherwise, all translations of French texts were undertaken by the author.

11 'Ah, those prisms. It must be said that you and Pierre have the secret, since I search vainly for them elsewhere. You have shown their beauty and explained their meaning and, thanks to you, we now know what architecture is.' (Letter from Raoul La Roche to Le Corbusier, 1 January 1927 (FLC P5(1)151).

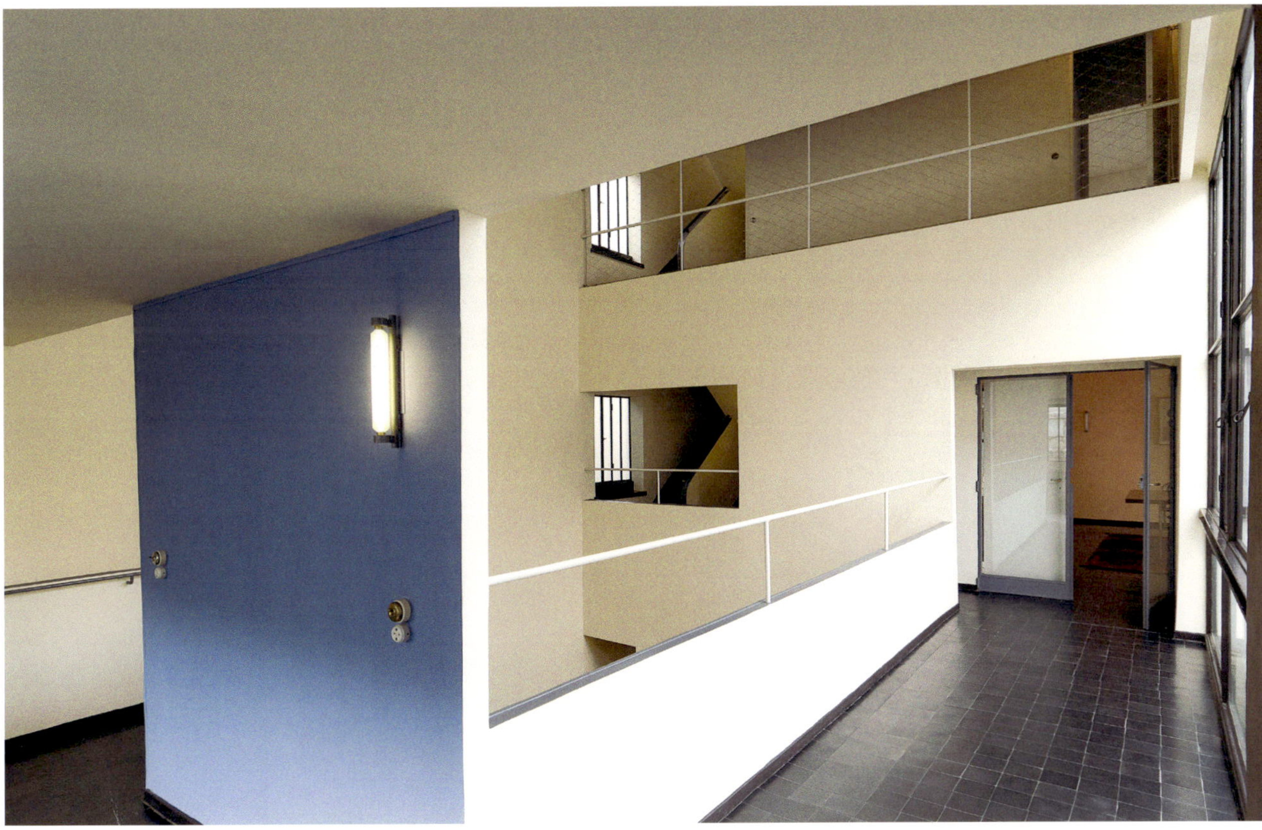

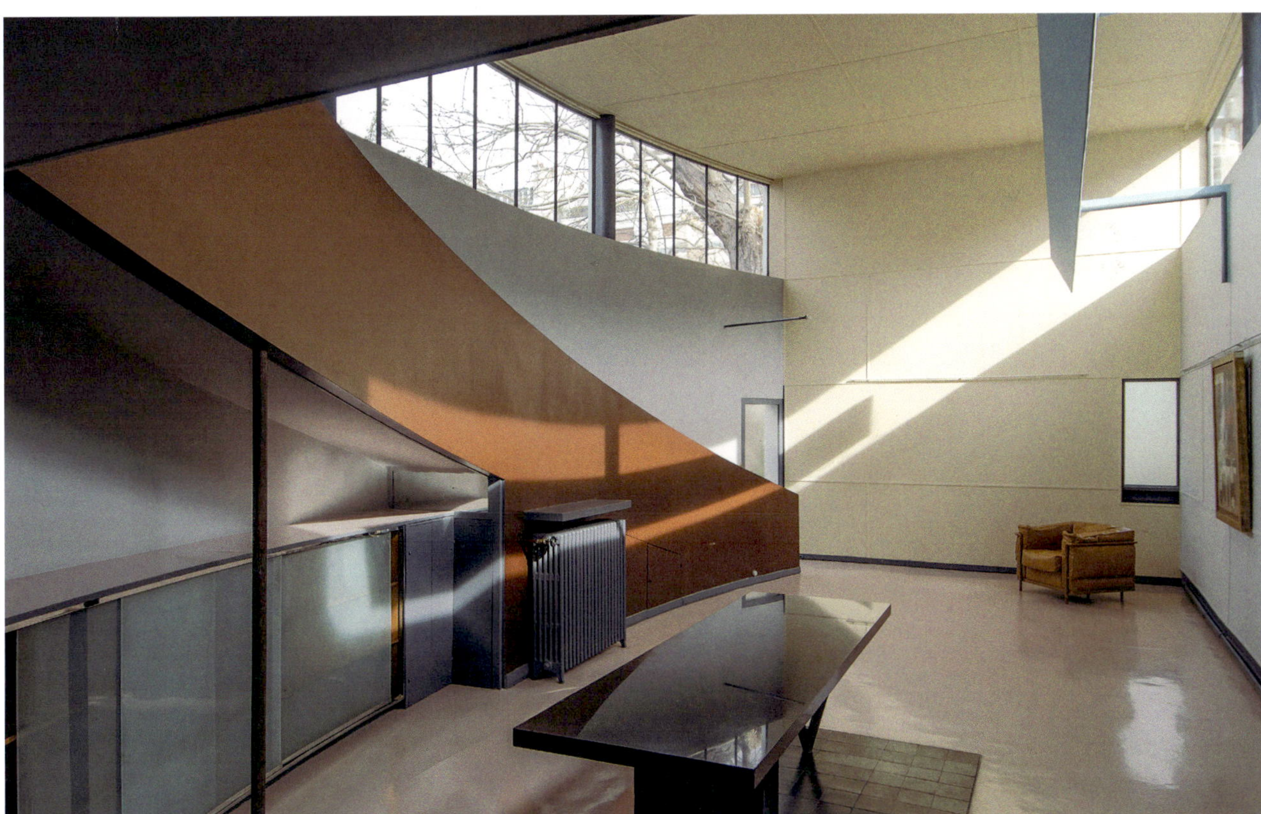

Le Corbusier and Pierre Jeanneret, Villa La Roche, Paris, bridge crossing the hall, 1923–1925.

Le Corbusier and Pierre Jeanneret, Villa La Roche, gallery (following changes of 1928).

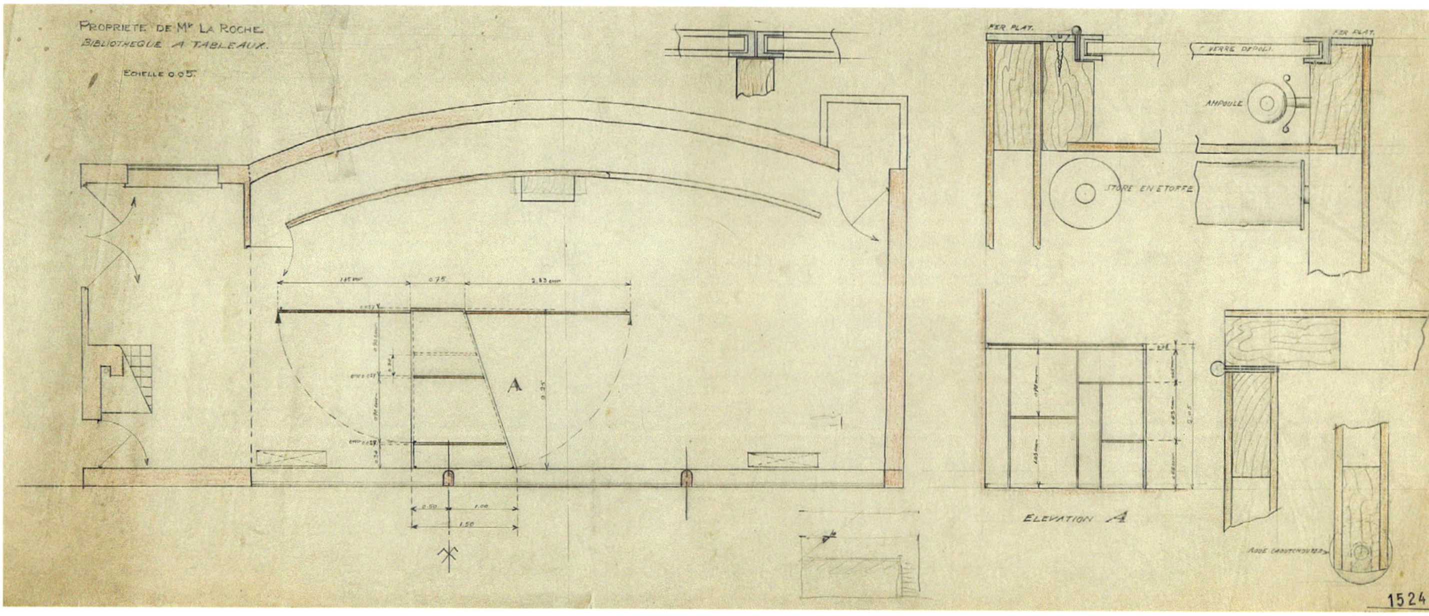

Le Corbusier and Pierre Jeanneret, design for picture store to occupy the painting gallery in the Villa La Roche, April 1925.

in a large cupboard and brought out a few at a time for concentrated attention. He went so far as to design such a fitment, some 2.25 m × 1.50 m at its widest point and 2.05 m high, which would have effectively divided the picture gallery into two. What is astonishing in this scheme is that the painting store would not only have seriously damaged the function of the space for showing La Roche's fabulous collection of Cubist and Purist paintings, but it would also have destroyed the architectural effect. As La Roche said, in the letter rejecting the scheme, 'this would create another antechamber and I have enough of those already.'[12]

Paintings did have an important role in Le Corbusier's interiors however. Le Corbusier had the Esprit Nouveau pavilion,[13] photographed in 1925 with paintings by Fernand Léger, Amédée Ozenfant and himself on the walls and a Lipchitz sculpture outside. This was an argument against 'decoration', a challenge to the Exposition des arts décoratifs et industriels modernes in which the pavilion was sited. Modern man had no need for 'decoration'; what he needed was music, literature and art. This was the formula, then: pure architecture and pure art. Where could mural painting fit in?

A first step, for Le Corbusier, was polychromy. Le Corbusier had always used colour in his buildings, and especially in the interiors. He saw it as part of the control of light entering the building through the large windows provided by the new structural principles and striking the walls in different ways during the day. Colour could

12 'The more I think about it, the more it seems a shame to place it in the middle of the paintings gallery (if it is still to be one) thus dividing it into two parts; this would create another antechamber and I have enough of those already.' Letter from Raoul La Roche to Le Corbusier, 12 May 1925, FLC P5(1)57, and letter from Le Corbusier to Amédée Ozenfant, 16 April 1925 (FLC P5(1)208).

13 The Esprit Nouveau pavilion was a model home, designed by Le Corbusier and Pierre Jeanneret to be stacked together in apartment buildings and built for the 1925 international exhibition Exposition des arts décoratifs et industriels modernes in Paris.

accentuate these effects or act in counterpoint (or 'fugue') with the natural light. But the old rules of applying colour in interiors no longer applied. Rooms in the new architecture were no longer self-contained boxes, allowing one to be painted red, another blue. Spaces opened into each other. A wall might belong to two spaces at once. He described his approach in an important article written after the completion of the Villa La Roche:

> *For several years I have thought that the polychromy of the house interior must be dictated by the luminosity of the walls. The overarching, general rules apply: warm tones in bright light, cold tones in the shadows. I have experimented with counterpoint and fugue in order to animate the interior by responding to the modulations of light. Once again, I am celebrating the phenomenon of light.*[14]

Le Corbusier's exploitation of the effects of colour approaches the pictorial art of the artist and seems to move away from the conventional dynamics of Purist architecture, with the stress on volumes:

> *What if I painted a red wall surrounded by white, or a blue ceiling above white walls? Or if I join at right angles a burnt umber wall to a white one. In truth, my house will not appear white until I have deployed in appropriate places the active force of colours and values.*[15]

The use of the word 'values', an artist's word, demonstrates the merging of the painterly and the tectonic in Le Corbusier's thinking. But from the creation of spaces modulated by colour to the addition of figurative mural paintings to wall surfaces was a step that Le Corbusier found very difficult to take.

Monumental painting

Large canvases and murals had always had a prestigious place in French culture. There are a number of reasons for this. 'High' art – the kind of painting that won prizes and would be bought by the state – was invariably large. This was partly because the subject matter of the most prestigious paintings – mythological, classical, religious or historical scenes – required a large surface and partly because painting big was a recognition of the status of the artist. Secondly, large public paintings – typically murals or frescoes – could be used to raise social or political issues and form the taste and opinion of the general public.[16] Thirdly, painting on walls could be seen as part of the aim of producing a *Gesamtkunstwerk* – a total work of art. These issues, much discussed in the nineteenth century, were

---

14 Le Corbusier (1926). 'Notes à la suite', *Cahiers d'Art*, 1, pp. 46–52, p. 48.
15 Ibid., p. 49.
16 Technically, Renaissance frescoes were painted onto wet plaster, so none of the paintings discussed in this book conform to this definition. Le Corbusier however often used the term 'fresque' to describe his mural paintings.

revived in the 1920s and especially in the 1930s. Le Corbusier actively engaged in these debates.
Émile Zola had argued, in his novel *L'Œuvre*,[17] that the responsibility of the modern artist was to paint huge pictures, in order to inspire the working classes but also to test the mettle of the artist. Painting big required courage. The failure of his character Claude Lantier to achieve this, and the madness and suicide which followed was the central plot of his novel. Artists are said to 'paint for themselves', but in the end they have to sell their work to live. Historically, success came by establishing a reputation by winning prizes at the annual *salons*. From the arrival of the Impressionists and the creation of the Salon des Indépendants in France (1884), the attention of progressive artists veered from competing for a place in the Louvre to capturing the admiration of the private clients and the galleries and dealers who supplied them.[18] The revolution of artistic language in Picasso and Braque's invention of Cubism, between 1909 and 1914, was largely sustained by private dealers such as Daniel Kahnweiler, without any significant exposure to the general public. 'Dealer art' was art intended for the home and was typically small in scale and intimate or neutral in subject matter. Instead of the great subjects of history, mythology or religion, modern artists typically represented still lives, portraits or landscapes. It was painting this kind of subject that successive 'movements' in modern art succeeded each other into the early 1920s, from Impressionism, Post-Impressionism, Fauvism, Orphism, Cubism and Purism. Avant-garde artists, supported by specialist dealers, could afford to 'paint for themselves', confident that knowledgeable clients would discover their work.

The artist Le Corbusier

In order to understand Le Corbusier's mural paintings we must trace his earlier development as an artist. In particular, we need to understand the frame of mind, increasingly bitter and frustrated, that governed his artistic activity in the 1930s. During the early 1920s, under the guidance of Amédée Ozenfant, Le Corbusier – or Jeanneret as he still signed his paintings – had a measure of *succès d'estime* as a painter. That is, the exhibitions to which he contributed provoked the usual kind of controversy due to any new 'movement', but they were accepted into the ranks of the avant-garde, hanging alongside the Cubist painters in the Galerie de l'Effort Moderne of Léonce Rosen-

17 Zola, E. M. (1974) [1886]. *L'Œuvre [S.l.]*, Paris, Garnier-Flammarion.

18 In fact, the development of 'dealer art', typically consisting of portraits, still life and landscapes, had developed much earlier: Antwerp had become a centre for such dealers in the sixteenth century. It was in France, however, that 'dealer art' challenged 'high art' for prestige and importance.

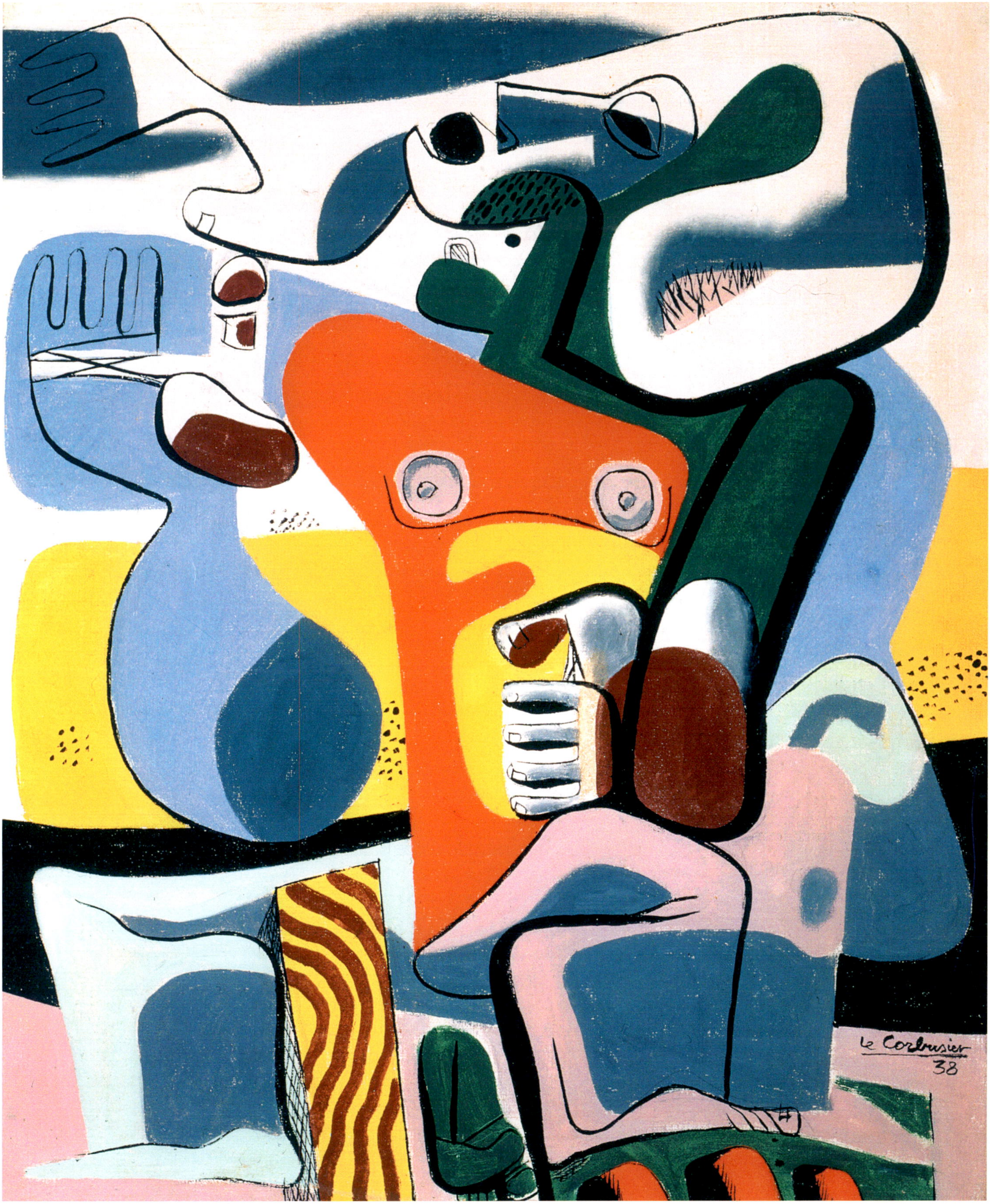

Le Corbusier, *Étreinte II* (Embrace II), 1938.

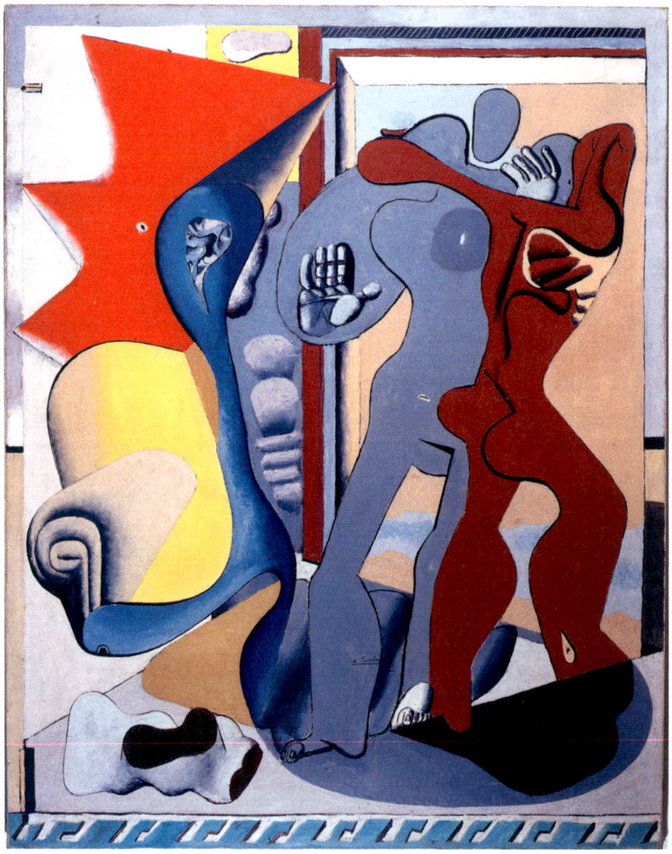

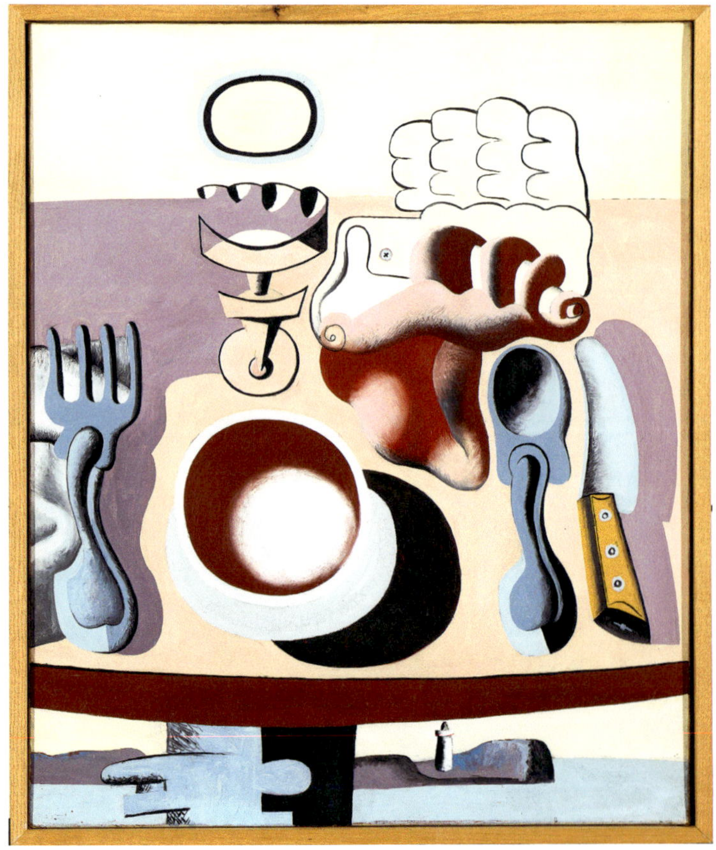

Le Corbusier, *Femme grise, homme rouge et os devant une porte* (Grey woman, red man and bone before a door), 1931.

Le Corbusier, *Le déjeuner près du phare* (Lunch near the lighthouse), 1928.

berg.[19] The magazine *L'Esprit Nouveau*, which they edited from 1920 to 1924, helped, as did the two books on art that they published: *Après le Cubisme* (1918) and *La Peinture moderne* (1925).[20] These books gave a theoretical structure to their work which was broadly consistent with the theories of modern architecture proposed in *Vers une Architecture* (1923). They stressed precision and geometrical proportion and preferred everyday, industrially produced objects for their subject matter.

Following his split from Ozenfant in 1925, however, Le Corbusier virtually stopped exhibiting. And his painting moved away from the great themes of modernity, industrialisation and standardisation. His centre of inspiration moved from the city to the coast, from Paris to the Bassin d'Arcachon, where he and his partner Yvonne Gallis took their holidays every year from 1926 to 1936.[21] He became fascinated with natural objects – seashells, fragments of driftwood,

19 The first exhibition by Ozenfant and Jeanneret was held at the Galerie Thomas on 22 December 1918. A second exhibition at the Druet gallery (January–February 1921) was enthusiastically reviewed by the critic Maurice Raynal. Léonce Rosenberg went on to invite the two artists to contribute to an exhibition at the Galerie de l'Effort Moderne (2–25 May 1921) alongside the work of Picasso, Braque, Gris and other Cubist artists. Rosenberg also included their work in exhibitions in Amsterdam and Barcelona.

20 Ozenfant, A. and C. E. Jeanneret (1918). *Après le Cubisme*, Paris, Éditions des Commentaires; and A. Ozenfant and C. E. Jeanneret *(1925). La Peinture moderne*, Paris, Éditions G. Crès et Cie.

21 Benton T. and B. Hubert (2015). *Le Corbusier. Mes années sauvages sur le bassin d'Arcachon* Paris, Ibep; and T. Benton (2013). 'Atlantic Coast: Nature as Inspiration', in J.-L. Cohen (ed.), *Le Corbusier: An Atlas of Modern Landscapes*, New York, Museum of Modern Art, pp. 162–167.

butcher's bones or bricks eroded by sea and wind. He was increasingly apt to see in these objects substitutes for the human body and he liked to juxtapose them with nudes, often specifically the body of Yvonne.

For Le Corbusier, an exhibition of his work in the Kunsthalle Zürich in January 1938 marked a big step in terms of public exposure. Between 1926 and 1938, he had developed a completely personal style which gave him great satisfaction. These paintings, many of them based on sketches made at Le Piquey, on the Bassin d'Arcachon, reveal a sensuality and absorption in natural forms not seen before in his work. His 1928 painting *Le déjeuner près du phare* (Lunch near the lighthouse) |ill. p. 28|, for example, includes the lighthouse at nearby Cap Ferret and suggests the pleasures of eating associated with the voluptuous form of a seashell.

The exhibition, and the purchase of one of his Purist paintings by the Museum of Modern Art in New York, did boost his confidence a little.[22] In a letter to his mother on 23 January 1938, he claimed 'On dit que c'est sensationnel'('They say it's sensational') and he warmly acknowledged the lecture given by Maurice Raynal on 20 January.[23] Raynal's critique was published in the *Journal des Beaux-Arts*, January 1938 and reprinted in *L'Equerre*.[24] Two days later, writing to Marguerite Tjader-Harris, he claimed that Raynal had said: 'This Corbusier, behind his rough exterior, is a sensitive man.' And he went on, coquettishly, 'What do you think about this, what [...] do you know about it.'[25] A few weeks later, however, in an undated letter to his mother, he claimed that his exhibition had been received in total silence: 'In any case, I am convinced that they will never take me seriously as a painter in my lifetime.'[26] To make matters worse, his mother visited the exhibition and expressed her disapproval, to the extent that Albert, Le Corbusier's older brother, intervened to try to soften her criticisms.[27] I believe that this experience hardened Le Corbusier's attitude to his painting. Instead of thinking of it as something private and personal, he was prepared to go public, irrespective of the opinion of the critics. As Maurice Raynal put it:

> *The monk has left his monastery to go on crusade. The artist has been cast out from his ivory tower to enter the lists. An art of joy and satisfaction in beatitude has been replaced by an art of anxiety, need and conflict. [...] The man has taken*

---

22 The Museum of Modern Art purchased his *Nature morte à la pile d'assiettes et au livre* (Still life with a pile of plates and a book), which had been exhibited in New York in 1935.

23 On 17 January 1938 he had told his mother that the exhibition was an 'unexpected success' (FLC R2(1)244).

24 FLC X1(13)69.

25 FLC E3(10)30. Le Corbusier had a brief affair with the wealthy widow Marguerite Tjader-Harris in 1935 during his lecture series in the USA. They remained in contact by letters until his death.

26 Collection Jornod. Letter cited in J. Petit (1970). *Le Corbusier lui-même*, Genève, Éditions Rousseau.

27 Letter from Albert Jeanneret (1886–1973) to their mother, 21 March 1938 (Collection Jornod). See J.-P. Jornod and N. Jornod (2005). *Le Corbusier (Charles-Édouard Jeanneret): Catalogue raisonné de l'œuvre peint*, Milan, Skira, p. 157.

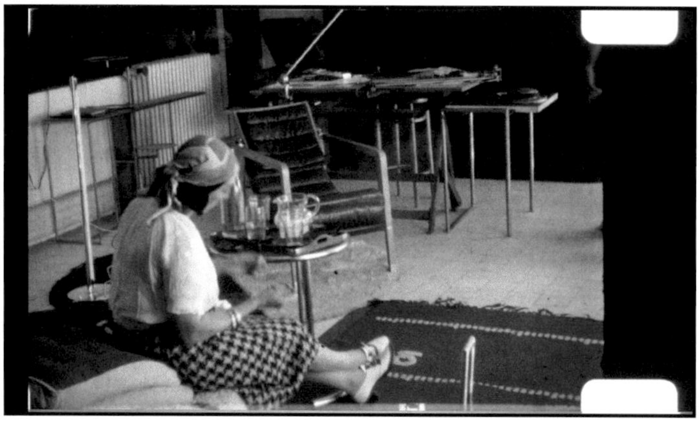

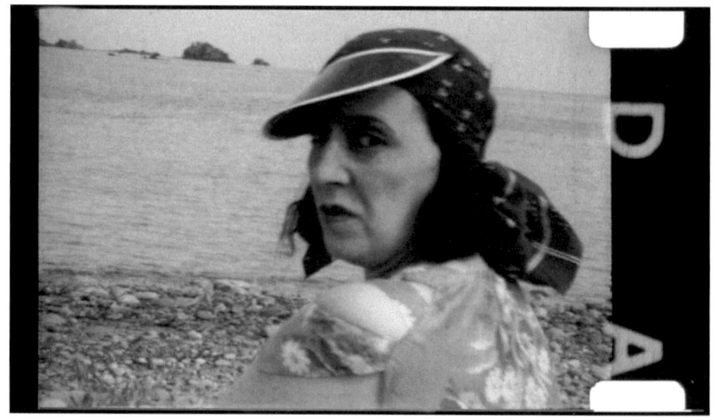

Le Corbusier, Yvonne in the living room of E1027, April 1938, photograph taken with his 16 mm cine camera.

Le Corbusier, Yvonne on the beach at Plougrescant, Brittany, July 1937.

> *over from the artist. He no longer pays his dues to art, as before. He demands that art pay its debt to him, to help him express his moral and physiological demands.*[28]

In the course of the 1930s, Le Corbusier's painting had become more strident. This may have been connected with his political attitudes which were becoming more right-wing. He sympathised with the violent anti-governmental clashes which took place on the streets of Paris on 6 February 1934 as a result of the Stavisky affair.[29] But more importantly, the thirties was a period of frustrating struggle for Le Corbusier, when his international reputation and his popularity as a lecturer and author did not prevent his architectural commissions from drying up almost completely. Between 1933 and 1939 he built almost nothing. As he wrote to his friend Marguerite Tjader-Harris, 'I have become a symbol. It doesn't feed you well'.[30]
On 3 November 1934, he complained to his mother about the sordid bureaucratic dealings which he thought blocked his success and he ended his letter:

> *Fernand Léger came round for the day on Sunday. A great fellow, strong, healthy, subtle, true. He was astonished by the torment, the explosiveness, the violence of my painting. Of course, I am exploding here because everywhere else I have to keep my fist in my pocket.*[31]

In his article accompanying the Zürich exhibition, Raynal described Le Corbusier's character in terms that undoubtedly encouraged him to continue on this path:

> *Violent, selfish, stubborn, fond of a drink, tetchy, disinterested, erudite, nature lover, spiritual, biased, enemy of the*

---

28 Raynal, M. (1938). 'Le Corbusier peintre', *Beaux Arts*, LXXV(264). *Croisade* was also the name of a book published by Le Corbusier defending modern architecture from the criticisms of its enemies. Le Corbusier (1933). *Croisade ou le crepuscule des Academies*, Paris, 1933.

29 The Stavisky affair was a financial scandal that caused political turmoil for the radical socialist government when it was revealed that Prime Minister Camille Chautemps had protected the embezzler Alexandre Stavisky, who died suddenly in mysterious circumstances. Right-wingers staged large anti-government demonstrations on 6 February 1934 in Paris, during which fifteen demonstrators were killed by the police. Even a right-wing *coup d'état* seemed a possibility at the time.

30 Letter from Le Corbusier to Marguerite Tjader-Harris, 8 March 1938 (FLC E3(10)30).

31 Letter from Le Corbusier to his mother, 3 November 1934 (FLC R2(1)208).

> *cliché; all of these, whether you consider them faults or virtues, are eminently aesthetic. [...] Skies, seas, mountains, serpents, women, weapons, ropes, locks, blood gushing forth with its full symbolic force, but always formal. Le Corbusier, restless traveller that he is in zeppelins and ocean liners, says that the skies, the sea and the mountains are a memory of childhood like the difficulties of tackling a complicated job. The psychoanalyst might find a similar explanation for the locks. The ropes and the women represent all the difficulties of succeeding, widows of his enemies, jealousy and betrayals. And this is where the temperament of Le Corbusier the man explodes with full effect. Straight talking, violence and force saturate and nourish these spontaneous paintings.*[32]

Most of his paintings from the late 1920s and early 1930s depict natural forms and/or women either alone or in pairs. But there is also a series of paintings which show a man and woman together, in front of an open door in what appears to be a more conflictual relationship. In *Femme grise, homme rouge et os devant une porte* (Grey woman, red man and bone before a door) |ill. p. 28| and a similar painting *Femme noire, homme rouge et os* (Black woman, red man and bone)[33] the woman's hand is upraised, flat on the picture plane, as if in rejection.[34] We know that his relationship with Yvonne was becoming strained. She suffered from bouts of depression and seems to have been drinking too much. Imprisoned in the apartment he had designed in Boulogne-sur-Seine, she felt isolated from her usual haunts on the Left Bank. Although Le Corbusier never ceases to write in glowing terms about her to his mother, he also admitted that Yvonne was passing through the menopause, and it was clear from something he wrote to Marguerite Tjader-Harris in 1936, that the couple no longer made love.[35]

Several Anglo-Saxon critics have described Le Corbusier's mural paintings in E1027 as explicitly erotic, thus reinforcing the idea of his 'rape' of the house.[36] Le Corbusier's interest in the nude does not

---

32 Raynal, M. (1938). 'Le Corbusier peintre', op. cit. Le Corbusier was well aware of current psychoanalytical theory, possessing several of the books by Dr. René Allendy including Allendy, R. (1931). *La psychanalyse; doctrines et applications*, Paris, Denoël et Steele, dedicated to him by the author.

33 (FLC 98).

34 In a number of drawings on this theme, the struggle is even more apparent (see FLC 0246, 1260, 1426 and others).

35 Writing to Marguerite Tjader-Harris from Rio de Janeiro on 8 July 1936, he admitted: 'I haven't made love since 13 December. It's crazy' (FLC E3(10)15). 13 December 1935 was when he was with Marguerite. And on 19 December he wrote to his mother about Yvonne: 'Furthermore, it is the beginning of the change of life with the depression that comes with it. Nature is mysterious; it works slowly to make changes in the body that have an effect on the psyche. We must understand all that. Men are stronger and, at the age of 50, are at the height of their powers.' FLC R2(1)233). On 8 December he again wrote to Marguerite claiming 'The other life – the one which is active at night – has been almost completely set aside.' (FLC E3(10)26).

36 Peter Adam describes them as 'overtly sexual'. He adds: 'It was rape.' See P. Adam (2000). *Eileen Gray: Architect/Designer: A Biography*, New York, Harry N. Abrams, p. 311.

distinguish him from most artists of the twentieth century, but it is true that there is something unsettling about his work of the 1930s. It is interesting to note what he wrote to his mother after an argument in 1937: 'An American psycho-analyst, on seeing my paintings commented: "You are in conflict with your mother, something that has still not been resolved."'[37] That Le Corbusier was aware that he had a distinctive psychic personality is revealed by a graphological test that he commissioned from the Centre de synthèse des méthodes psychologiques et des graphologues français et étrangères in June 1948.[38] This document, whose scientific credentials are perhaps questionable, certainly reflects Le Corbusier's self-image:

> *The author engages too much in the external life to be able to find a higher level of equilibrium. [...] He has no access to his soul. He lacks introversion [...] His is an affective and loving character. He attaches himself to people and things. Very sensitive to criticism because he has a secret and hidden desire to be approved and admired. [...] The handwriting expresses a very strong anality. Furthermore, since there is clear evidence of a self-castration complex, it is likely that the author underwent, at the age of 6, 7 or 8 years old, a regression to an anterior anal state. [...] Anality that has subsequently been sublimated (intellectual curiosity, human philosophy, sociology, decorative arts, sculpture, architecture).*[39]

In another series, entitled *Étreinte* (Embrace, 1938), Le Corbusier represents a more harmonious relationship between male and female bodies. These paintings are based on sketches of a woman sitting on the knee of a man, who embraces her tenderly and protectively. Naïma and Jean-Pierre Jornod in their *Catalogue raisonné* read this series as a representation of Le Corbusier and Yvonne, and this hypothesis is sustained by their similarity to the painting of 1939, entitled *Adieu Von*.[40] This painting hung in his Paris apartment until his death, and, when Yvonne died in 1957, Le Corbusier added the inscription 'Adieu Von 1939–1957'. *Étreinte II* |ill. p. 27| is of particular interest because it was dedicated to Maurice Raynal, no doubt in gratitude for his support in Zürich.

Le Corbusier kept abreast of new developments in Parisian avant-garde art. Picasso's increasingly vigorous and jagged compositions must have made an impression. He was certainly struck by Picasso's mural *Guernica* in the Spanish Pavilion at the International Exhibi-

---

37 Letter from Le Corbusier to his mother, 19 February 1937 (FLC R2(1)149).

38 Collection Jornod. J.-P. Jornod and N. Jornod (2005). *Le Corbusier: L'œuvre peint*, op. cit., vol. 2, pp. 1050–1061, note 23. At this time, he was insisting that all of his assistants undergo a graphological test.

39 Ibid., p. 1055, p. 1060.

40 *Adieu Von 1939–1957* (FLC 4).

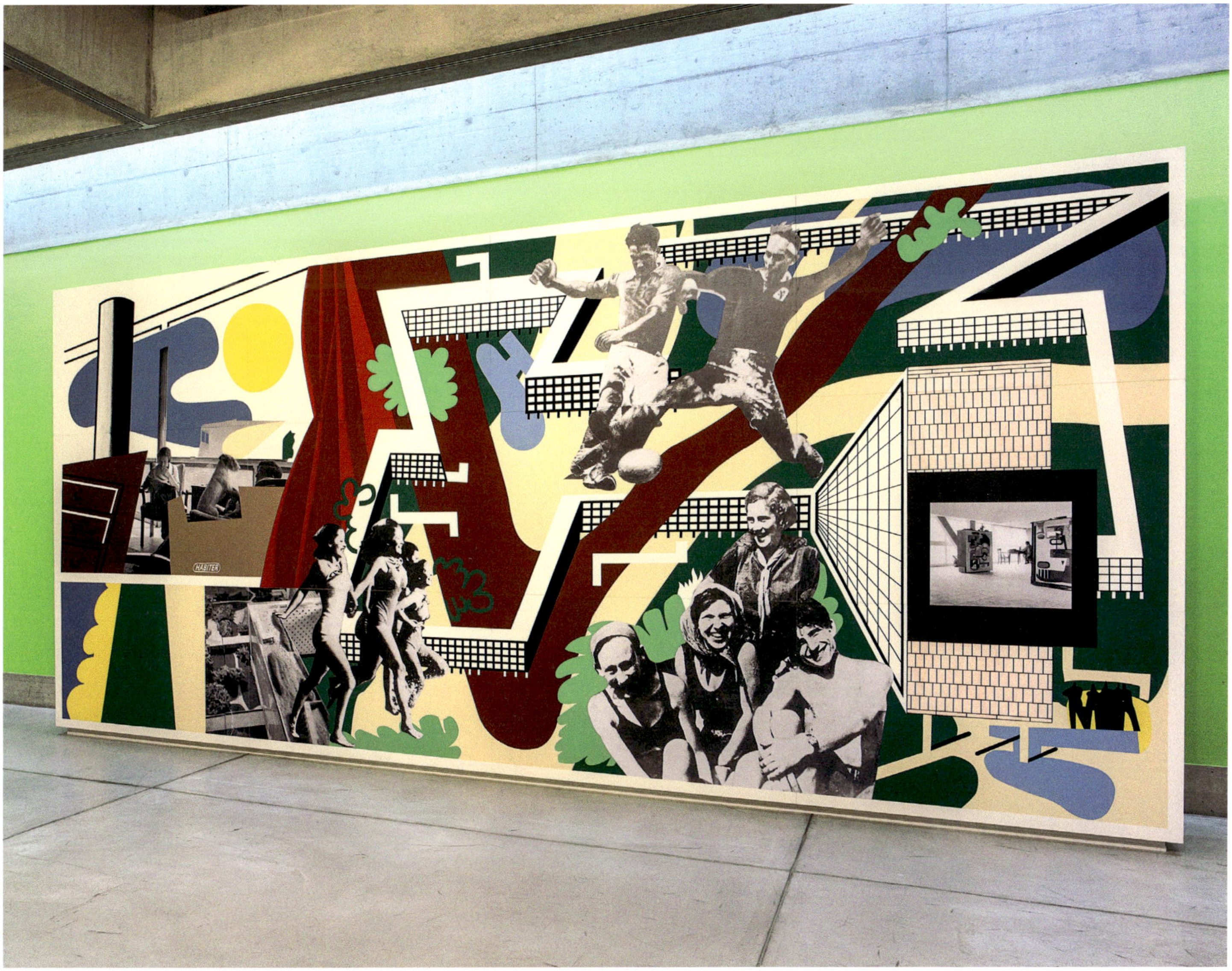

tion in Paris in 1937.[41] After the discipline of Cubism and Purism, a more expressive approach to painting had become generally accepted in Parisian art circles. And, as Raynal had indicated, Le Corbusier's work was becoming increasingly personal at the same time that it began to receive wider public attention. His decision to paint mural paintings in 1935–1936 came at a decisive moment, both in his growing need for recognition as a painter and as a means of expressing his most intimate feelings.

Le Corbusier, *Habiter* (Living), photocollage, Pavillon des Temps Nouveaux, Paris, 1937 (reconstruction Arthur Rüegg, 2019).

41 The World Exhibition Exposition Internationale des Arts et Techniques dans la Vie Moderne was held from 25 May to 25 November 1937 in Paris. Both the Palais de Chaillot and the Palais de Tokyo were created for this exhibition.

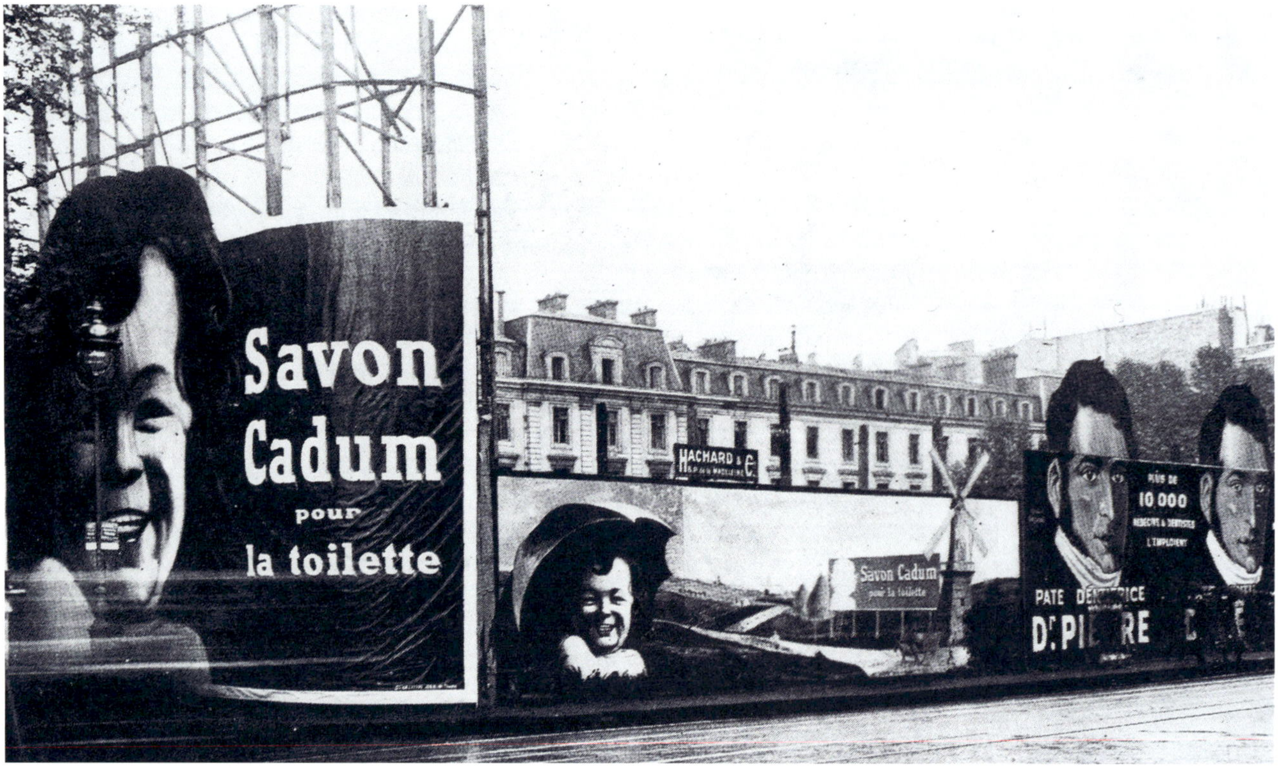

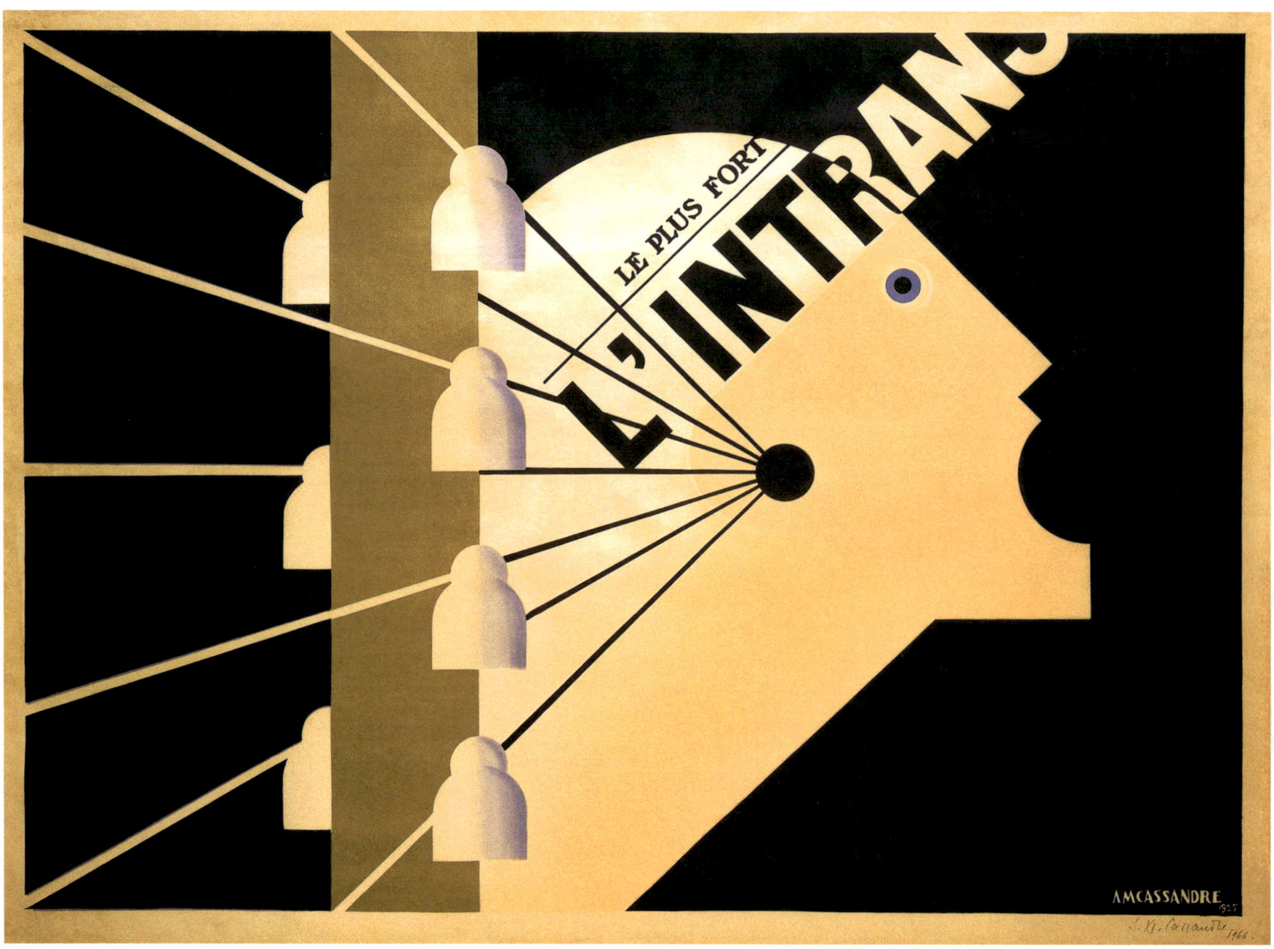

Advertisement for Bébé Cadum soap, Paris.

A. M. Cassandre, Poster *Le plus fort: L'Intransigeant*, 1925.

The Pavillon des Temps Nouveaux

To add to his frustrations, in 1937, in order to participate in the International Exhibition in Paris, Le Corbusier was obliged to join the group 'Jeunes 1937' (Youth 1937). This was a group of leftist architects that had been promoting a politically engaged strategy for the exhibition since 1935. Several members of Le Corbusier's office in the Rue de Sèvres were leading members of this group, including André Masson, Jean Bossu, Charlotte Perriand and even Le Corbusier's cousin Pierre Jeanneret.[42] Recalling this difficult period in 1940, Le Corbusier wrote:

> *In 1935, as* La Ville Radieuse *was being published – a book that was a decisive moment in my life – Charlotte Perriand tried to group together my young people and set them against me in order to publish a book 'anti* Ville Radieuse' *(Sert, Weissmann, Bossu, Beaugé, later Pellak etc.).*[43] *Pierre did not take my side but followed this movement. [...] Bossu wrote me a letter full of incredible insults. I showed this letter to Pierre and Charlotte. They did not share my astonishment.*[44]

Bossu's letter did indeed go beyond a political commentary to attack Le Corbusier in person:

> *I am indignant and astounded by your behaviour which is taking on the instinctive reflexes of an animal and I believe that I am not sufficiently brutal and cruel to serve the cause of truth. [...] My dear Corbu, you have missed out on something in your life, you have forgotten that a man's faith can only be built on generosity. [...] Why this bitterness, this disgust for anything alive and developing, anything that responds to natural forces? [...] You are always saying that you never engage with politics, but it's precisely then that you do. Your whole life has consisted of manoeuvres based on politics.*[45]

Le Corbusier understandably took this as a personal attack. 'In 36-37, Pav.T.Nx [the Temps Nouveau Pavilion at the 1938 International Exhibition], it was a battle against me, a real betrayal at a time when I was so seriously ill and loaded with such a responsibility.'[46]

---

42 Udovicki-Selb, D. (1997). 'Le Corbusier and the Paris Exhibition of 1937: the Temps Nouveaux Pavilion', *JSAH*, 56(1), pp. 42–63. See also J. Barsac (2005). *Charlotte Perriand: un art d'habiter, 1903–1959*, Paris, Norma, pp. 140–144.

43 This book eventually emerged as Sert, J. L. (1942). *Can Our Cities Survive? An A.B.C. of Urban Problems, Their Analysis, Their Solutions, Based on the Proposals Formulated by the Congrès Internationaux d'Architecture Moderne*, Cambridge, Mass., Harvard Univ. Press.

44 Collection Jornod. See J.-P. Jornod and N. Jornod (2005). *Le Corbusier: L'œuvre peint*, op. cit., annexe 1.12, pp. 1038–1042, note 23.

45 Georges Blanchon archives, cited in J. Barsac (2005). *Charlotte Perriand: un art d'habiter*, op. cit., p. 173, note 33. Le Corbusier's movement to the right during the 1930s has been much debated. The book by François Chaslin (2015). *Un Corbusier*, Paris: Seuil, has been challenged by several scholars. See R. Baudoui, ed. (2020). *Le Corbusier 1930–2020: polémiques, mémoire et histoire*, Paris, Tallandier.

46 Collection Jornod. See J.-P. and N. Jornod (2005). *Le Corbusier: L'œuvre peint*, op. cit., annexe 1.12, pp. 1038–1042, note 23. Le Corbusier was indeed ill in 1937 and spent several weeks in Brittany in July to recover.

PL. 9

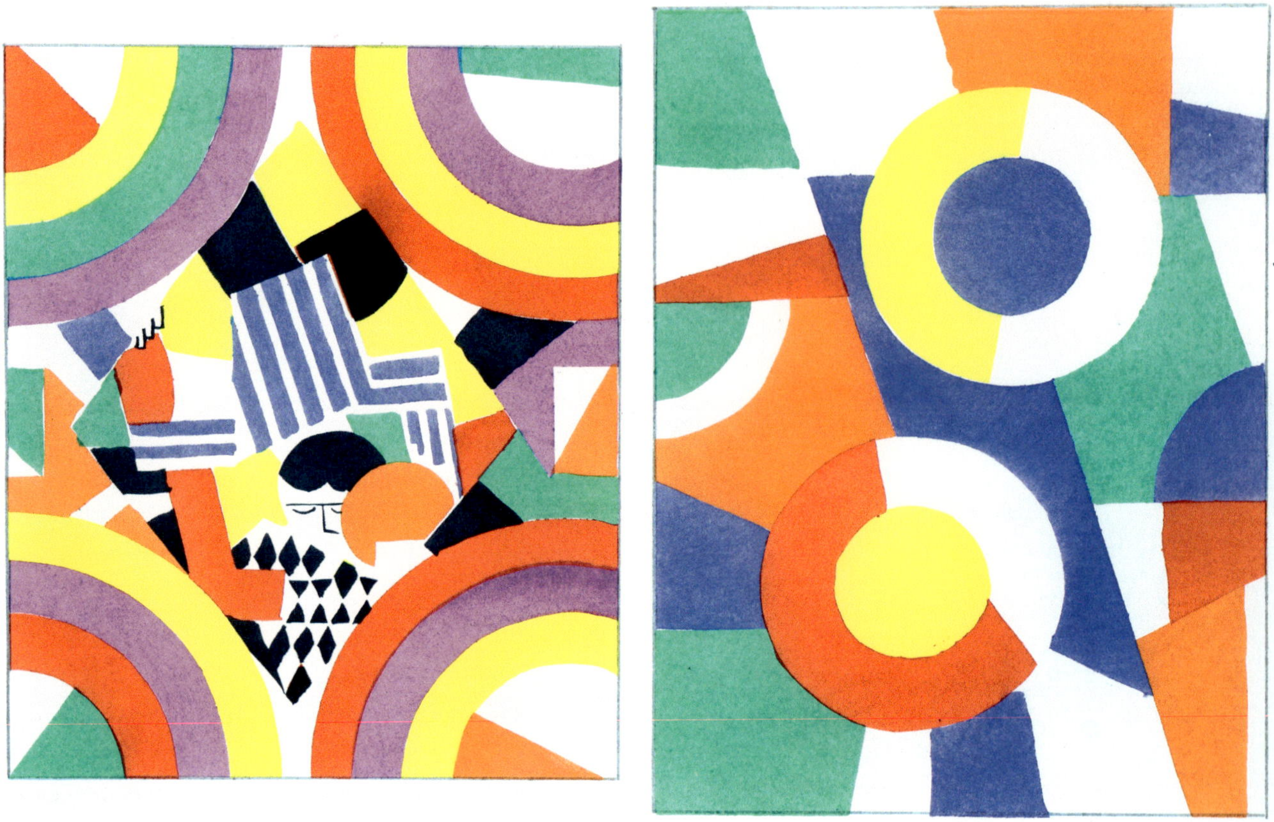

Fernand Léger, Decorative project for a music hall and project for an exterior fresco for a hotel, *L'Architecture Vivante*, autumn 1924.

Le Corbusier had plenty of experience of conflict with the authorities or with political movements, whether on the right or left. He had used these disputes to establish his credentials as prophet and martyr. But this conflict in the heart of his own studio affected him in a different way. He was particularly unsettled by the silence that developed between himself and Pierre:

> *From 1933 or 1932, Pierre abandoned almost completely his friendly relations with Yv (Yvonne) and myself – a striking contrast with the situation before. Politics came between us. [...] Pierre is a violent, introverted man, stubborn with a weak character. He has not been able to control his private life, make decisions or set limits to the possible. He has been overwhelmed.*[47]

Despite this discord, the Temps Nouveaux pavilion, designed by Le Corbusier and his assistants, was one of the successes of the exhibition. This was in part due to the gigantic murals and photocollages intended to stimulate political debate. Le Corbusier contributed a giant mural collage called *Habiter* (Living) |ill. p. 33| that juxtaposed photographs of happy people playing sport with images of his studio and an apartment in the building he had just designed in Boulogne-sur-Seine. The backdrop is a version of the *Ville Radieuse*, the radiant city, where long blocks of apartments are deployed around green

47 Collection Jornod, ibid.

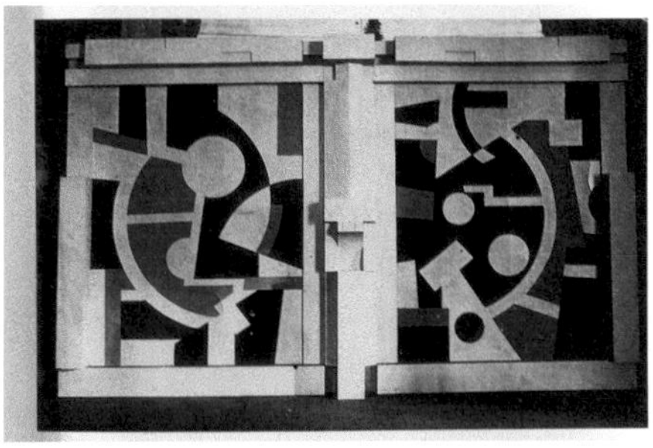

Fernand Léger and József Csáky, Project for a hall, Salon des Indépendants, 10 February–11 March 1923.

spaces and playing fields.[48] In this mural, Le Corbusier followed the practice of Fernand Léger in combining photocollage with a flat painted background that did not disrupt the plane of the wall.

Mural painting

Mural paintings, like all public art, raised the issue of popular taste and comprehension. Following the theory of the Realist movement in the 1870s and 1880s, artists should depict subjects of social concern in such a way that everyone could understand and be motivated by them. In the early days of the Russian Revolution, many artists abandoned easel painting for public works, from the propaganda trains (steam trains that toured across the USSR) of the *Proletkult* to street pageants (theatrical propaganda plays in which hundreds and sometimes thousands of workers staged heroic moments from the history of the revolution) and the design of clothing and furniture. As the communist regime developed, and especially in the 1930s, the doctrine of Socialist Realism was developed, requiring artists to address the widest possible audience with stimulating and encouraging paintings which conformed to a political agenda and employed traditional styles. Mural art played an essential role in this process and many artists tending towards communism felt challenged by the Soviet example to create a viable alternative which might inspire the working class without abandoning the principles of modern art. The example of Picasso has been much discussed in this context, and his mural *Guernica* at the Spanish Republican pavilion in 1937 was seen by some as a triumphant example of how to combine a powerful message of political protest with an eminently modern form of expression.[49]

Fernand Léger and Le Corbusier: a constructive dialogue

The problem for many modern artists was how to paint public murals that retained the avant-garde principles of their other work, even if this meant that they would be more difficult to understand for the general public. In 1913, Léger wrote of the 'social task to

48 Le Corbusier (1933). *La Ville Radieuse*, Boulogne, Éditions de l'Architecture d'Aujourd'hui. – Throughout the 1930s, Le Corbusier had developed the idea of a new, ideal city with a clear zoning of functions. Discussions at the Fourth CIAM meeting on board the *SS Patris* bound for Athens were incorporated in his book which in turn influenced the Athens Charter. The first English translation was published in 1967 under the title *The Radiant City: Elements of a Doctrine of Urbanism to be Used as the Basis of Our Machine-Age Civilization*, New York, Orion Press.

49 See R. Golan (2009). *Muralnomad: The Paradox of Wall Painting, Europe 1927–1957*, New Haven, Yale University Press, p. 62.

assist architecture in its popular expressiveness' but it wasn't clear to him how the 'decorative fresco could accomplish this'.[50]

Léger was untypical of many modern artists, since subject matter – that of the modern city – was very important to him. Le Corbusier and Ozenfant also claimed that their paintings represented the products of the machinist era – industrially produced bottles, glasses, carafes and plates.[51] But they were more concerned with achieving a disciplined and harmonious arrangement of forms than evoking the modern city. Fernand Léger defended the incorporation of modern imagery into art and the extension of art into contemporary forms of popular culture. The problem was how to make the necessary but difficult transition into the field of popular culture and public entertainment or, as Léger put it: 'the dangerous space [that is] difficult to cross' but 'must be crossed.'[52] Fernand Léger was quoted by Louis Chéronnet, a design critic, praising the posters of A. M. Cassandre, for their contribution to the 'spectacle of the street'.[53] To illustrate his point, Léger compared a poster for the soap firm Bébé Cadum with a Cassandre poster for the magazine *L'Intransigeant* |ill. p. 34|. Whereas the realistic imagery of the Bébé Cadum poster created a perspectival void in the wall, Cassandre's poster (1925), with its flat figurative space and geometric construction, contributed to the architectural values of the street. In this sense, Cassandre's poster was like a mural that affirmed the wall rather than destroying it.

Léger was tempted to try to intervene in an architectural project, and in 1923, he collaborated with the sculptor and interior designer József Csáky on a pair of doors for a hallway |ill. p. 37| which were exhibited as a full-scale mock-up at the Salon des Indépendants (10 February–11 March 1923).

Only a black and white image of this project remains, but we can form an idea of what Léger's design would have looked like from a number of sketches he did for mural paintings in this period, some of which were published by Jean Badovici in the autumn 1924 edition of *L'Architecture Vivante*. Léger's brightly coloured abstract forms were framed by a subtle relief frame designed by József Csáky |ill. p. 36|. The critic Waldemar George criticised this scheme in exactly the same terms which Léger later used to criticise the Bébé Cadum poster.[54] According to George, Léger's brightly coloured geometric forms would have destroyed the flat surface of the wall and this was exacerbated by Csáky's neo-Cubist frame.

---

50 Léger, F. (1913). 'The Origins of Painting and its Representational Value', cited in C. J. Green (1976). *Léger and the Avant-Garde*, New Haven, Yale University Press, p. 28, note 168.

51 Ozenfant, A. and C.-E. Jeanneret (1921). 'Le Purisme', *L'Esprit Nouveau*, 4, pp. 369–386.

52 Fernand Léger (1925). 'The Spectacle of Objects' in F. Léger (1965). *Fonctions de la peinture*, Paris, Gallimard. Published in English in 1973 as *Functions of Painting*, New York, Viking Press.

53 A quotation from an interview with Léger, cited in L. Chéronnet (1926). 'La publicité moderne: Fernand Léger et Robert Delaunay', *L'Art Vivant*, p. 800.

54 I gratefully acknowledge Anna Vallye for this insight: Vallye, A., et al. (2013). *Léger: Modern Art and the Metropolis*, Philadelphia, Philadelphia Museum of Art in association with Yale University Press, p. 28.

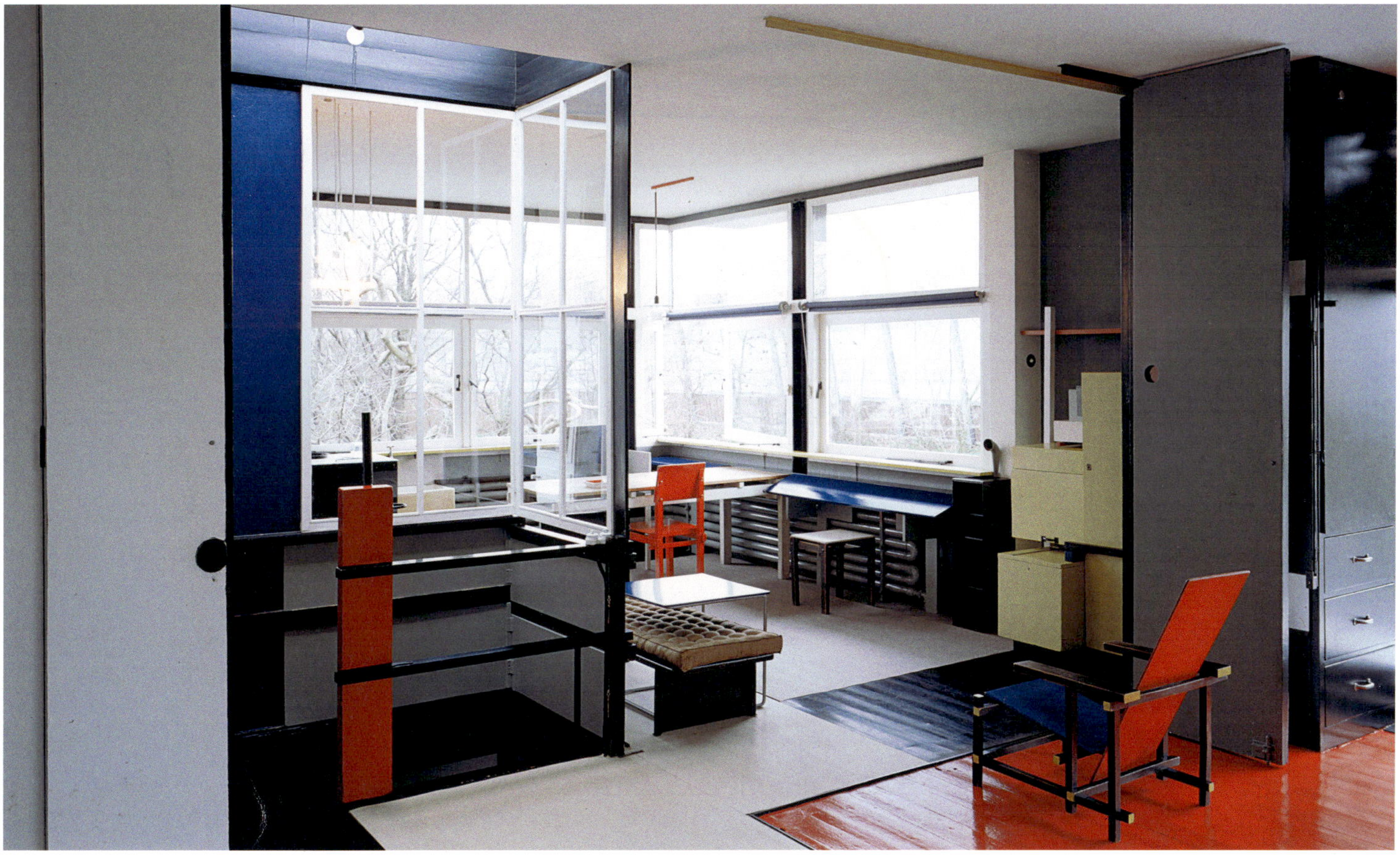

Gerrit Rietveld and Truust Schröder, Schröder House, Utrecht, 1923–1924.

In a dialogue with Léger, Le Corbusier also criticised this project, 'You accept, therefore, that coloured surfaces should remain intact or nearly so and that they should never be decorated in the way you attempted with Csáky at the last Salon des Indépendants.' To which Léger replied, 'I agree perfectly: that was an error. Walls must be left whole so that they become part of the [spatial] equation as entities.'[55] The key word in Le Corbusier's comment is 'decorated'. Modern architecture, for him, could not be decorated, and art that stooped to decoration was no longer art.[56]

Le Corbusier went on to point out that a work of coloured architecture would mean that the artist could not sign it. In other words, it would have become architecture. In a lecture in 1933, Léger took the opposite view. For him any work of polychromy belonged to the domain of the artist:

> *Architects, you would like to forget that artists have been brought into the world to destroy dead surfaces, to make them liveable and to avoid the too absolute solutions of architects.*[57]

55 Le Corbusier (1923). 'Salon d'automne; Architecture', *L'Esprit Nouveau*, No 19, December 1923, unpaginated.

56 These arguments were spelled out in detail in Le Corbusier's essays, published in *L'Esprit Nouveau* in 1924 and as a book in 1926: Le Corbusier (1926). *L'art décoratif d'aujourd'hui*, Paris, Éditions G. Crès et Cie.

57 Léger, F. (1933). 'Le mur, l'architecte, le peintre' in F. Léger (1965). *Fonctions de la peinture*, op. cit., p. 180. This lecture was given at the Kunsthaus in Zürich in May 1933 and again in the same year at the Fourth CIAM conference, in the presence of Le Corbusier.

He is claiming that artists could play a key role in mitigating the cold and brutal impact of modern architecture. It is notable that he refers to this as 'to destroy dead surfaces'. Only painters, he insists, have the skill to distribute colour in architecture.[58] He went on to propose an agreement between artist and architect:

> *'Mister painter', you would say in your haughty tone, 'I want here 3m50 × 1m25 of* living colours.' *'Fine, mister Architect', the artist would say modestly, 'that's what you'll get.' We have to create a three-way agreement: wall – architect – painter.*[59]

But Léger concluded by explaining that architects – and it was obvious that he was referring to Le Corbusier – did not want this agreement.

The revelation of de Stijl

This discussion had been given further relevance by the exhibition of the Dutch de Stijl group in Léonce Rosenberg's L'Effort Moderne gallery in October 1923.[60] The Dutch architect Cor Van Eesteren and the de Stijl artist Theo Van Doesburg had collaborated on an exhibition of paintings, architectural drawings and coloured architectural models. Le Corbusier strangely criticised the use of colour on exteriors, although he used some exterior colour in all of his buildings from the 1920s, sometimes discreetly as in the case of the Villas Stein-de Monzie or Savoye, or very explicitly in his housing estate at Pessac. But he was of the opinion that the de Stijl experiments with colour in the interior were worth studying closely. His polychrome treatment of the Villa Cook was an example |ill. p. 43|. But the discussion is still one of pure coloured architecture or pure easel painting. As Le Corbusier put it, Léger's art was profoundly influenced by architecture, the city and the place of colour in both. But he went on: 'This painting is sister to architecture. There lies its import. But it remains, profoundly, painting.'[61]

Two people on whom the de Stijl exhibition had a lasting effect were Jean Badovici and Eileen Gray. The respect was mutual. Gray's display at the Salon des Artistes Décorateurs in 1923 – the so-called Monte Carlo apartment – was much admired in Holland.[62] Badovici published the work of the de Stijl group in Holland and he and Gray went to visit their work, including the recently completed Schröder house by Gerrit Rietveld and Truus Schröder in Utrecht

---

58 'You would like to deploy colour yourselves. Allow me to remind you that in a period such as ours, where everything is specialised, it is an error on your part.' Ibid, p. 182.

59 Ibid.

60 Bois, Y.-A. and B. Reichlin (1985). *De Stijl et L'architecture en France*, Brussels, Mardaga.

61 Le Corbusier (1929). 'L'Architecture et Fernand Léger', in 'Fernand Léger', *Sélection. Chronique de la vie artistique*, cahier 5, Antwerp, February 1929, pp. 21–24.

62 The Monte Carlo suite was published in *Bouwkundig Weekblad* in 1923 and in the prestigious journal *Wendingen* in 1924, with an article by Jean Badovici and an introduction by the de Stijl architect Jan Wils. J. J. P. Oud wrote Gray a postcard praising her work, see P. Adam (2000). *Eileen Gray: Architect/Designer. A Biography*, op. cit, pp. 163–169.

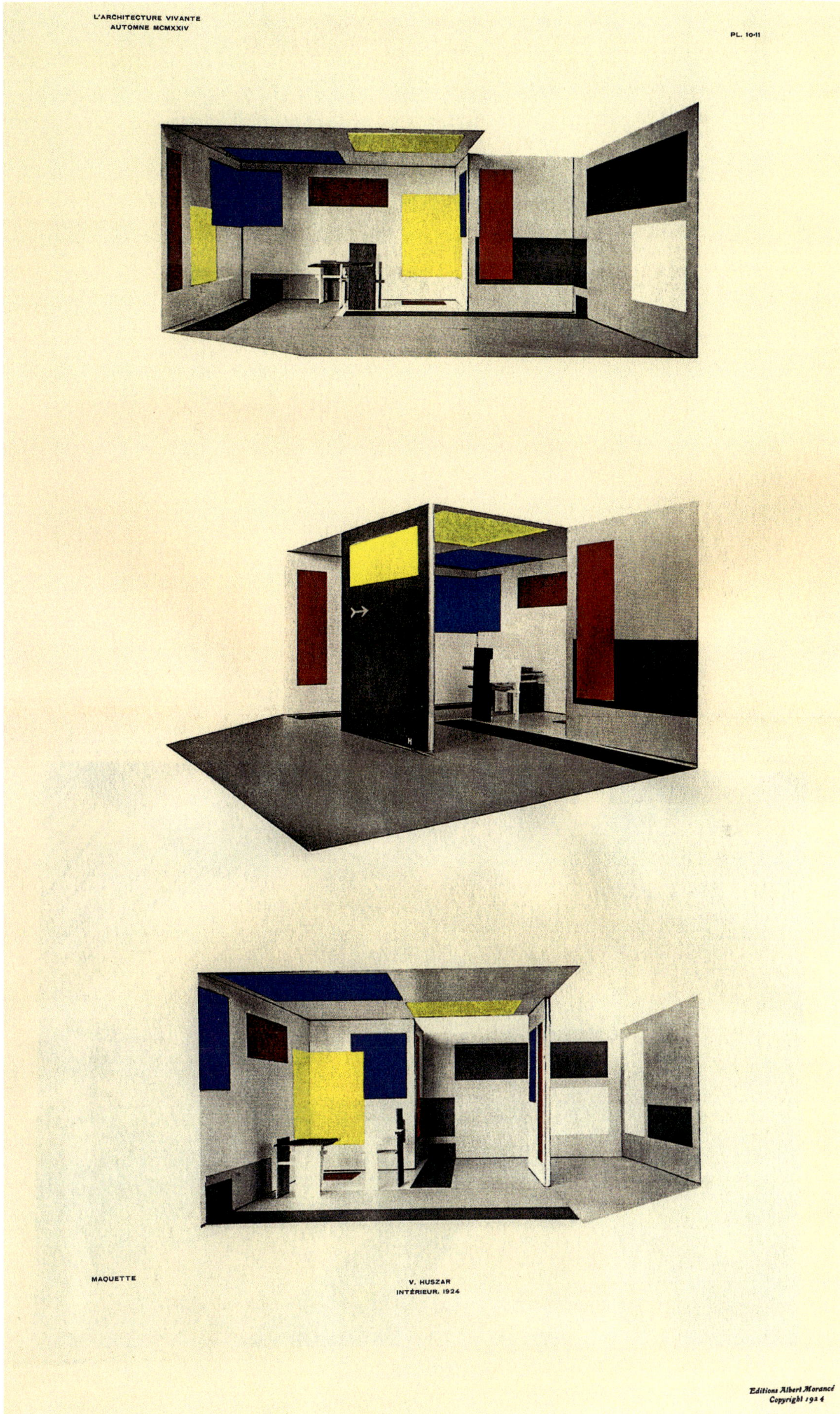

Vilmos Huszár and Gerrit Rietveld, interior shown at Greater Berlin exhibition, 1923.

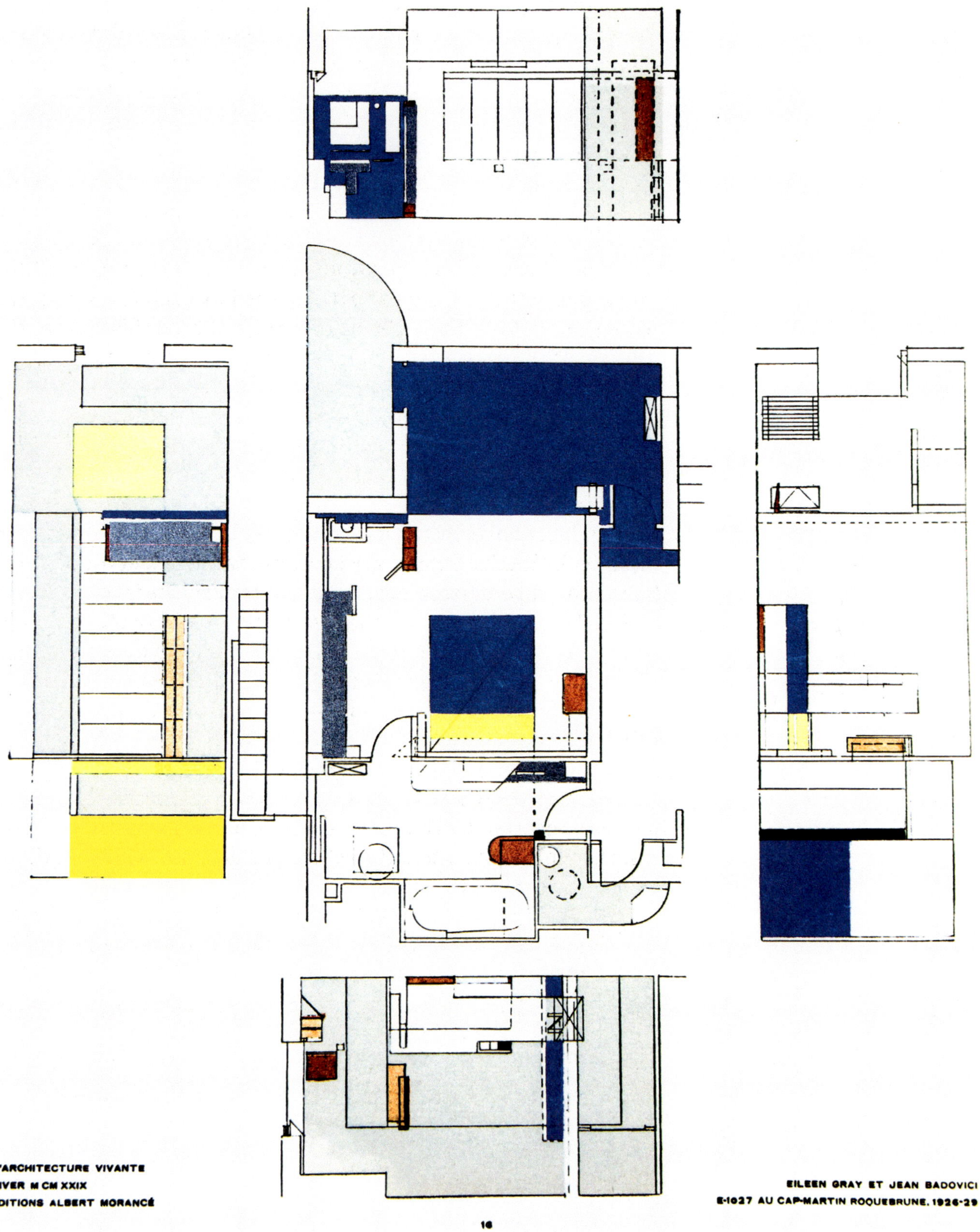

Eileen Gray and Jean Badovici, plan and elevations of the master bedroom, E1027, *L'Architecture Vivante*, 1929.

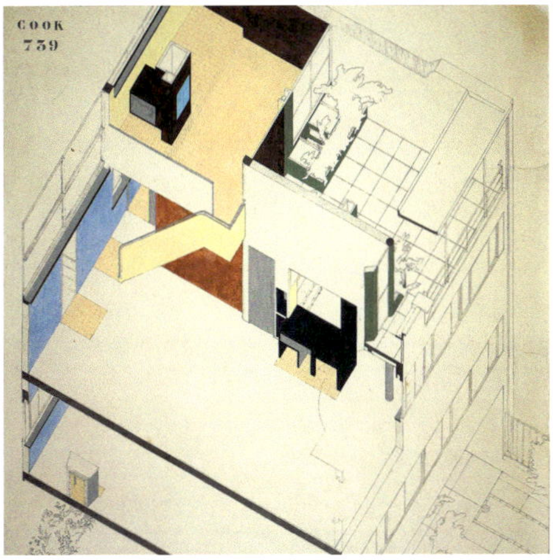

Le Corbusier and Pierre Jeanneret, axonometric study of Villa Cook, Boulogne-sur-Seine, 1928.

(1923–1924) |ill. p. 39|, which had been represented in the Léonce Rosenberg exhibition in model form. They also visited Berlin where they may have seen the room designed by Vilmos Huszár and Gerrit Rietveld for the Greater Berlin exhibition of 1923 |ill. p. 41|. At any rate, the interior was published in colour by Badovici in 1924 in *L'Architecture Vivante.*

But if Van Doesburg and Van Eesteren, Vilmos Huszár and Gerrit Rietveld experimented with the marriage of painting and architecture, Piet Mondrian had quite a different opinion: 'Even if art is indivisible, the expressive possibilities of each of the arts are different. These possibilities have to be discovered by each art within the limits of their field.'[63] Le Corbusier normally shared this view of the separation of the arts into distinct disciplines, which makes his desire to take over the role of architectural colourist more surprising.

Eileen Gray was trying to learn about architecture from Badovici and took lessons in architectural draughtsmanship from his friend Adrienne Gorska. A schematic model of an architectural design by her was included in the *Wendingen* article about her work. Gray was clearly interested in the use of abstract colour planes as a means of articulating interior spaces because when she and Badovici published the special issue of *L'Architecture Vivante* in 1929 dedicated to E1027, they used a *pochoir* technique to add planes of colour to the walls, floors and ceilings in imitation of the de Stijl movement. Furthermore, recent archaeological research has uncovered an abstract polychromatic treatment on the north wall of the living room of E1027 |ill. p. 44 and 45|[64]. This was beholden to de Stijl in its general principles, but not in the colours used. Instead of the red, yellow and blue of the de Stijl canon, she picked from her own range of colours, inspired by the red-brown colour of the earth at Cap-Martin, the blue of the sea and a yellow perhaps derived from the stonework of the terraces.

By the time that the special issue of *L'Architecture Vivante* was published in 1929, the walls of the living room had been painted white or off-white and the polychrome treatment covered over. The parts of the floor in the master bedroom coloured blue in the plan were carried out in black tiles. Similar planes of black or grey were inscribed in the tiling of the salon, in other rooms and on the terrace in the garden as an indication of different spheres of activity.

63 Mondrian, P. (1917). 'Neo-Plasticism in Painting', *de Stijl*, 1, 1, p. 6.

64 Pierre-Antoine Gatier discovered traces of colour on the north wall of the living room and reconstructed a polychrome treatment in brown, blue, yellow and pink in 2010. In the subsequent restoration campaign (2015-2022), it was decided to paint over this polychrome treatment in order to restore the effect as reproduced in the photographs of 1929.

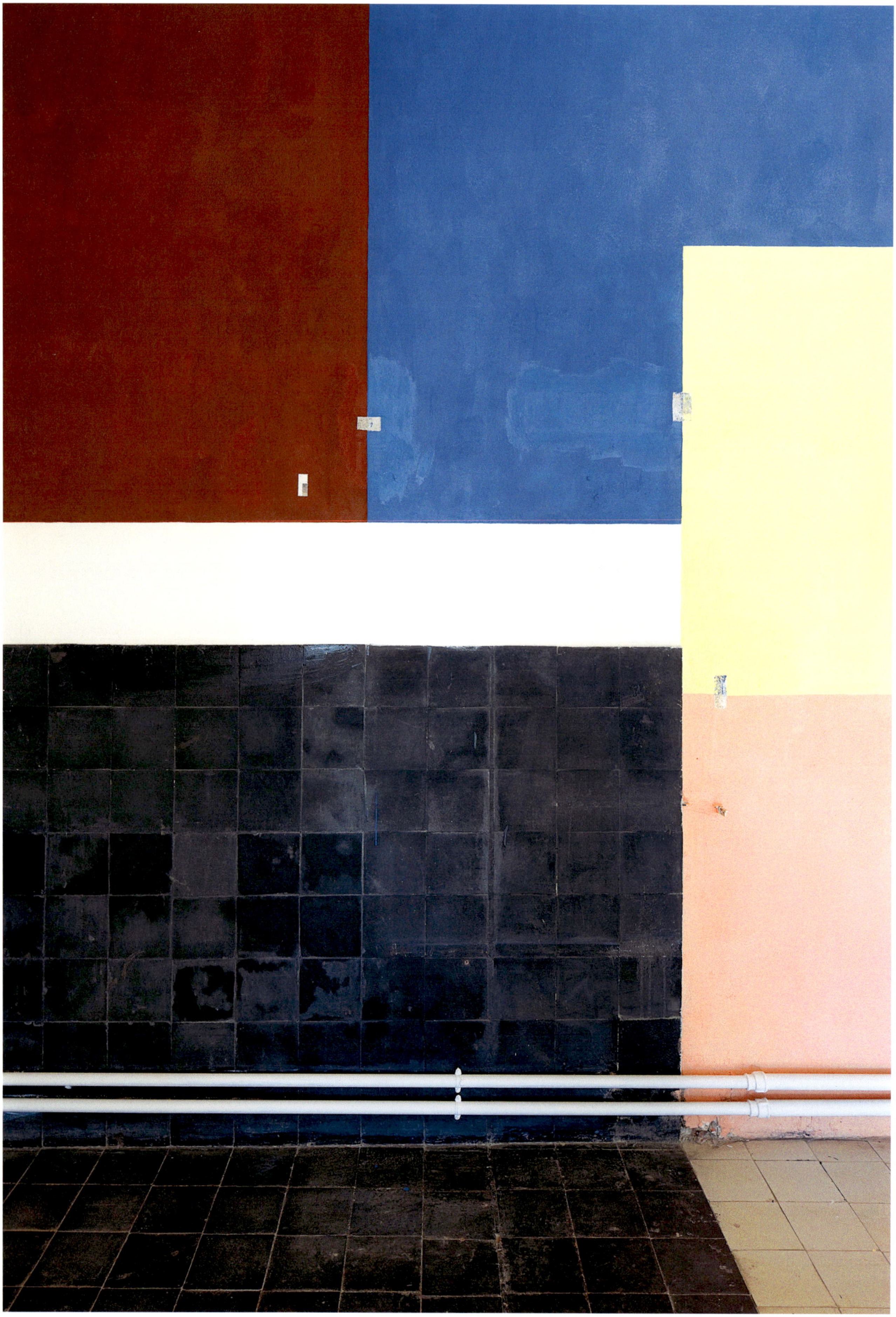

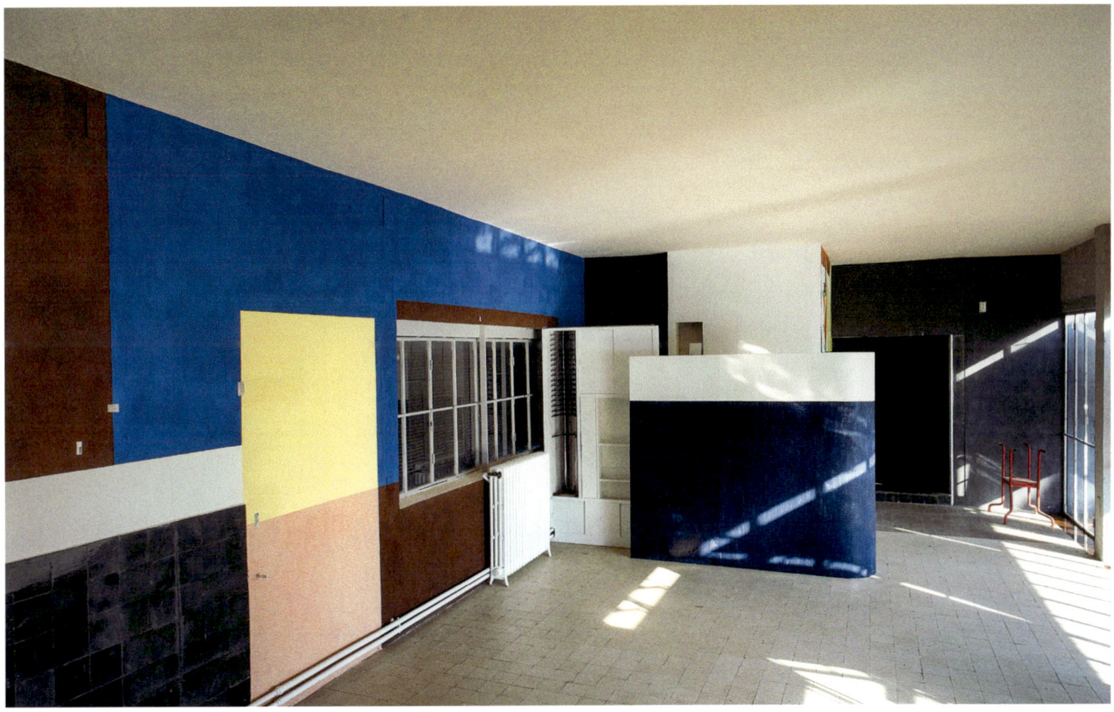

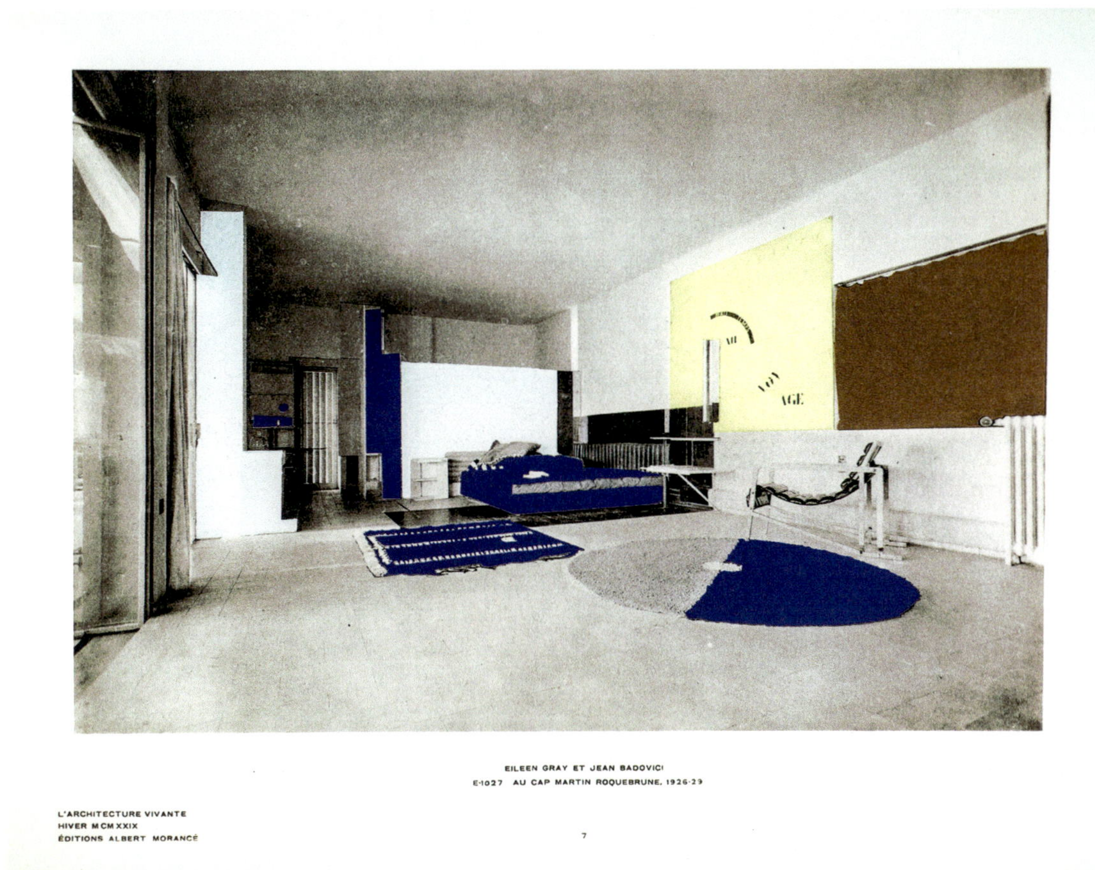

EILEEN GRAY ET JEAN BADOVICI
E-1027 AU CAP MARTIN ROQUEBRUNE. 1926-29

L'ARCHITECTURE VIVANTE
HIVER MCMXXIX
ÉDITIONS ALBERT MORANCÉ

7

Detail of the north wall of the living room in E1027.

North wall of the living room in E1027 showing the polychrome treatment of the wall by Eileen Gray and Jean Badovici reconstructed by architect Pierre-Antoine Gatier, during his restoration of the villa (2006–2010; photo 2012).

Eileen Gray and Jean Badovici, photograph of the living room in E1027, overlaid with *pochoir* colour scheme, *L'Architecture Vivante*, 1929.

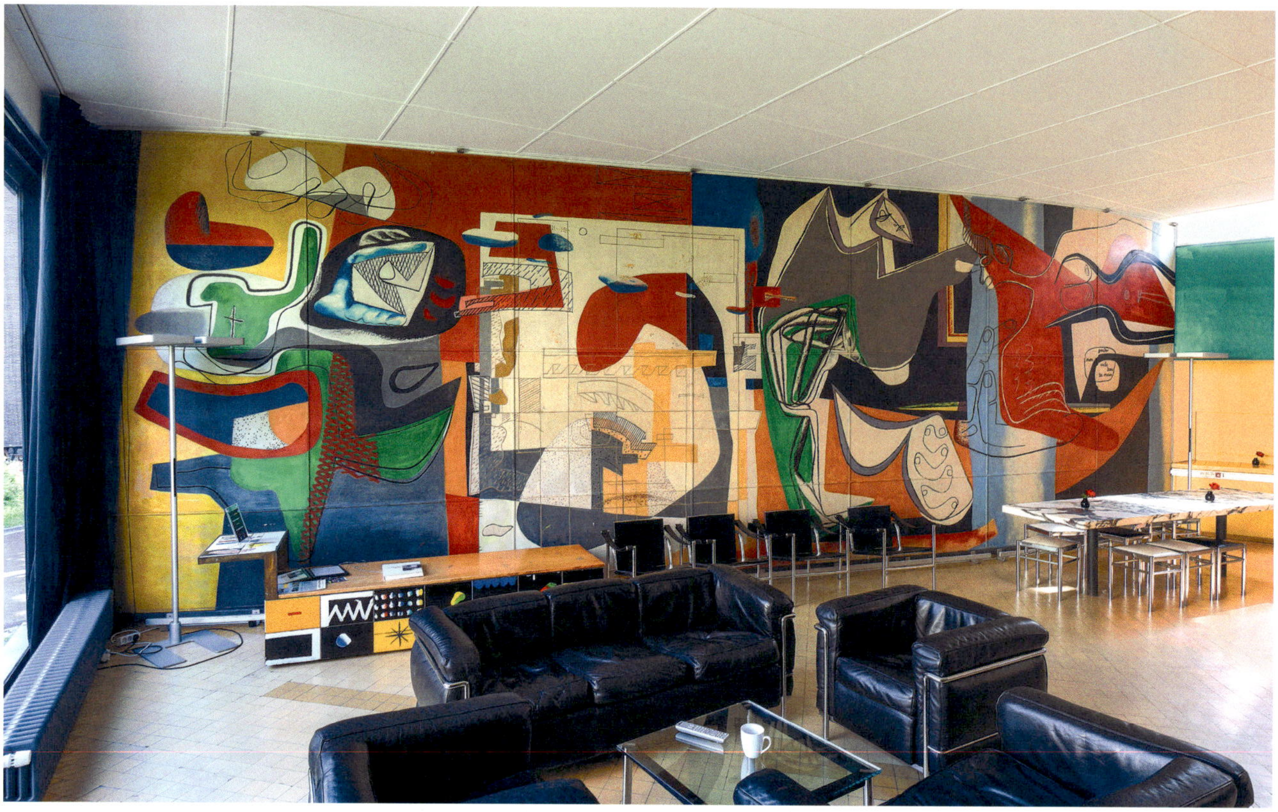

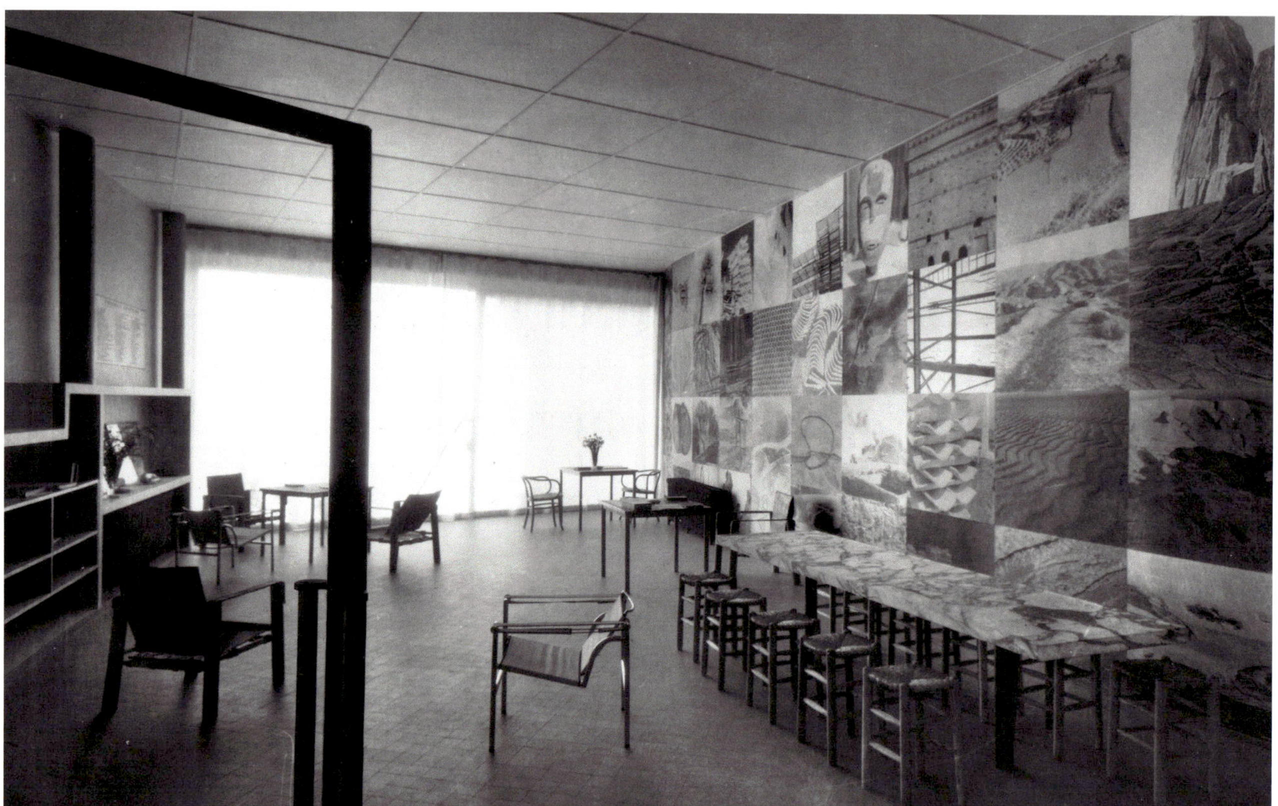

Le Corbusier, mural in the Swiss Pavilion, 1948.

Le Corbusier and Pierre Jeanneret, common room of the Swiss Pavilion, Cité Universitaire, Paris, showing the photomural of 1933.

Mural art as propaganda

The 1930s was a great period for mural artists, from the Social Realists in Russia to the wide range of artists who worked for the fascist regime in Italy. The mural had become a key vehicle of propaganda. At the same time, in the 'democratic' countries, a taste for mural painting was fostered by the large expanses of wall offered up both by modern architecture and by the dominant style of stripped classicism. The International Exposition of 1937 was a riot of mural decoration, from socialist and communist photo-murals to the decorative treatments derived from the Art Déco tradition of the 1920s. Le Corbusier's Pavillon des Temps Nouveaux was no exception, hammering home a message of social reform and urban renewal with large collaged murals |ill. p. 33|.

Le Corbusier was invited to give a lecture at a prestigious conference, the Sixth Convegno Volta in Rome, in October 1936. The theme of the conference, 'Relationships between Architecture and the Figurative Arts', was of particular interest in Fascist Italy, where the propaganda role of sculptural reliefs and mural paintings was taken very seriously. Le Corbusier's intervention was to once again reject any large-scale figurative painting in works of architecture, calling on the architect's deployment of polychromy, aided by the palette of coloured wallpapers which he had recently designed for the Swiss manufacturer Salubra, as the only remedy.[65] Only the architect could achieve this:

> *[the artist] disqualifies the wall, blows it up, makes it explode, taking away its very existence. [...] Architectural polychromy does not kill the walls, it shifts them around in space and reorders them in terms of importance.*[66]

And in an article published in *L'Architecture d'Aujourd'hui* in 1935, he again asserted the autonomy of architecture: 'Architecture by itself supports total lyricism. Architecture alone can express a whole idea.'[67]

But he went on to suggest that a collaboration with painting and sculpture might be possible. However, this collaboration required tact. Both the architecture and the work of art must be respected:

> *The work of art is a presence. The work of art is exactly like the presence of a host in a house. You have to listen to him. It may give you immense pleasure to listen to him.*[68]

---

65 An overview of Le Corbusier's work for Salubra can be found in A. Rüegg, ed. (2016). *Le Corbusier. Polychromie architecturale. Color Keyboards from 1931 and 1959* (sec., revised edition), Basel, Birkhäuser.

66 Le Corbusier (1936). 'Les tendances de l'architecture rationaliste en rapport avec la collaboration de la peinture et la sculpture', *Convegno di arti*, pp. 107–119. Cited in R. Golan, (2009). *Muralnomad: The Paradox of Wall Painting*, op. cit., p. 62.

67 Le Corbusier (1 July 1935). 'Sainte alliance des arts majeurs, ou le grand art en gésine', *La bête noir*, Paris.

68 Ibid.

Although Le Corbusier was still thinking primarily of works of art – easel painting – he may already have been thinking about the tapestries and mural paintings which he would begin to design next year. Gradually, his ideas about large-scale painting evolved.[69]
Here, it is worth noting the intervention that Le Corbusier and Pierre Jeanneret made on the curved wall of the Swiss Pavilion in the Cité Universitaire in Paris in 1933. Instead of mural painting, they turned to photomontage |ill. p. 46|. This work responded to the popularity of this technique at the time, but also to Le Corbusier's newfound interest in natural forms. The photomontage, which covered the whole wall, presented two advantages: it did not create a 'hole' in the wall and, due to the subject-matter, avoided any criticism of being 'decorative'. Indeed, the *Gazette de Lausanne* accused the architects of materialism (implying communism) and an act of propaganda leading to 'corruption of minors'.[70] Le Corbusier gleefully reproduced this article, published on 28 December 1933, in the second volume of his *Œuvre complète* in 1937. The photomural was damaged during the war and Le Corbusier replaced it with a mural based on four of his paintings, in 1948.

Medieval art: model for mural painting?

In 1929, Le Corbusier suggested that figurative fresco painting might have a role in architecture. In a text praising Léger's discovery of a new idiom in the machines of modern life and the spectacle of the street, Le Corbusier dropped a tantalising hint:

> *This is a new art [Léger's work]. And this art existed once before, when painting was near to architecture – masterful, correct and magnificent play of forms brought together in light: masterful and magnificent play of coloured forces moving on the surface of a wall.*[71]

This seems to be a reference to the fresco and mosaic cycles which the young Le Corbusier had sketched and described in his first trips to Italy in 1907 and 1911. He admired the medieval frescoes of the Campo Santo in Pisa, the work of Giotto and his assistants in Santa Croce Florence and, above all, the work of Orcagna in Orsanmichele.

---

69 Arnoldo Rivkin traces the progression of Le Corbusier's ideas about the synthesis of the arts. See A. Rivkin (1987). 'Synthèse des Arts; un double paradoxe', in J. Lucan (ed.), *Le Corbusier une encyclopedie*, Paris, Centre Georges Pompidou, pp. 286–291.

70 Le Corbusier (1937). *Le Corbusier et Pierre Jeanneret Œuvre Complète 1929–1934*, Zürich, H. Girsberger, p. 76. Reprint (1995) Willy Boesiger (ed.), *Le Corbusier Œuvre Complète. Volume 2 1929–34*, Basel, Birkhäuser.

71 Le Corbusier (1929). 'L'Architecture et Fernand Léger', in 'Fernand Léger', *Sélection. Chronique de la vie artistique*, op. cit., pp. 21–24.

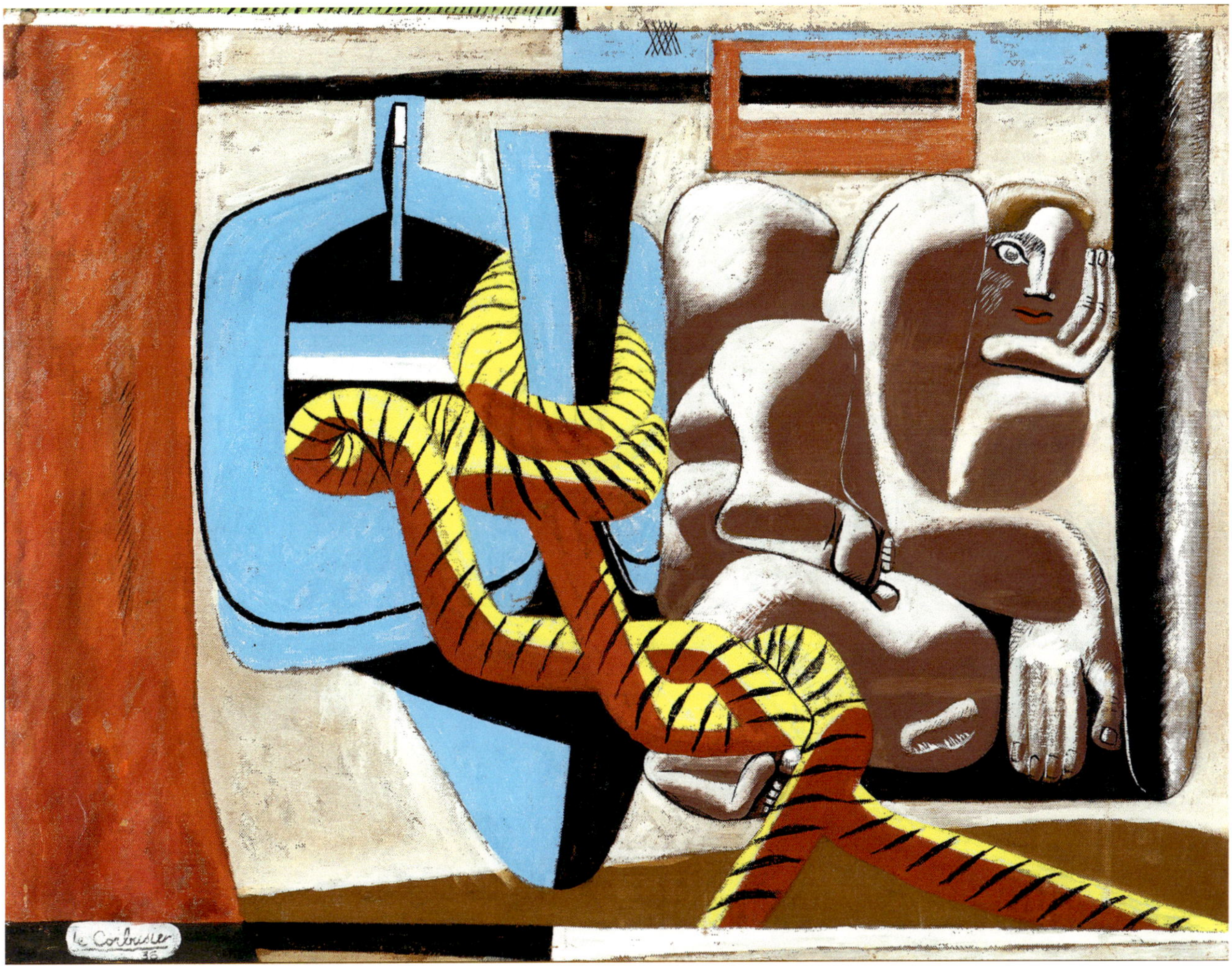

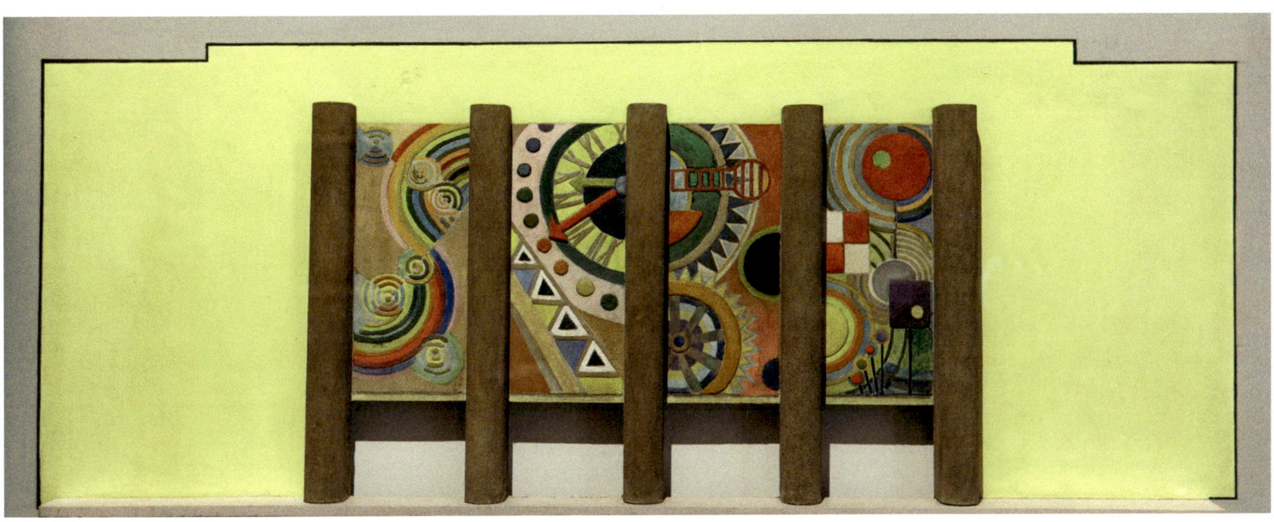

Le Corbusier, cartoon for the Marie Cuttoli tapestry, 1935.

Robert Delaunay, study for the side wall of the Railways Pavilion at the International exhibition, Paris, 1937.

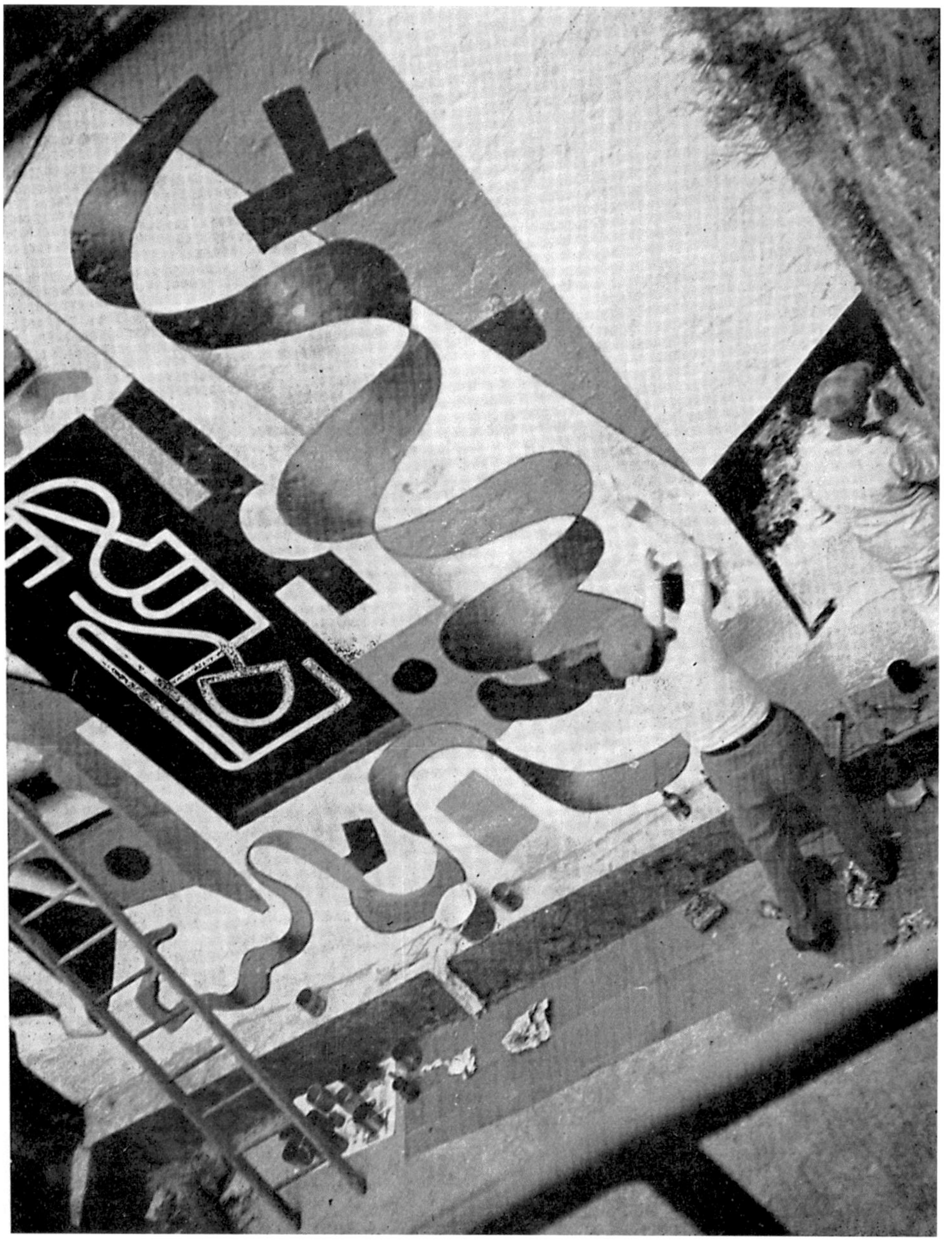

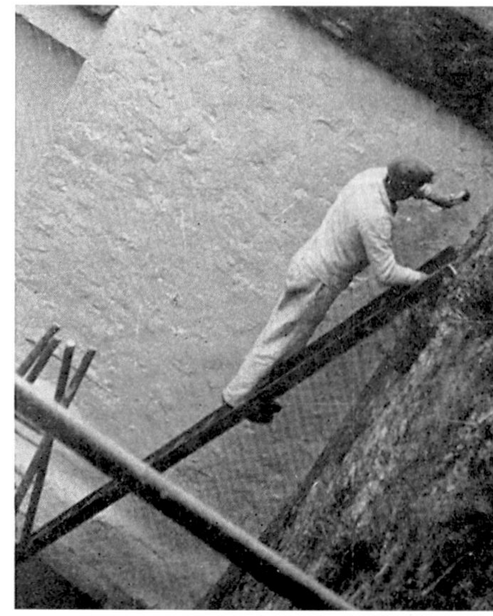

Fernand Léger working on his mural in the courtyard of Badovici's house in Vézelay, published in Badovici's article 'Peinture murale ou peinture spatiale', *L'Architecture d'Aujourd'hui*, March 1937.

Fernand Léger at work published in Badovici's article 'Peinture murale ou peinture spatiale', *L'Architecture d'Aujourd'hui*, March 1937.

Le Corbusier, sequence of 16 mm film images shot between 30 October and 4 November 1936 of Léger's mural in Badovoci's house at Vézelay, painted the year before.

Le Corbusier's continuing interest in Romanesque frescoes is revealed in a letter to Yvonne on 27 March 1932, at the end of a busy trip to Mallorca and Barcelona:

> *So, this morning I finally visited the frescoes in the Catalan museum. These paintings knocked me out. This is what I am looking for. Mediterranean antiquity: it leads to our work. I am picking up confidence again.*[72]

Although it was probably the graphic abstractions used in Catalan painting that interested him, the theme of large-scale mural painting was also relevant. These paintings, painstakingly removed from churches in Catalonia, had just been installed in the National Museum in Barcelona in settings which reproduced the walls and vaults on which they had been painted. The curators of the Musée des Monuments Historiques in Paris followed this development closely and began a campaign of faithful copies of medieval French paintings, which were installed in the Trocadero.[73] In 1937, a fresco museum was installed in the recently constructed Palais de Chaillot and, as in Barcelona, whole sections of the churches where these frescoes originated were reproduced in three dimensions. The point was to differentiate mural painting – as an art of three-dimensional space – from easel painting.

Renaissance art: a model for a total work of art?

Le Corbusier also began to become interested in Renaissance frescoes. On 27 July 1939, writing to his South African friend, the architect Rex Martienssen, he recalled a conversation that he had had in 1936 with Bertie Landsberg on the ocean liner *Conte Biancamano*. Landsberg was the owner of Palladio's Villa Foscari ('La Malcontenta', 1558–1560), with its frescoes by Battista Franco and Giambattista Zelotti. Le Corbusier suggested to Martienssen that he and his friends could design a modern version of the villa:

> *I told him [Landsberg]: it would be possible for anyone with a reasonable sum of money to build a villa in the spirit of the Renaissance villas of Palladio, with me as architect and my friends as painters and sculptors. The aim would be to create the most perfect imaginable work. The owner could even live in another house nearby but he would have a kind of twentieth century jewel which would be famous worldwide. It would allow those of my generation (the over-50s)*

---

72 Letter from Le Corbusier to Yvonne, 27 March 1932 (FLC R1(12)356-358).
73 Golan, R. (2009). *Muralnomad: The Paradox of Wall Painting*, op. cit., pp. 74–77, note 38.

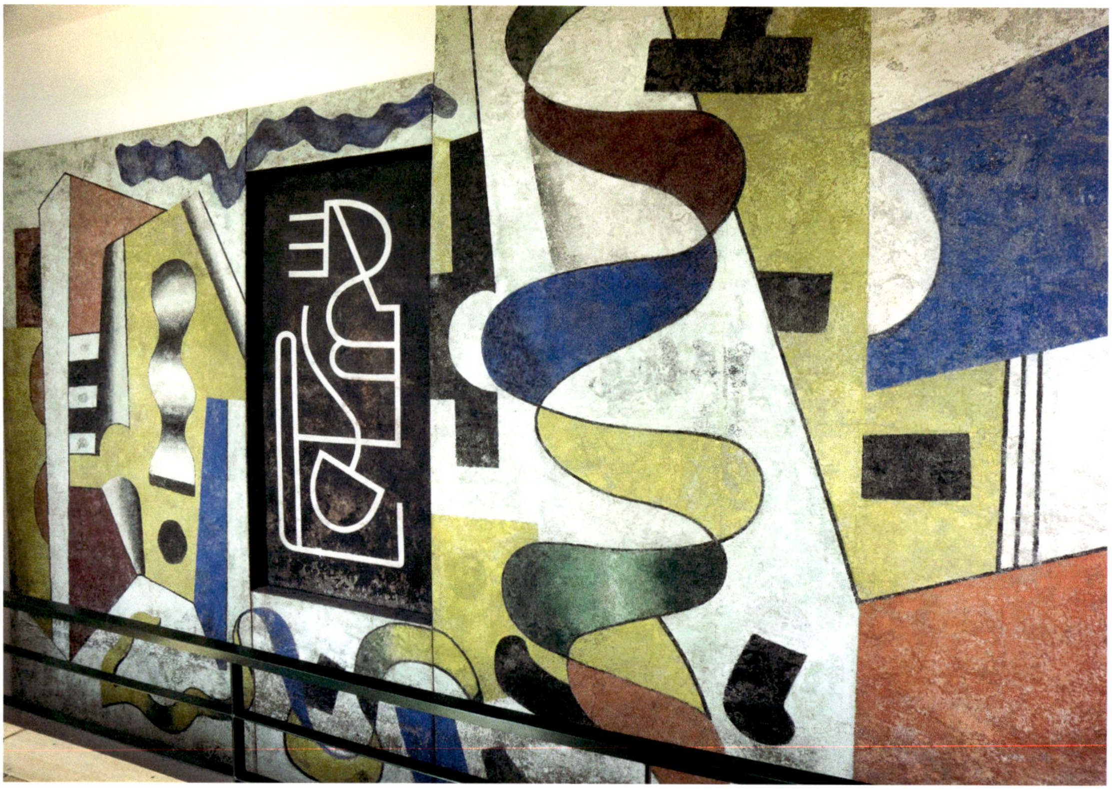

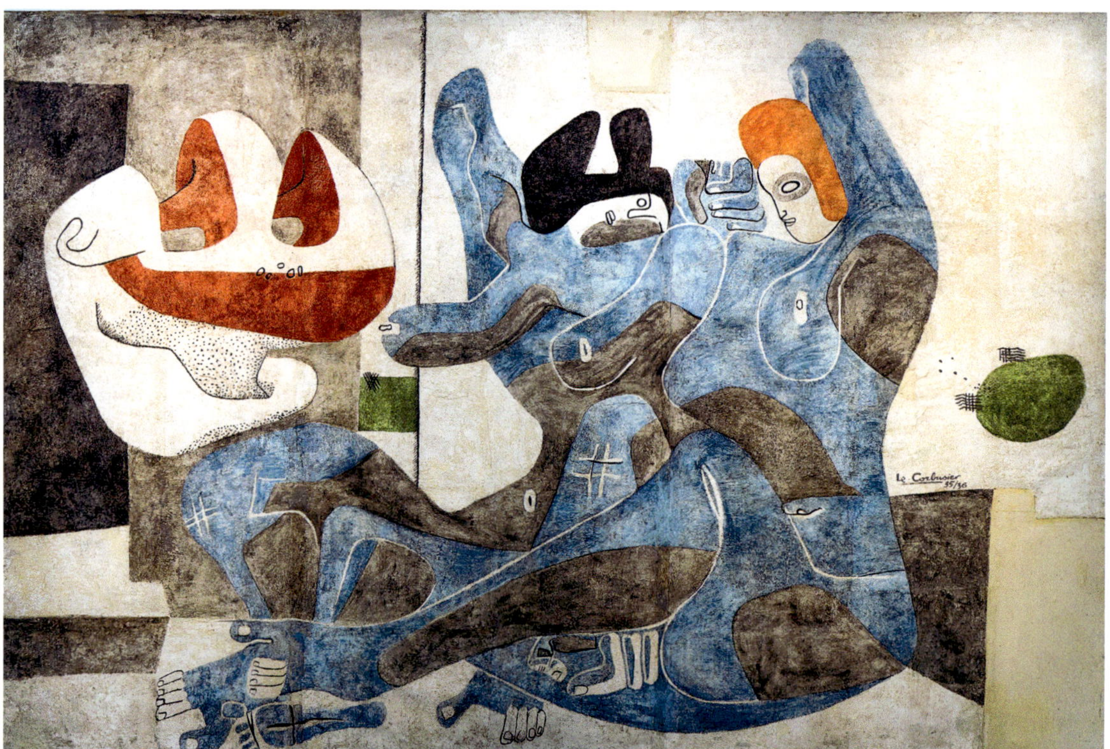

Fernand Léger, mural painting in the courtyard of Badovici's house in Vézelay, 1935.

Le Corbusier, mural painting in Badovici's house in Vézelay, April 1936.

> *who represent a longstanding artistic tradition to make a work of art truly of this time that will not come again.*[74]

It is worth noting that Le Corbusier had just completed the first two mural paintings in the villa E1027 when he advocated this *Gesamtkunstwerk* on the model of Palladio.

In praise of public art

As a measure of Le Corbusier's evolving ideas in the 1930s, he wrote a thoughtful piece about Robert Delaunay's huge coloured murals in the Railway Pavilion at the 1937 exhibition |ill. p. 49|.[75] Praising the strategy of offering large wall surfaces to some of the best modern painters in Paris, he remarked on the difficulty of this 'forced marriage' between artist and architect. One problem was the very nature of public art. Delaunay and his collaborators were singled out for praise in this piece, however, because they responded best to the challenge of decorating a huge space with great swathes of colour, where 'the colour scheme was organised by a colourist who understands how colour can contribute to space and lyricism. All this, through well-judged colour relationships, expresses joy and a kind of explosion and space expansion.'[76] The secret of Delaunay's work, for Le Corbusier, was that his work was placed equally between architectural polychromy, with its space enhancing and controlling potential, and easel painting.

Interestingly, Le Corbusier ended this short piece with an uncharacteristic expression of self-doubt:

> *If I have analysed certain precise feelings prompted by various effects of polychromy, paintings and coloured sculptures, it is also true that I remain puzzled by the problem of mural painting in architecture. Forgive me for my indecision; it's a product of the real debate I have with myself. I think it necessary to continue these experiments, and success may be achieved precisely when there is a coming together, when talents of a similar kind could find a unity between painting and architecture.*[77]

---

74 Letter from Le Corbusier to Rex Martienssen, 27 July 1939 (FLC E2(14)596). Le Corbusier had stayed in the Villa Malcontenta in 1935. Rex Martienssen wrote about E1027 in glowing terms in 1941. See P. Adam (2000). *Eileen Gray: Architect/Designer. A Biography*, op. cit., p. 219, note 28. According to Adam, Martienssen visited E1027 with Le Corbusier in 1938.

75 Four-page typescript entitled 'Robert Delaunay; A propos de peintures murales à l'exposition de 1937' and dated 7 December 1937 (FLC A3(1)182).

76 Ibid.

77 Ibid.

Tapestries: itinerant mural paintings?

A monumental medium in which artists effectively painted pictures at the scale of the mural was the tapestry. Marie Cuttoli, who ran a gallery called Maison Myrbor, commissioned designs from a number of leading artists including Picasso and Léger and turned to Le Corbusier in 1936.
The latter produced a cartoon |ill. p. 49| based on his painting *Femme, cordage, bateau et porte* (Woman, rope, boat and door, 1935). Twenty-five years later, Le Corbusier coined the term 'muralnomad' to describe the use of tapestries by people who can expect to move from one apartment to another.[78] According to him, a tapestry should not be like a painting; it must be architectural in scale; it should touch the floor and rise above viewing height. But it can be rolled up and transported from house to house. By this stage, Le Corbusier's scruples about figurative art occupying wall surfaces had disappeared. It is fascinating to note that, when asking an assistant to look at photographs of the murals, he referred to them as the 'mural tapestries of the Badovici villa'.[79]

The first mural: Léger, Vézelay and Badovici

In 1935, Jean Badovici asked his friend Fernand Léger to paint the wall of a half-open courtyard in one of the old stone properties he had acquired and restored in Vézelay |ill. p. 52|.[80] Léger prepared a cartoon and engaged the local sign painter Raoul Simon to transfer it onto the wall. Not to be outdone, on 4 April 1936, Le Corbusier told his mother:

> *I have four days at Easter to go to Vézelay to paint two walls. Twice the area of your wall in the living room. An unpaid commission, obviously! This is how one can create one's work these days. I am delighted to attack these walls.*[81]

---

78 Le Corbusier (1960). 'Tapisseries muralnomad', *Zodiac*, 7, pp. 57–63.
79 Note from Le Corbusier to his assistant Henry Bruaux, 2 September 1960 (FLC E1(5)148).
80 The village of Vézelay, in the region Bourgogne-Franche-Comté, was a historically important pilgrimage destination and a point of departure on the Way of St James. In 1840, Eugène Viollet-le-Duc headed the restoration work on the Benedictine abbey, founded in 858, which had become dilapidated. The restoration effort marks the beginning of modern monument preservation. Badovici acquired eight properties in the historic village, proposing to create a colony of artists and writers. He spent more and more of his time there as his professional career in Paris declined. Others who bought houses in Vézelay included the Nobel prize-winning author Romain Rolland, Georges Bataille and the editor of *Cahiers d'Art*, Christian Zervos.
81 Letter from Le Corbusier to his mother, 4 April 1936, Collection Jornod. J.-P. Jornod and N. Jornod (2005). *Le Corbusier: L'œuvre peint*, op. cit., p. 153.

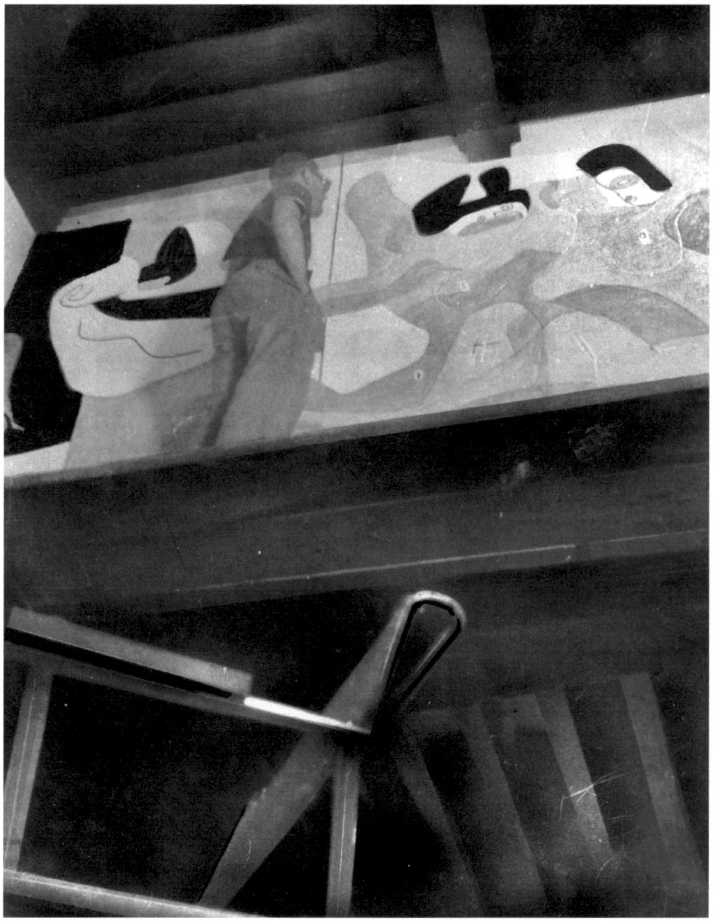

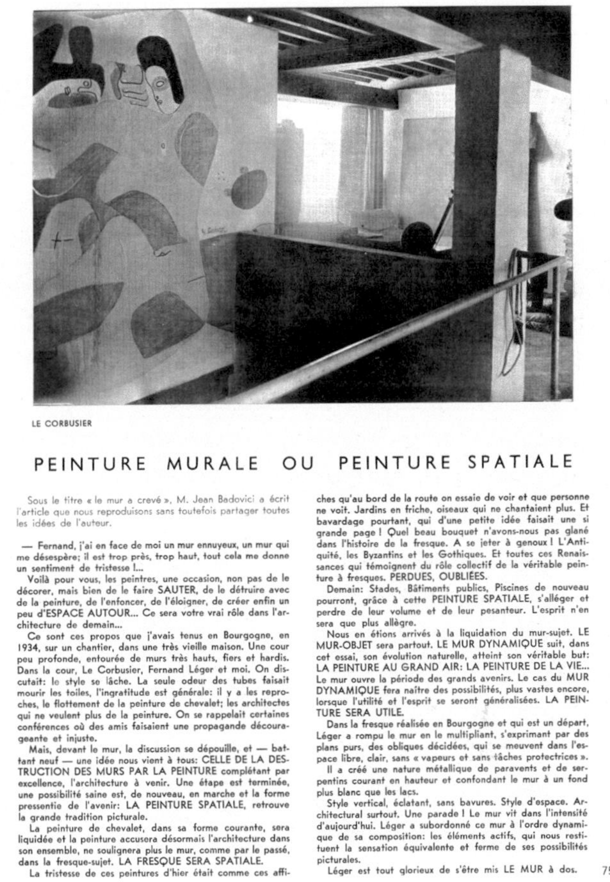

LE CORBUSIER

PEINTURE MURALE OU PEINTURE SPATIALE

Sous le titre « le mur a crevé », M. Jean Badovici a écrit l'article que nous reproduisons sans toutefois partager toutes les idées de l'auteur.

— Fernand, j'ai en face de moi un mur ennuyeux, un mur qui me désespère; il est trop près, trop haut, tout cela me donne un sentiment de tristesse !...

Voilà pour vous, les peintres, une occasion, non pas de le décorer, mais bien de le faire SAUTER, de le détruire avec de la peinture, de l'enfoncer, de l'éloigner, de créer enfin un peu d'ESPACE AUTOUR... Ce sera votre vrai rôle dans l'architecture de demain...

Ce sont ces propos que j'avais tenus en Bourgogne, en 1934, sur un chantier, dans une très vieille maison. Une cour peu profonde, entourée de murs très hauts, fiers et hardis. Dans la cour, Le Corbusier, Fernand Léger et moi. On discutait: le style se lâche. La seule odeur des tubes faisait mourir les toiles, l'ingratitude est générale: il y a les reproches, le flottement de la peinture de chevalet; les architectes qui ne veulent plus de la peinture. On se rappelait certaines conférences où des amis faisaient une propagande décourageante et injuste.

Mais, devant le mur, la discussion se dépouille, et — battant neuf — une idée nous vient à tous: CELLE DE LA DESTRUCTION DES MURS PAR LA PEINTURE complétant par excellence, l'architecture à venir. Une étape est terminée, une possibilité saine est, de nouveau, en marche et la forme pressentie de l'avenir: LA PEINTURE SPATIALE, retrouve la grande tradition picturale.

La peinture de chevalet, dans sa forme courante, sera liquidée et la peinture accusera désormais l'architecture dans son ensemble, ne soulignera plus le mur, comme par le passé, dans la fresque-sujet. LA FRESQUE SERA SPATIALE.

La tristesse de ces peintures d'hier était comme ces affiches qu'au bord de la route on essaie de voir et que personne ne voit. Jardins en friche, oiseaux qui ne chantaient plus. Et bavardage pourtant, qui d'une petite idée faisait une si grande page ! Quel beau bouquet n'avons-nous pas glané dans l'histoire de la fresque. A se jeter à genoux ! L'Antiquité, les Byzantins et les Gothiques. Et toutes ces Renaissances qui témoignent du rôle collectif de la véritable peinture à fresques. PERDUES, OUBLIÉES.

Demain: Stades, Bâtiments publics, Piscines de nouveau pourront, grâce à cette PEINTURE SPATIALE, s'alléger et perdre de leur volume et de leur pesanteur. L'esprit n'en sera que plus allègre.

Nous en étions arrivés à la liquidation du mur-sujet. LE MUR-OBJET sera partout. LE MUR DYNAMIQUE suit, dans cet essai, son évolution naturelle, atteint son véritable but: LA PEINTURE AU GRAND AIR: LA PEINTURE DE LA VIE... Le mur ouvre la période des grands avenirs. Le cas du MUR DYNAMIQUE fera naître des possibilités, plus vastes encore, lorsque l'utilité et l'esprit se seront généralisées. LA PEINTURE SERA UTILE.

Dans la fresque réalisée en Bourgogne et qui est un départ, Léger a rompu le mur en le multipliant, s'exprimant par des plans purs, des obliques décidées, qui se meuvent dans l'espace libre, clair, sans « vapeurs et sans tâches protectrices ».

Il a créé une nature métallique de paravents et de serpentins courant en hauteur et confondant le mur à un fond plus blanc que les lacs.

Style vertical, éclatant, sans bavures. Style d'espace. Architectural surtout. Une parade ! Le mur vit dans l'intensité d'aujourd'hui. Léger a subordonné ce mur à l'ordre dynamique de sa composition: les éléments actifs, qui nous restituent la sensation équivalente et ferme de ses possibilités picturales.

Léger est tout glorieux de s'être mis LE MUR à dos.

75

Le Corbusier painting his fresco in Badovici's house at Vézelay, April 1936.

Le Corbusier's mural in Badovici's house, April 1936, illustrated in Badovici's article 'Peinture murale ou peinture spatiale', *L'Architecture d'Aujourd'hui*, March 1937.

In the event he was only able to paint one of the murals, which he confirmed on 15 April: 'Finished my fresco – 3 ½ × 2 ½ metres. A success. Happy to have made this attempt.'[82] Between 30 October and 4 November in the same year he returned to Vézelay and filmed Léger's mural but not his own |ill. p. 50|.

This painting |ill. p. 52|, which is located on a wall at first-floor level overlooking the double-height space that Badovici had created, represents two nudes and a large seashell on a table. A preparatory sketch includes an erotic visual pun that Le Corbusier attributes to Badovici |ill. p. 58|.[83] Le Corbusier often discusses seashells in a sensual way. In his *Poème de l'angle droit* (1955) he introduces the section 'C4 Flesh' with a lithograph of a nude next to the same seashell and on page 89 he writes:

> *Tenderness! Seashell. The sea has never stopped sending us their happy, harmonious remains on the beaches. The hand fondles, the hand caresses, the hand slides. The hand and the shell love each other.*[84]

82 Letter from Le Corbusier to his mother, 15 April 1936, Collection Jornod, ibid., p. 132.

83 'La vie est dure; la vie est belle' (Life is hard; life is beautiful) (FLC 4579). This note accompanies an erotic sketch on Le Corbusier's sketch for the mural: FLC 4579. The pun turns on the similarity between the words *'vie'* (life) and *'vit'* (penis).

84 Le Corbusier (1955). *Poème de l'angle droit. Lithographies originales [de l'auteur]*, Paris, Teriade (impr. de Mourlot frères), p. 89.

There are some points to note in these events. It is clear that Léger has gone further than Le Corbusier in attempting a distinctly mural form of art, responding to the form of the wall allotted to him and working with abstract forms. His mural both explodes the solid surface of the wall and illuminates an otherwise dark and dingy corner. Le Corbusier's painting, although not copied specifically from any of his previous paintings, is more classically a 'picture'. Secondly, Le Corbusier finds it impossible to discuss mural painting without using aggressive language. He is pleased to have 'attacked' the walls. In August 1939, he will tell Badovici that he is keen to 'dirty the walls' of E1027.[85]

The context for this aggressive language was a discussion that Jean Badovici recorded in an article entitled 'Peinture murale ou peinture spatiale' in March 1937.[86] Badovici used the heading 'the wall has collapsed'. He reports a conversation with Léger and Le Corbusier, as if standing in front of the wall that Léger had painted in the courtyard of his house:

> *'Fernand, I have before me an annoying wall, a wall that drives me mad. It's too close, too high; it's depressing. [...] Now, here's a challenge for you painters, not to decorate the wall but to EXPLODE it, destroy it with painting, make it go away, in short, create some SPACE around it. [...] This is going to be your real role in the architecture of tomorrow.' [...] But, standing in front of this wall, the conversation branched out and – brainwave – a new idea came to all of us: THE DESTRUCTION OF WALLS BY PAINTING. Thus completing to perfection the architecture of tomorrow.*[87]

In its emphasis on the power of colour to create spatial effects, this passage can be compared with Le Corbusier's views on polychromy. But the language is much more violent and now, instead of being critical of exploding the wall, it had become positive. Badovici went on to make a claim which Le Corbusier, committed as he still was to easel painting, would certainly not have accepted:

> *Easel painting, in its current form, will be liquidated and painting will become architectural in essence. [...] THE FRESCO WILL BECOME SPATIAL.*[88]

In his article, Badovici included a mosaic from Torcello Cathedral |ill. p. 57|, in reference to Le Corbusier's discussions with Léger about medieval mural painting and he claimed that there were similarities between the abstract forms in Léger's paintings and medieval illuminated manuscripts. Referring to Le Corbusier's mural in his house, Badovici anticipated possible criticisms of the effect of murals on architecture with a strange argument:

---

85 Letter from Le Corbusier to Jean Badovici, 3 August 1939 (FLC E1(05)34).

86 Badovici, J. (1937). 'Peinture murale ou peinture spatiale', *L'Architecture d'Aujourd'hui*, March 1937, p. 75.

87 Ibid.

88 Ibid.

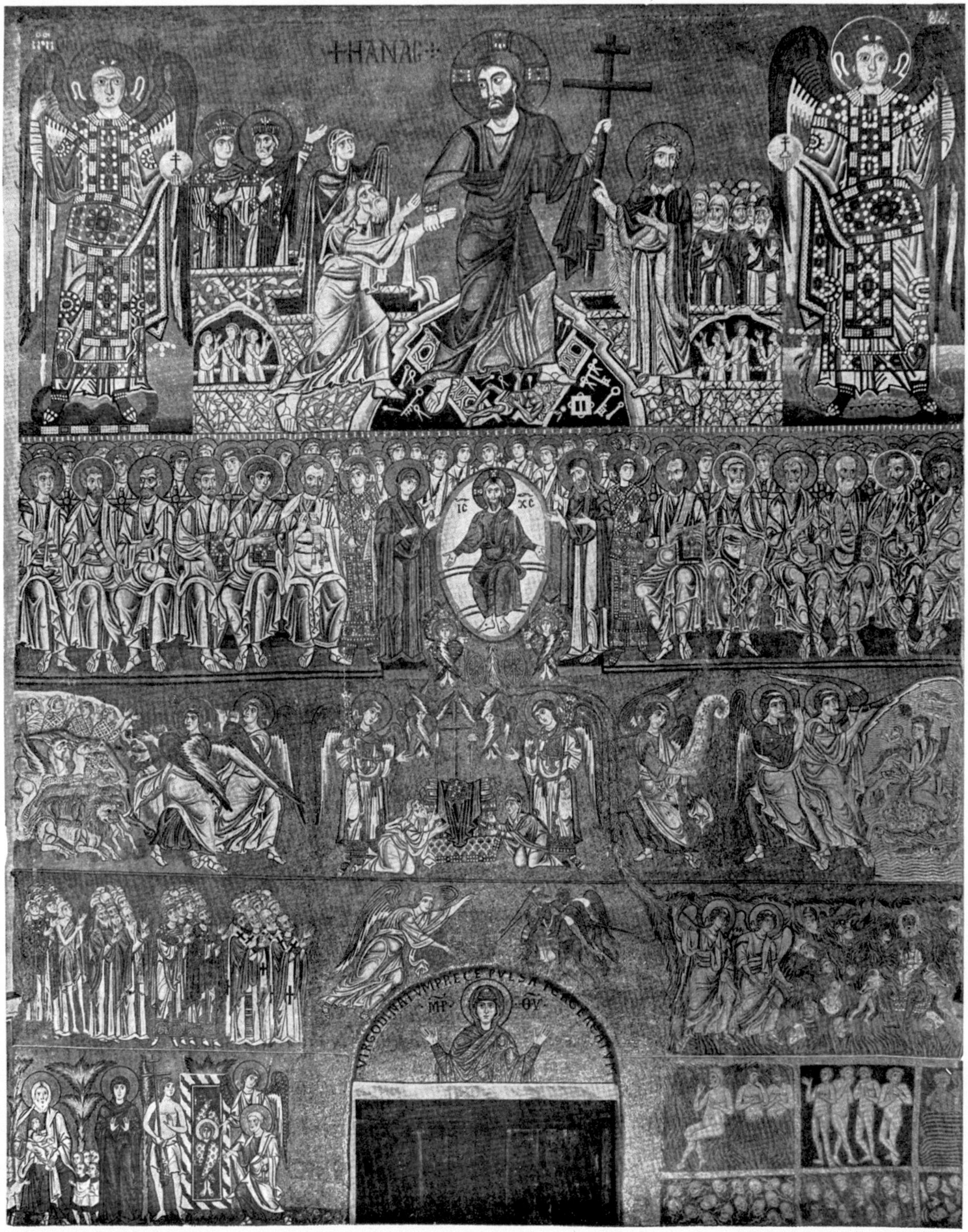

ART MURAL (12me SIECLE) CATHÉDRALE DE TORCELLO

Mosaic from Torcello Cathedral, in Badovici's article 'Peinture murale ou peinture spatiale', *L'Architecture d'Aujourd'hui*, March 1937.

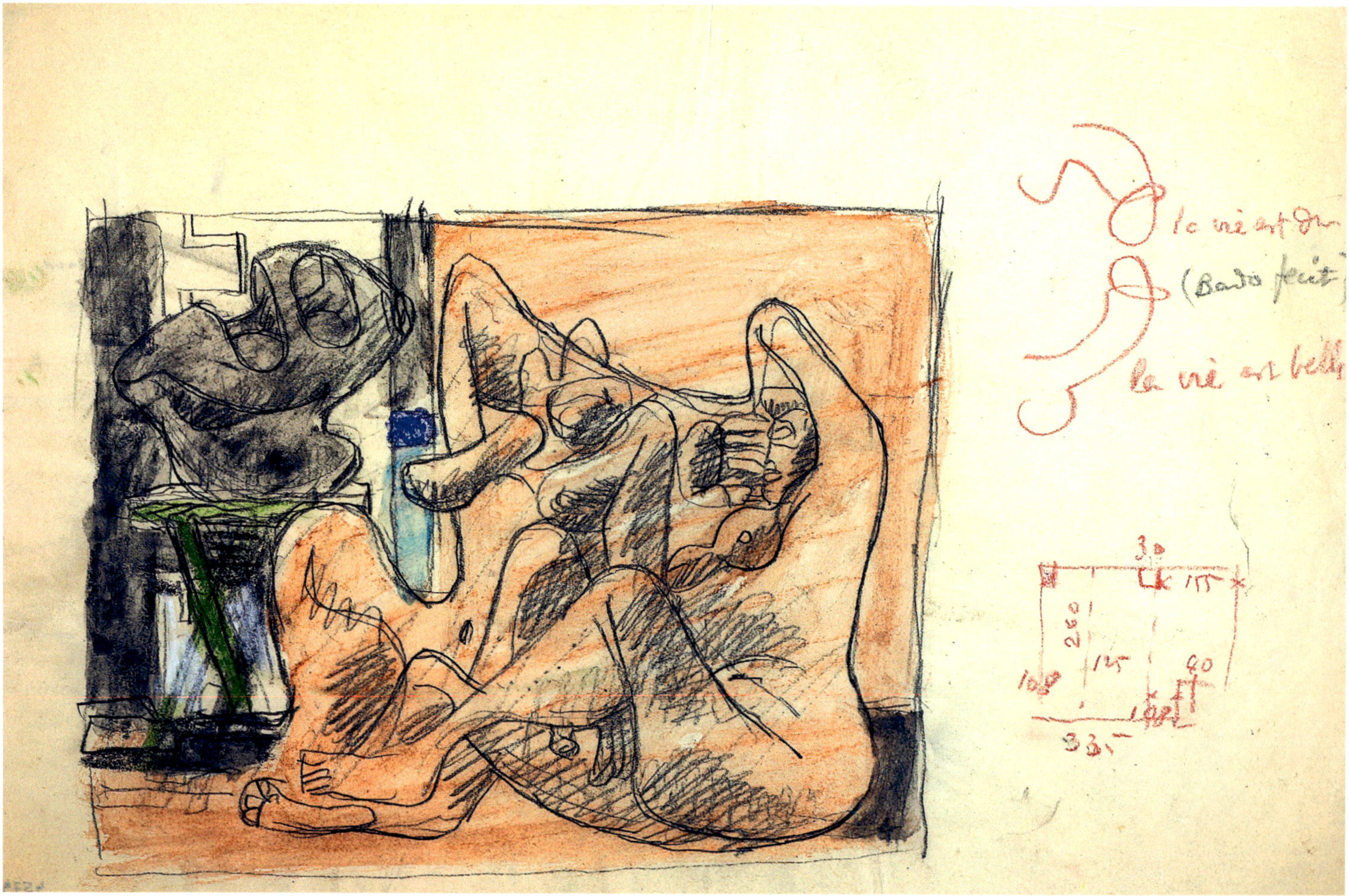

Le Corbusier, preparatory sketch for his mural in Vézelay. On the right he added a visual erotic pun, which he attributes to Badovici: 'Life is hard, life is beautiful.'

> *The mural is situated in a place which, although at the centre of the house, is a place of passage; IN NO WAY DOES IT DISTURB. The fresco does not impose itself on you; to see it you have to look upwards.*[89]

Clearly, we have travelled some distance from claims of a harmonic relationship between painting and architecture. The best that can be hoped for is that the painting does not upset the architectural effects too much. And Badovici emphasised the personal aspect of the work:

> *Le Corbusier's first fresco, carried out in Burgundy, is that of a living man. It's the new 'Holy Family' of our day. The composition was accompanied by his pipe, his box of matches, a bottle of wine and a packet of tobacco. Because Le Corbusier has an instinct for the good things and benefits from 'atmosphere'.*[90]

Badovici clearly welcomed this painting as a personal signature in his house. He also claimed that it was a 'painting of life', which in the terminology of Léger and other artists of the Left, had political connotations, suggesting an opposition to formalism. During a de-

89 Ibid.
90 Ibid.

bate at the Maison de Culture in Paris entitled 'The dispute over realism', Léger had confirmed the leftist aspirations of the meeting, arguing for the political engagement of artists.[91] Le Corbusier, who followed Léger to the rostrum, called his talk 'Destiny of painting' and took a considerably more formalist line, referring to 'the great song of plastic lyricism'.[92] It is clear that Le Corbusier had little interest in using his murals for political purposes. For him they were 'pictures'.

From these debates and discussions all the ambiguities and contradictions of the E1027 murals can be predicted.

91 Léger's contribution was called 'Le nouveau réalisme continue' and originally published in *La querelle du réalisme: deux débats organisés par l'Association des peintres sculpteurs de la Maison de la culture* (1936). Paris, Éditions Sociales internationales. Reprint 1987: Paris, Cercle d'Art.

92 Le Corbusier (1936). 'Destin de la peinture', in *La querelle du réalisme*, Paris, Cercle d'Art, 1987, pp. 110–123.

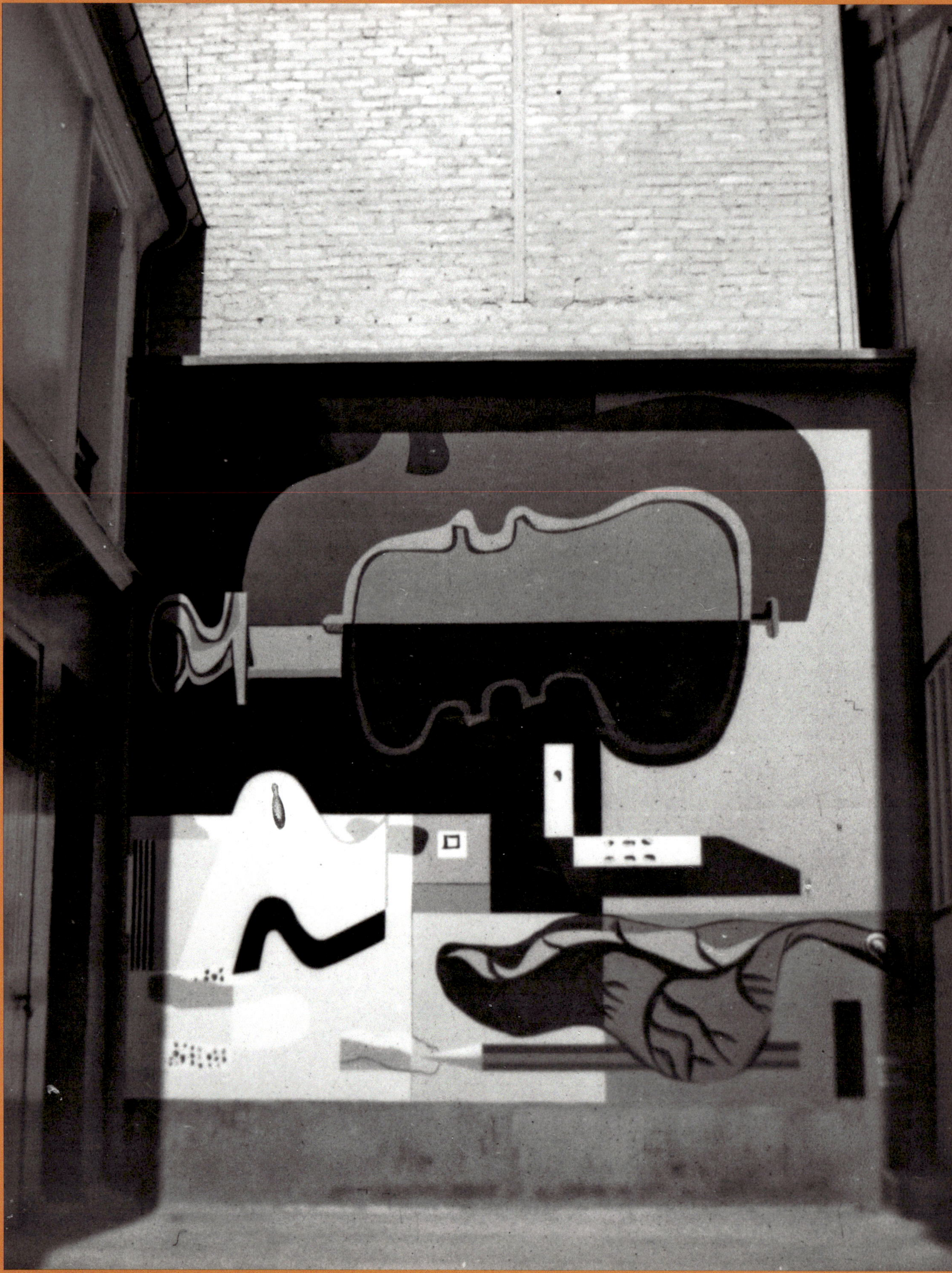

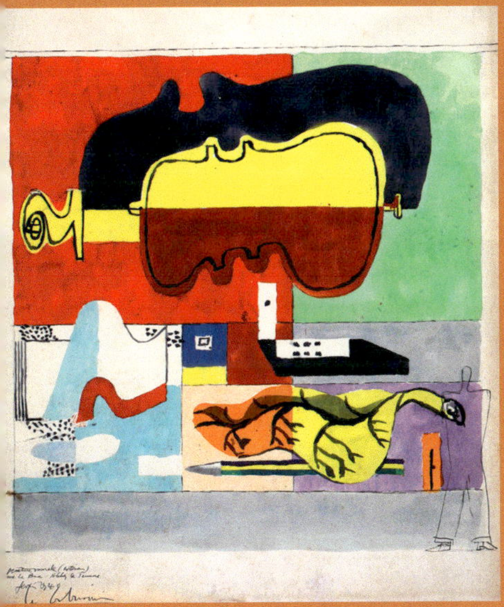

The mural in the Rue Le Bua

In 1938–1939, Le Corbusier worked on the restoration of two old buildings in the Rue Le Bua in the XXth arondissement in Paris to accommodate the Centre de réhabilitation de jeunes chômeurs (Centre for rehabilitation of young men out of work). This was part of the Centre for the Study of Labour founded in January 1938 by Philippe Serre, Under-Secretary of State in the Blum government.[I] For one of the courtyards in the Centre Le Corbusier designed a mural that the painter Raoul Simon executed on the basis of a cartoon.[II]
Raoul Simon began work on the mural in January 1940 but the composition probably dates from six months earlier.[III] It was based on a much older Le Corbusier painting, *La nature morte au violon rouge* (Still life with red violin), 1920, which had been included in his exhibition in Zürich in January 1938.[IV] The cartoon given to Raoul Simon was a watercolour that Simon followed faithfully. Once again, Le Corbusier makes no effort to establish a relationship between his composition and the architectural space. The painting dominates the end wall and 'explodes' the wall. This seemed justifiable to Le Corbusier, given the simplicity of the project.

Photograph of Rue Le Bua mural, 1940.

Le Corbusier, watercolour sketch for a mural for the Centre de réhabilitation de jeunes chômeurs, Rue Le Bua, Paris, 1939–1940.

I Two drawings document this very functional project (FLC 31838 and 31839).
II See Le Corbusier's diary (FLC F3(6)5 folios 59r and 65r).
III 'Simon from Vézelay began today to lay on some brilliant colours in the centre for adolescents that we are furnishing in Ménilmontant.' (Letter from Le Corbusier to his mother and brother, 4 January 1940, cited in R. Baudoui and A. Dercelles, eds. (2013). *Correspondance, tome II. Lettres à la famille 1926–1946*, Gollion, Infolio éditions, p. 646, note 79.
IV Listed as number 4 in the list of paintings labelled 'Zürich Kunsthaus' in the diary (FLC F3(6)5, folios 60v-64r).

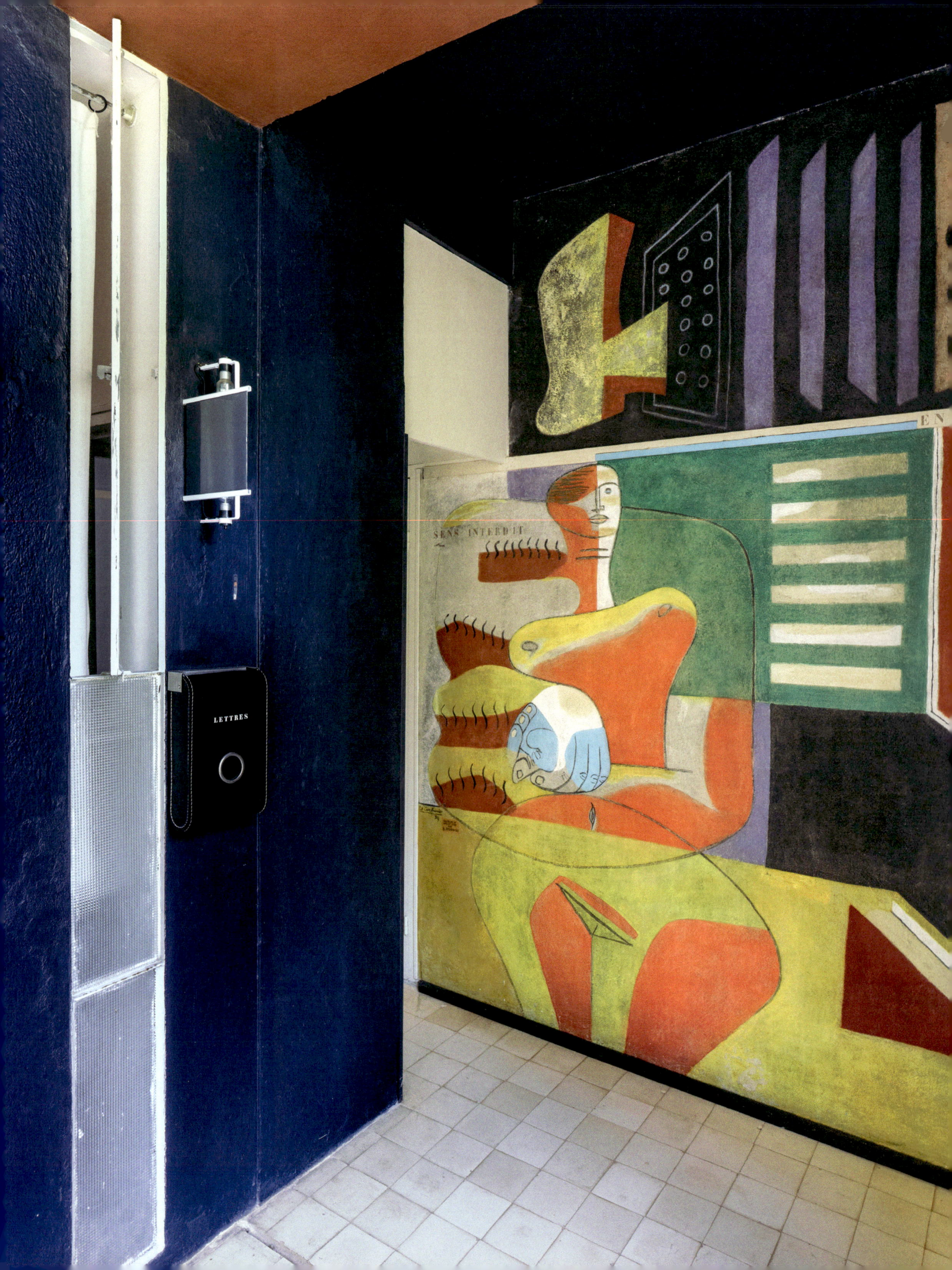
LETTRES
SENS INTERDIT

PAINTING E1027

To believe the received historiography, Le Corbusier visited E1027 (ironically termed 'baraque')[93] regularly in the 1930s. However, a detailed study of his diaries and correspondence demonstrates that he visited only once before 1938. He wrote to Marguerite Tjader-Harris about this trip in March 1937, and his presence was confirmed in a letter from Pierre Guéguen to Badovici on 14 April 1937.[94] In his diary, he noted the train times to Roquebrune.[95]

But Roquebrune was not the only place on the Côte d'Azur that Le Corbusier and Yvonne visited. On at least two occasions they stayed with Madame Pégurier, for whom Le Corbusier had offered to design a villa.[96] Two letters addressed to Le Corbusier and Yvonne at her villa in St Tropez from July 1928 are evidence of these visits.[97] It was during this stay that Le Corbusier suffered his terrible accident while swimming in the harbour. A speedboat 'made mincemeat' of me, as Le Corbusier said. The prow of the boat split open his skull and the propeller gashed his thigh |ill. p. 74|. He spent thirty-three days in hospital and wrote detailed accounts of his experience to his mother.[98] Referring to his thigh, he told his mother that the wound was 'as long as *La Ville Radieuse*' (his book):[99]

> *From six in the evening on Saturday the 13th until nearly midnight I was cut up, sewn up and hammered by the saw-bones, without anaesthetic. The doctors complimented me.*[100]

This accident, which Le Corbusier referred to as the 'miracle of St Tropez' had a profound effect on him, to the point that, three years later, he introduced the manuscript of his book on urbanism – *Sur les quatre routes* – with a detailed description of the event.[101] He explains

Entrance to E1027, with Eileen Gray's lamp and letterbox and Le Corbusier's mural painting.

---

93 Le Corbusier and Badovici used the ironic title 'baraque' (shack) to describe Eileen Gray's finely articulated villa. It is important to note, however, that 'baraque' had a privileged connotation in Le Corbusier's vocabulary, signifying not only the simple vernacular structures that he greatly admired around the Bassin d'Arcachon, but also the cabin on Long Island where he and Marguerite Tjader-Harris consummated their affair in November 1935. In his letters to her for years after, he asks after the 'baraque', referring not to the structure but to the memory of their experience together.

94 FLC E3(10)28 and Getty Research Institute, 880412, Box 6.

95 (FLC F3(6)4 folios 9v and 10r.

96 In a letter to Mr Steele, Le Corbusier mentions these visits, 13 May 1937 (FLC I1(1)133).

97 See R. Baudoui and A. Dercelles, eds. (2013). *Correspondance. Lettres à la famille*, op. cit., p. 582. The letter from Mr G. Pellerson, of 19 July 1928, was redirected to Madame Pégurier's address in St Tropez.

98 23 August (FLC R2(1)263) and 21 September 1938 (FLC R2(1)264).

99 FLC R2(1)263.

100 Ibid.

101 FLC B3(12)242 ff. The editor of the book, Jean Paulhan, cut this passage but Le Corbusier later tried to reinsert it. See Guillemette Morel Journel (2010). *Le Corbusier, l'écrivain: arpenter sur les 4 routes*, PhD thesis directed by Prof. Jean-Louis Cohen, Paris, EHESS, 17 December 2010.

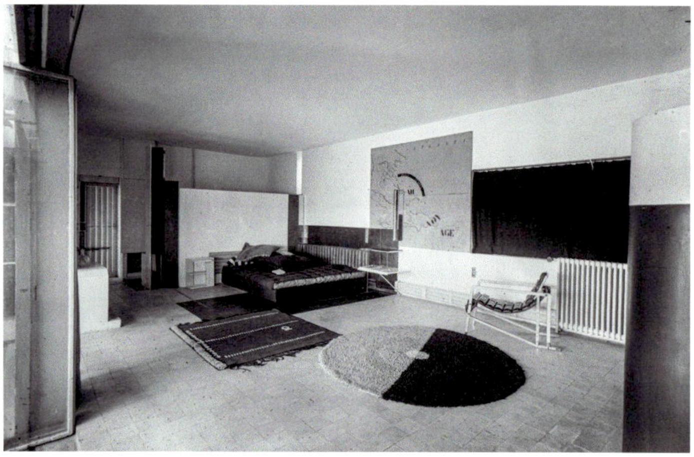

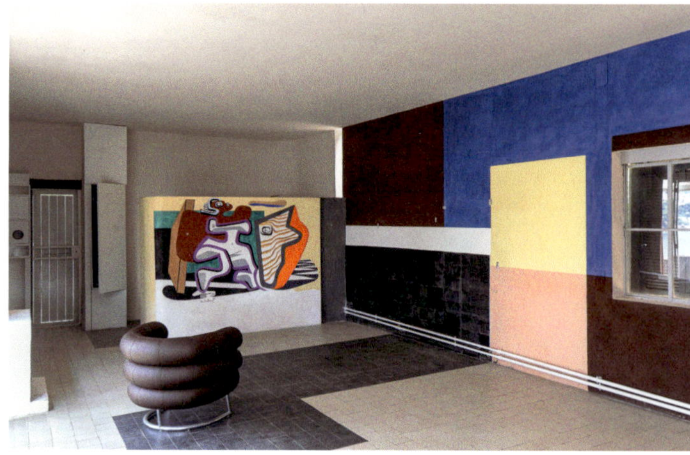

Eileen Gray, photograph of the E1027 living room, 1929.

E1027 living room as restored by Pierre-Antoine Gatier in 2010, before the insertion of a folding panel hiding Le Corbusier's mural and before the removal of the restored polychrome treatment on the north wall.

that the overwhelming experience of the accident and his suffering during the operation had changed him:

> *Instantly, he is transported onto another plane. The landscape is new, with unknown perspectives [...] it must be like someone who throws himself off a cliff, a tower or a pier before he hits the hard ground or deep water. It is crossing over, another side of life. Man finds himself face to face with his destiny.*[102]

This accident, combined with his sense of betrayal by his colleagues and the anxiety of the imminent approach of war, marks Le Corbusier's substantial moral destabilisation.

The first two murals

On 26 April 1938, after ten days spent in Algiers, Le Corbusier joined Yvonne and Badovici in E1027. He covered two walls in the villa E1027 with paintings, at Badovici's invitation. It was Badovici's house and Eileen Gray had left in 1932.[103] One of these was on the partition wall separating the living room from the shower room. The other – the so-called 'sgraffitte' – is located on a wall under the pilotis |ill. p. 73|. Both works are the product of a long trail of sketches and paintings. He wrote to his mother:

> *At Bado's place, five days in his delicious house, busy painting two murals which went very well and marked a significant progress for me. Don't imagine that I will return to graceful young women leaning on a balcony. It's not the time for that.*[104]

On 28 April, probably after completing one or both of his paintings, he wrote Gray a letter:

---

102 Ibid.

103 Badovici bought the site for the house on 26 March 1926 for 33,000 francs (Conservatoire des hypothèques de Nice, 2e Bureau, Acte No 67, vol. 140, No 86). The house was in his name from the outset.

104 Letter from Le Corbusier to his mother, 8 May 1938 (FLC R2(1)248).

First floor plan

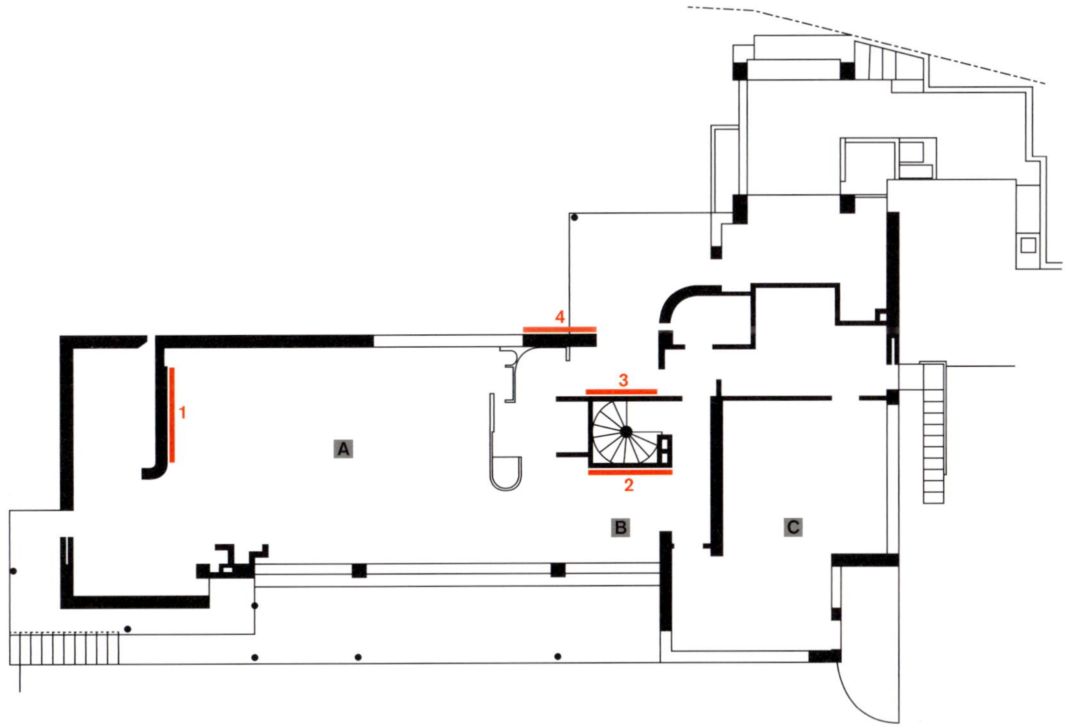

Ground floor plan

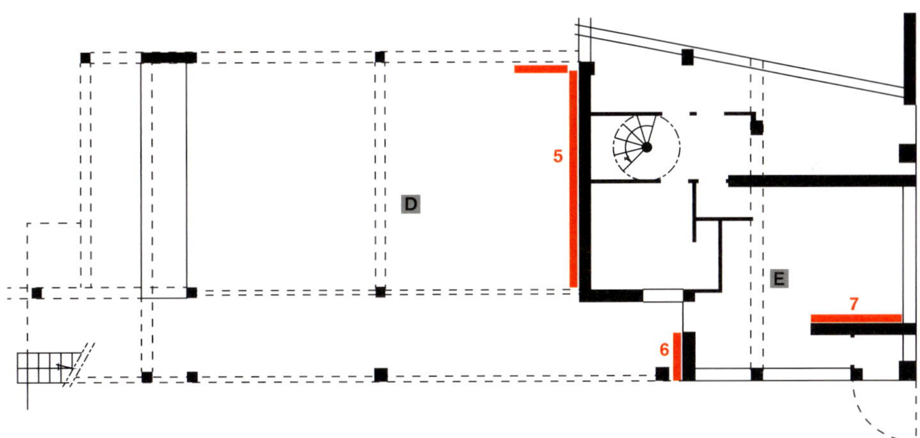

A Living room
B Dining area and bar
C Master bedroom
D Space under the pilotis
E Guest room

1 Mural in the living room, April 1938
2 Mural in the bar, August 1939
3 Mural in the entrance, August 1939
4 Mural to the right of the entrance, August 1939 (no longer existent)
5 'Sgraffitte' mural, April 1938
6 Mural by entrance to guest bedroom, August 1939 (no longer existent)
7 Mural in the guest bedroom, August 1939

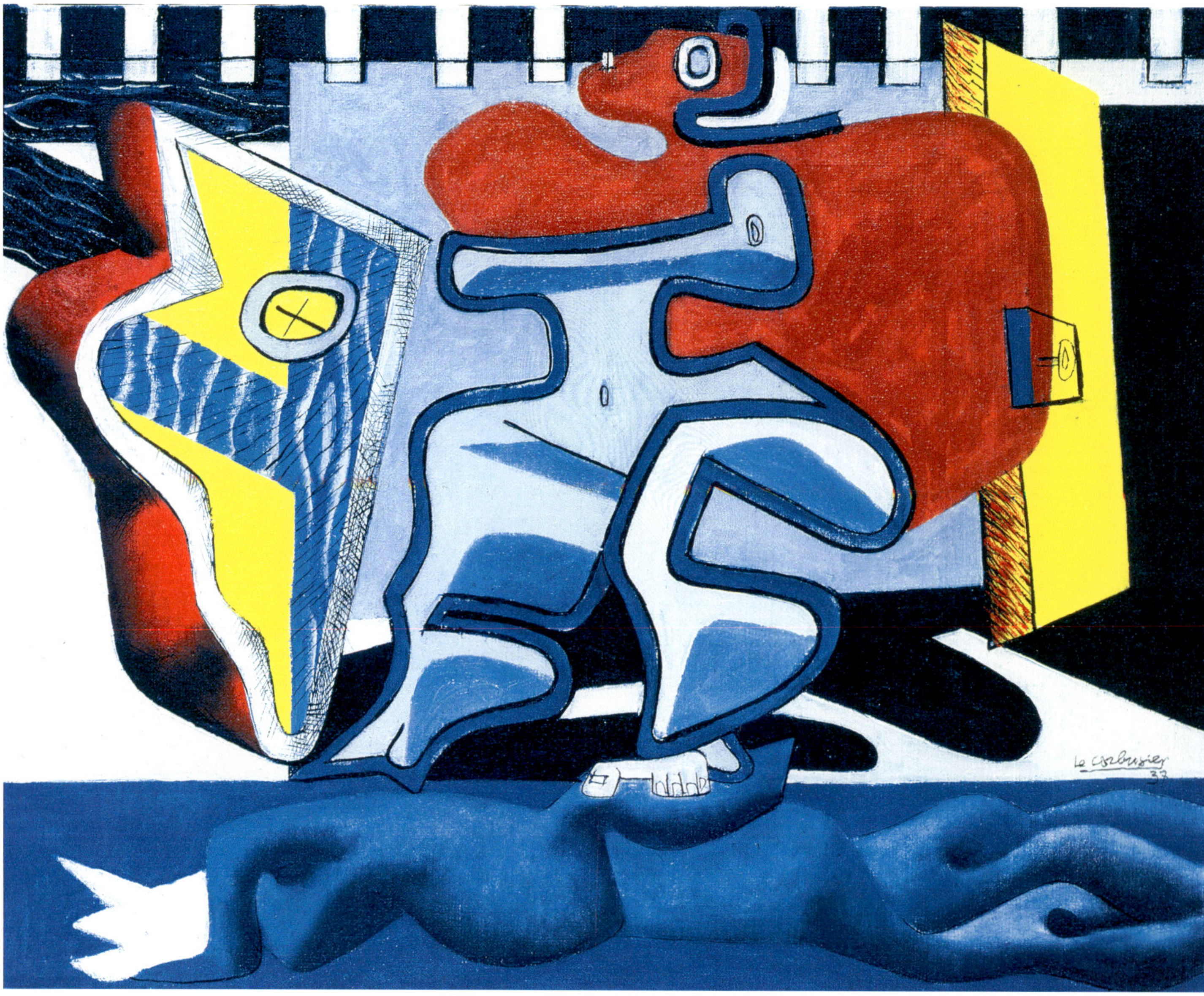

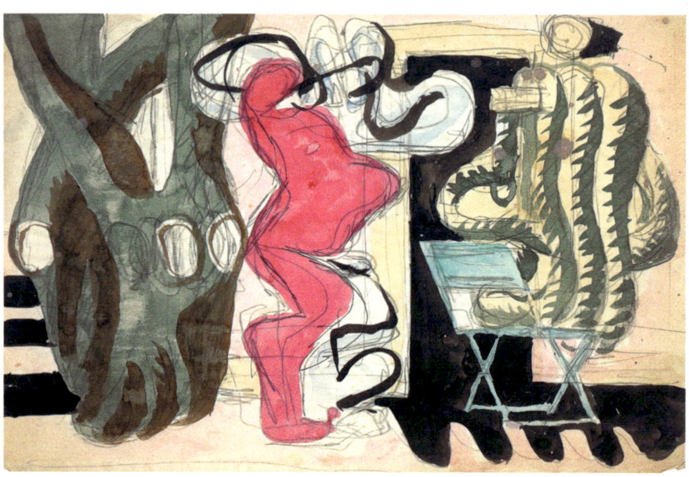

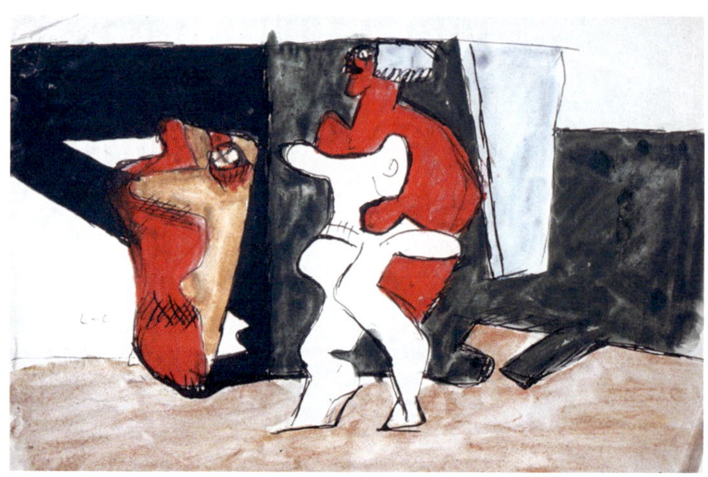

Le Corbusier, *Figure à la porte jaune* (Figure with yellow door), 1937.

Le Corbusier sketch for *Arbre, nu et cordage* (Tree, nude and rope), Le Piquey, ca 1932–1933.

Le Corbusier, sketch for *Figure devant une porte blanche* (Figure before a white door), ca 1937.

> *Chère mademoiselle*, I was extremely sorry to have arrived too late to be able to spend some time with you. My wife tells me that you wanted to heap gastronomic pleasures on us, among other things. I missed that, but above all your company. So I hope that you will give us the pleasure of visiting us in Paris. I would be happy to tell you to what extent these few days spent in your house have enabled me to appreciate the fine sensibility that has dictated all the details, inside and out, and has given the modern furniture – the equipment – such a dignified, charming and intelligent quality. On Sunday we are returning to Paris and hope to see you soon. Best regards from myself and from my wife.[105]

The polite formality of this letter, which is unlike any other letter by Le Corbusier to a woman, suggests that Le Corbusier did not know Eileen Gray well or at all.[106] It is very likely that he wrote it after painting one or both murals, prompted by a nervous Badovici who feared for Gray's reaction. In fact, she does not seem to have been aware of the murals until Le Corbusier published them in 1948. Le Corbusier referred to E1027 as 'your house'. There are no references to Gray in Badovici's correspondence, but he clearly told Le Corbusier of her important role in the design of the house.

With these mural paintings, Le Corbusier contradicted all the arguments he had supported since the 1920s. He seems to have opened himself up to Léger's criticism of the Bébé Cadum posters: using visual depth in a painting to create a hole in the wall. Instead of defending the rights of the architect to allow their walls to speak, he seems to have adopted the position of Léger and Badovici, 'to EXPLODE it, destroy it with painting, make it go away, in short, create some SPACE around it.'[107] In *New World of Space* (1948) he tried to finesse this position:

> The paintings created space in cramped places: at the entrance, within the porch and at the bar.[108]

But in general he is adopting the role of the artist over that of the architect, or rather introducing a dialogue:

> When you open the door to an artist you must allow him to speak. When he speaks, you listen. [...] This is the great danger of allowing walls to be painted.[109]

The painting in the living room of E1027 is a revised version of the paintings called *Figure à la porte jaune* (Figure with yellow door) |ill. p. 66| and *Figure devant une porte blanche* (Figure before a white door) |ill. p. 66|, both paintings having been exhibited in Zürich four

105 Letter from Le Corbusier to Eileen Gray, 28 April 1938 (FLC E2(3)478).

106 I know of no other letter from Le Corbusier to a woman addressed as 'chère Mademoiselle'. It is also surprising that he referred to Yvonne as 'my wife'. See also T. Benton (2017). 'E-1027 and the Drôle de Guerre', *AA files*, 74, pp. 123–154.

107 Badovici, J. (1937). 'Peinture murale ou peinture spatiale', op. cit.

108 Le Corbusier (1948). *New World of Space*, op. cit., p. 99.

109 Le Corbusier (1948). 'Unité', *L'Architecture d'Aujourd'hui*, 19, p. 49, cited by C. Constant (2000). *Eileen Gray*, London, Phaidon, p. 202.

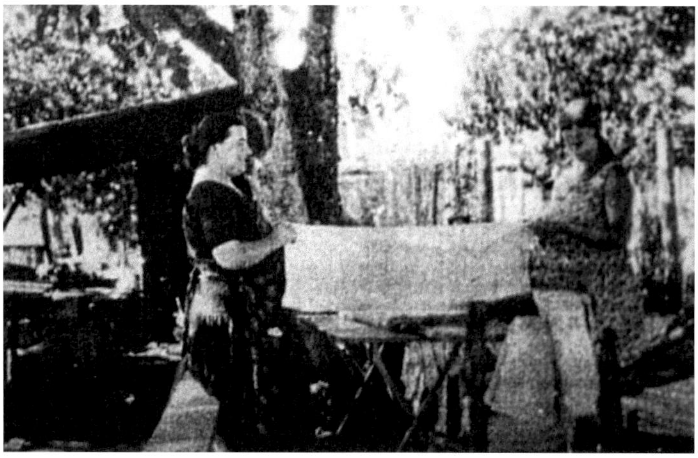

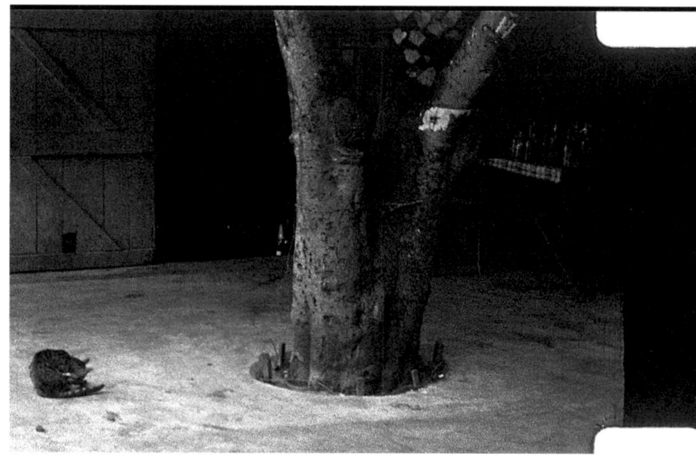

Madame Vidal and Yvonne in the courtyard of the Vidal house, Le Piquey, ca 1930.

Le Corbusier, photograph of the tree in the courtyard of the Vidal house, Le Piquey, September 1936.

months before. These works were themselves the end result of a series of studies relating a tree to a nude |ill. p. 69|. This tree was located in the courtyard of the Vidal house where Le Corbusier and Yvonne stayed at Le Petit Piquey on the Bassin d'Arcachon. A feature of this tree, barely recognisable in these paintings, was a large knot that Le Corbusier associated with a female breast. The woman's head is tilted back, with the hair net that Yvonne often wore. For some reason, Le Corbusier associated the living room mural |ill. p. 98| with Delacroix's painting *Dante et Virgile aux enfers* (Dante and Virgil in hell) in the Louvre. This mural is perhaps the least successful of Le Corbusier's paintings and it is notable that it is the only one he did not publish later. With its glaring colours and crude composition it is hard to defend the painting in context. It was executed with three or four pots of Ripolin house paint blended together and diluted with petrol. Le Corbusier was unable to equip himself with the oil paints with which he modulated the colours in the later murals.[110] The decision was taken in 2018 to disguise it behind a hinged panel, in order to preserve Gray's delicate colour scheme |ill. pp. 18–19, 64|.

The 'sgraffitte' under the pilotis

Under the pilotis on the lower-ground floor, Le Corbusier traced a monochrome linear composition of three women. Although Le Corbusier and Badovici refer to it as a 'sgraffitte', after the Italian term 'sgraffitto', it was not incised into the wall but drawn directly onto the rough cement-rendered wall and finished in black Ripolin paint. A misunderstanding arose because in 1978 a local artist, Jean Broniarski, made a copy on a plastered wall constructed in front of the original wall. This crude copy was traced from the projection of a

110 See the analysis of Marie-Odile Hubert, who restored the paintings: M.-O. Hubert (2015). 'La restauration des peintures', in T. Benton and M. Bougot (2015, sec. ed. 2021). *Le Corbusier Peintre à Cap-Martin*, Paris, Éditions du patrimoine, pp. 116–119.

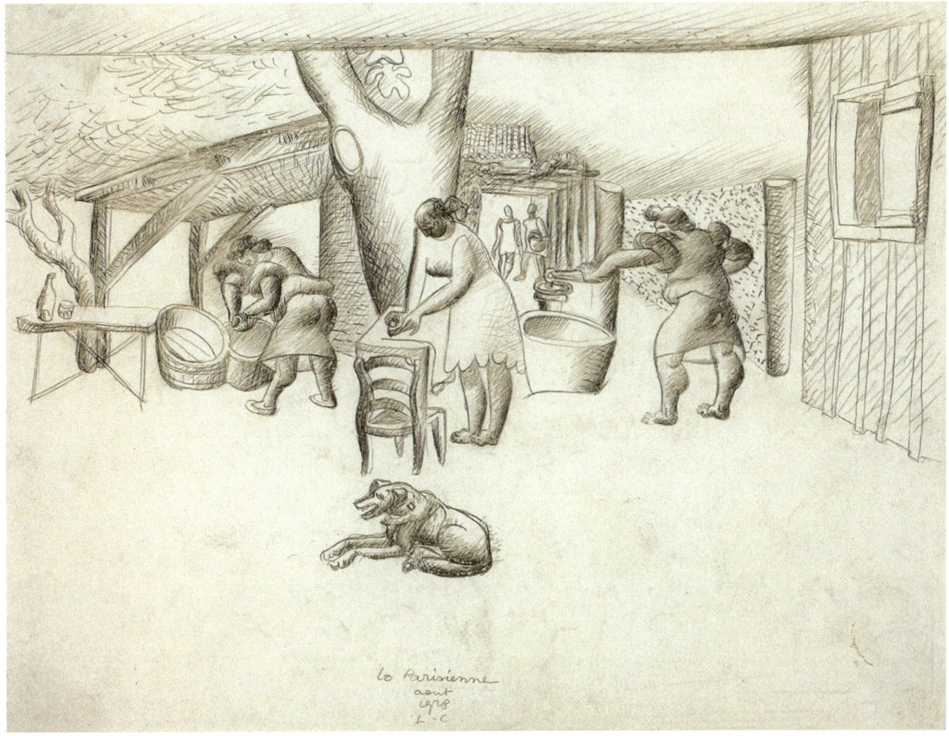

Le Corbusier, *La Parisienne* (Yvonne in the courtyard of the Vidal house), August 1928.

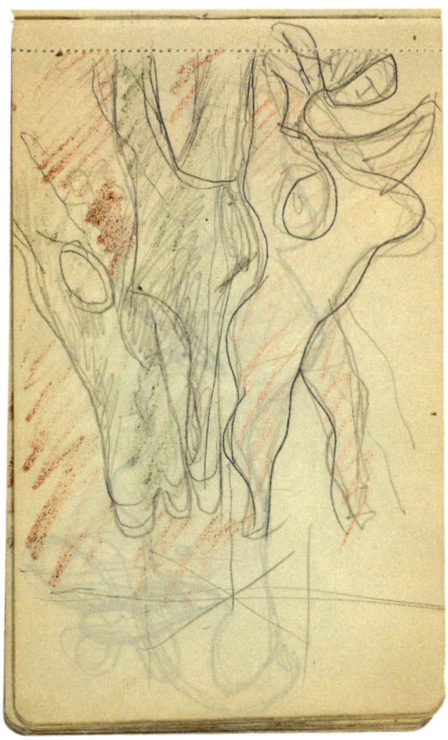

Le Corbusier, drawing of the tree in the courtyard of the Vidal house, with female nude, ca 1932–1933.

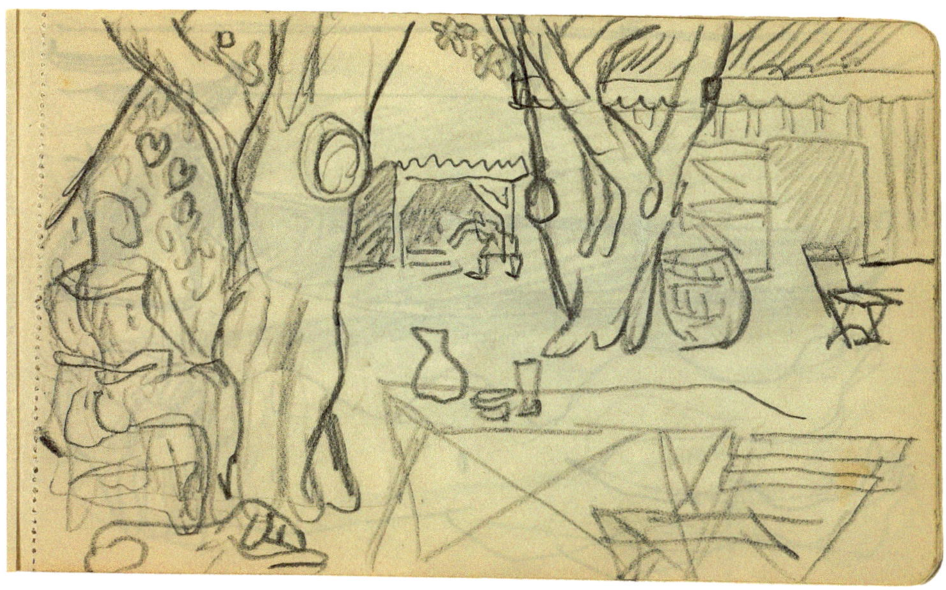

Le Corbusier, drawing of the courtyard of the Vidal house, 1932.

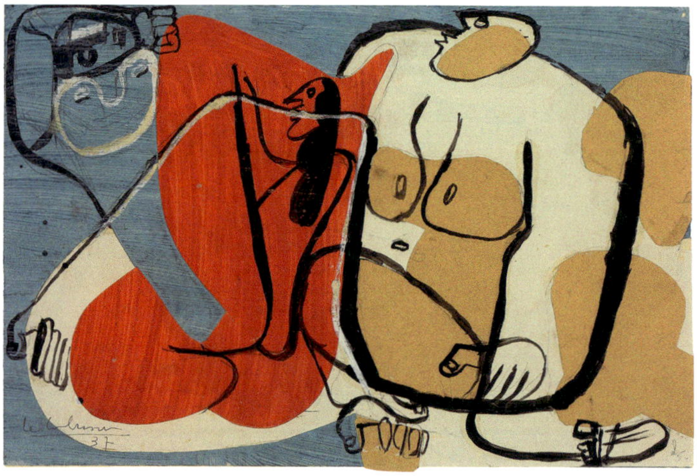

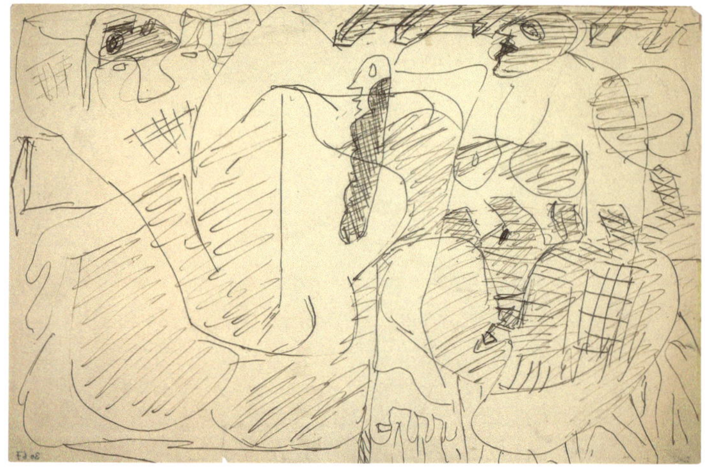

Le Corbusier, gouache study for *Trois personnages* (Three figures), 1937.

Le Corbusier, sketch of female nudes, 1937.

transparency and was indeed incised into the soft plaster. It is this copy, on which a squatter later picked out the swastika form on the right-hand figure, that has been discussed by Beatriz Colomina and others.[111]

The sources of this painting include a long list of compositions in which Le Corbusier tried to combine two or more female nudes, often overlapping the figures. The theme of these compositions was Le Corbusier's ideal of women, which he referred to as '*Tendresse*' (tenderness). In his book of lithographs *Poème de l'angle droit* (1955), the section C5 'Flesh' opens with the word '*Tendresse*' and focuses on the sensual pleasures of touch, blending the female form with seashells and other products of nature.[112] The 'sgraffitte' mural is flanked on the left by an outline, based on the grey and white pebbles from the nearby beach, that conforms to Le Corbusier's search for sensual form in natural objects. The imbrication of outlines derives from the concept of 'marriage of contours' that had already been a staple concept in the Purist paintings of Jeanneret and Ozenfant in the 1920s. The outlines of the three figures blend into an arabesque of lines. Although sensual in form, this painting has a quality of calm that hardly seems 'erotic'.

Beatriz Colomina has written about this mural as a direct attack on Eileen Gray and her sexuality, associating the composition with a series of nude drawings of Algerian prostitutes that Le Corbusier is supposed to have drawn in the 1930s.[113] According to her, Le Corbusier reproduced the colonisation of the Algerian 'other' as a colonisation and implied rape of Eileen Gray. There is no evidence that these drawings ever existed and, in any case, Le Corbusier bare-

111 See B. Colomina (1993). 'War on Architecture: E.1027 – House Designed by Eileen Gray at Cap Martin', *Assemblage*, 20, April, pp. 28–29. In this article, reprinted many times, Colomina suggests that Le Corbusier's intervention in the house was a personal attack on Eileen Gray and reproduced the colonial sexual oppression of women in Algiers. This influential publication is discussed in T. Benton (2017). 'E-1027 and the Drôle de Guerre', op. cit.

112 Le Corbusier (1955). *Poème de l'angle droit*, op. cit.

113 Colomina, B. (1993). 'War on Architecture: E.1027 – House Designed by Eileen Gray at Cap Martin', op. cit. Colomina based her research on S. von Moos (1987). 'Les femmes d'Alger', in D. Pauly (ed.), *Le Corbusier et la Méditerranée*, Marseille, Éditions Parenthèses, pp. 191–209.

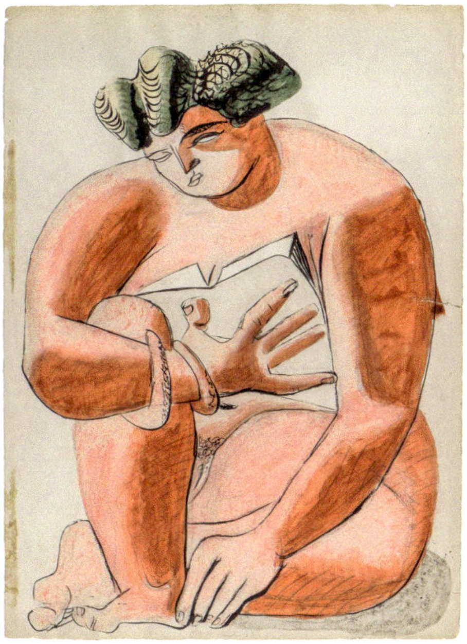

Le Corbusier, watercolour sketch of woman reading a book, ca 1936.

ly knew Gray at this point. Le Corbusier knew Badovici with the latter's mistress Madeleine Goisot, who was present in 1938 and again in 1939 and who was a close friend of Le Corbusier and Yvonne. Colomina based her argument on an article by an obscure Egyptian artist named Samir Rafi, but this article, which is full of mistakes, must be treated with extreme scepticism and there is no evidence of the frequent interviews Rafi claimed to have had with Le Corbusier. The drawings he illustrates as being the sole surviving sketches of Algerian women are now recognised as fakes, clearly drawn by Rafi himself in imitation of motifs in the E1027 mural.[114] As I have said, Le Corbusier's murals at E1027 cannot be defended on moral grounds, but they have little or nothing to do with Eileen Gray.

The source for the mural is the painting *Trois personnages* (Three figures), 1937. A coloured study for this painting |ill. p. 70 left| shows the composition and Le Corbusier made a number of sketches at Le Piquey in preparation for this study.[115] On two of the preparatory drawings for this painting |ill. p. 70 right|,[116] the timber roof of the Vidal establishment at Le Piquey, where Le Corbusier stayed on the Bassin d'Arcachon, can be identified |ill. p. 69 bottom right|. The fact that the preliminary sketches can be located at Le Piquey suggest that Le Corbusier was not thinking of Badovici, let alone Gray. Although the three figures in the 'sgraffitte' look female, the figure on the right could be a man. A visual pun, most clearly visible in the drawing on p. 73 top, plays with the ambiguity between the thumb of a hand and a penis. Marie-Louise Schelbert, who bought E1027 in 1960 after the death of Jean Badovici, liked to say that the painting represented Badovici, Eileen Gray and the child they never had. Although Mrs Schelbert never met either Badovici or Gray, it is possible that, unlikely as it may seem, Le Corbusier told her this story. On the other hand, a sketch in a notebook (Sketchbook B6) and a watercolour drawing |ill. p. 71| clearly show a woman in this posture and also indicate the origins of what Colomina takes to be a swastika, in the shape of a book. Days after completing this mural, Le Corbusier took 127 photographs of it with his cine camera.[117] These photographs show the rough surface of the cement-rendered wall. They also reveal traces of the charcoal lines drawn freehand onto the wall. They offer privileged insights into what he thought was important in the composition. For example, one of the photographs draws attention to the relationship between the head of the left-hand woman and the outline of the pebble on the wall on the left.

114 Rafi, S. (1968). 'Le Corbusier et les femmes d'Alger', *Revue d'histoire et de la civilisation du Maghreb*, pp. 50–66. See T. Benton (2017). 'E-1027 and the Drôle de Guerre', op. cit. Rafi also claimed that Le Corbusier made hundreds of drawings on tracing paper based on Delacroix's *Femmes d'Alger* and that this was a source for the mural. Again, none of these drawings exist and the similarities are not evident.

115 FLC 1196. The drawings FLC 3067, 1403, 494, 348, 142, 6152, 1430 and 1196 all deal with a similar theme and date from 1934–1938.

116 FLC 1403 and 3067.

117 Benton, T. (2013). *LCFoto: Le Corbusier: Secret Photographer*, Baden, London, Lars Müller, pp. 398–399.

The paintings of August 1939

On 3 August 1939, Le Corbusier wrote to Badovici announcing that he and Yvonne would like to visit him at Roquebrune. He continued: 'I have a furious desire to dirty your walls: ten compositions are ready, enough to daub everything.'[118] Five murals resulted from this campaign, of which two, on external walls, have since disappeared. In his diary, Le Corbusier noted, 'Cap-Martin: Badovici owes me: 81 + 17 + 38.50: loan 1,000, food 500 + 200 + 100.'[119] This tells us that Le Corbusier considered that Badovici should pay his expenses on materials and three weeks of upkeep. The note of resentment, that he was working as an artist unpaid by the client, led to further discontent after the war.

On 25 August 1939, Le Corbusier told his mother:

> *Worked passionately for a fortnight on large paintings with a barometer indicating 'variable', that is thundery, electric and hot: overwhelming. But I had strength in store and so here is this house, the size of 'Le Lac' [his mother's house], animated by strong and explosive paintings, of which some cover ten square metres. [...] This house is remarkable in an admirable location day and night.*[120]

The mural to the right of the entrance

In the 1930s, Le Corbusier frequently based his paintings on compositions from his Purist period (1920–1926). The origins of the mural to the right of the entrance |ill. p. 76| can be found in two still lives from 1926, *Bouteille et livre (rose)* (Bottle and book (pink), and *Table bouteille et livre* (Table, bottle and book), as well as *Nature morte aux deux bouteilles* (Still life with two bottles), 1928.[121] In 1939, he returned to this theme in two paintings, *Deux bouteilles et coquetier* (Two bottles and egg cup) and *Totem* (Totem) |ill. p. 74| which he dated '26–39'.[122] A sketch similar to the mural is annotated 'Vézelay 1939' |ill. p. 74| and seems to have been made after his stay at Roquebrune. The painting *Totem* reverses the composition and renders it flatter and more abstract. Someone, probably Madeleine Goisot, took several photographs of Le Corbusier at work in August 1939. In one photograph, we can see him sketching freehand on the wall, apparently consulting a little sketch in his left hand. The painting, exposed to the weather, had suffered by 1949, when Le Corbusier restored it. It eventually disappeared completely before he made his final restoration of the paintings in 1962.

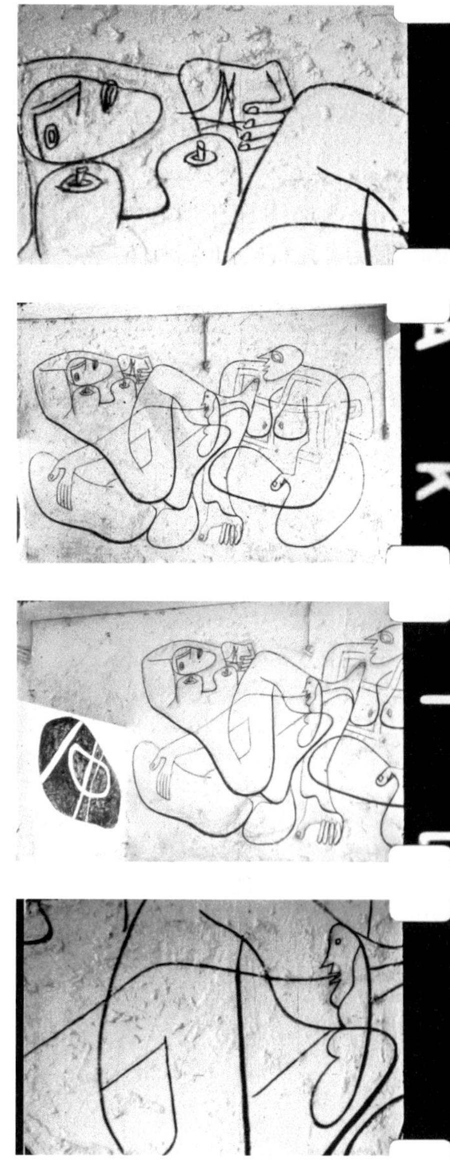

Le Corbusier, photographs of the 'sgraffitte' taken with his cine camera, May 1938.

Photograph of Le Corbusier's 'sgraffitte' at E1027, 1938.

Le Corbusier, still life (destroyed) located to the right of the main entrance of E1027, 1939.

Le Corbusier sketching the under-drawing of the still life to the right of the entrance.

---

118 FLC E1(05)34.
119 FLC F3(6)5 folio 67r.
120 FLC R(2)142.
121 FLC 143, 326 and 338, respectively.
122 FLC 153 and 236, respectively.

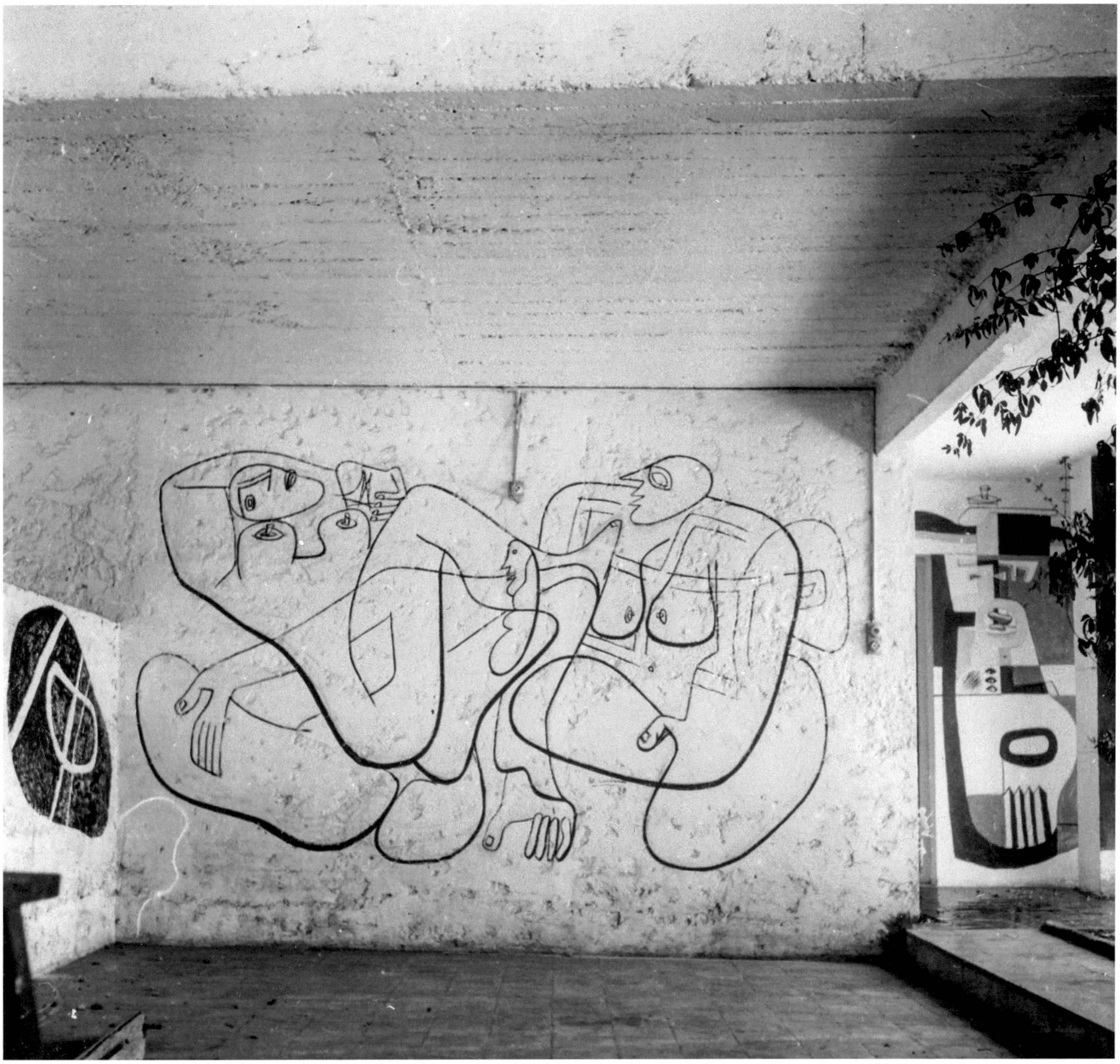

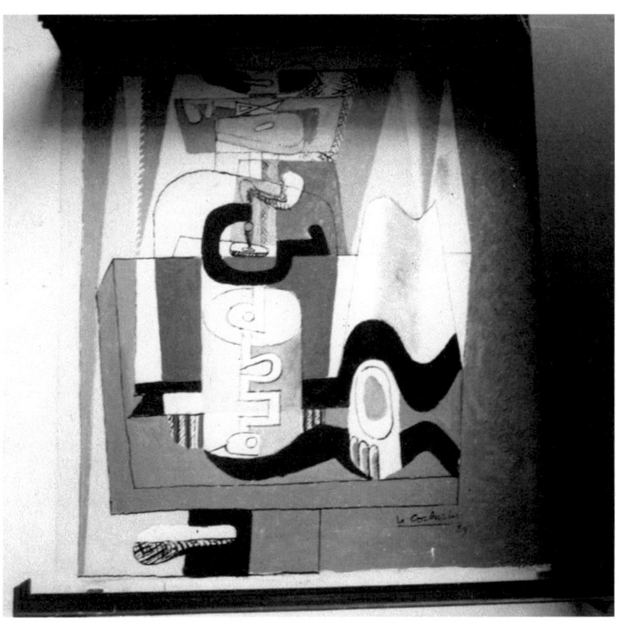

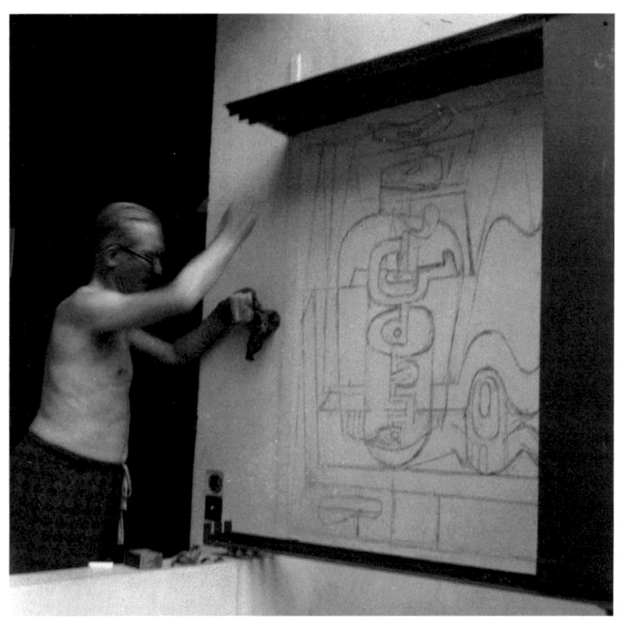

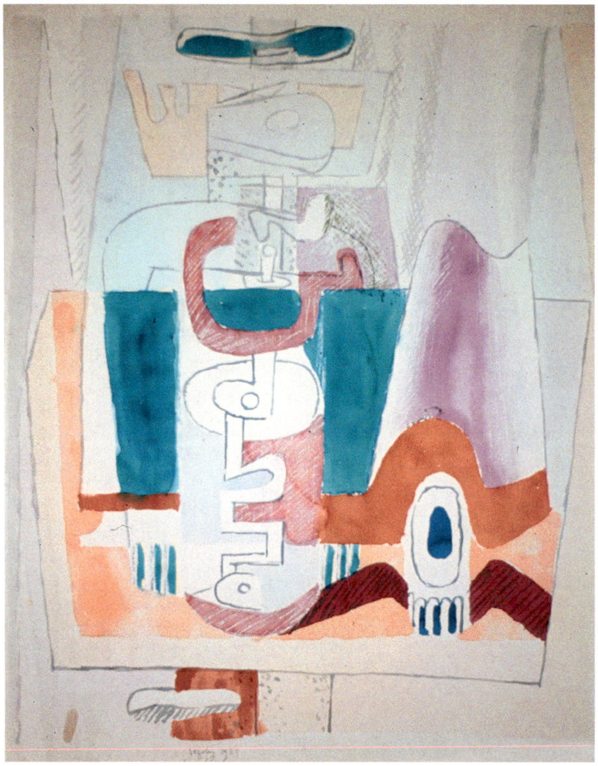

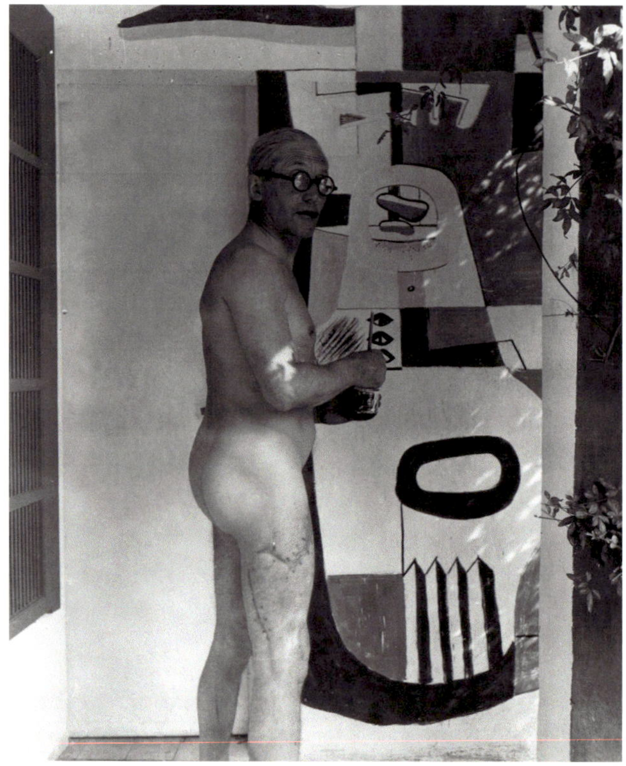

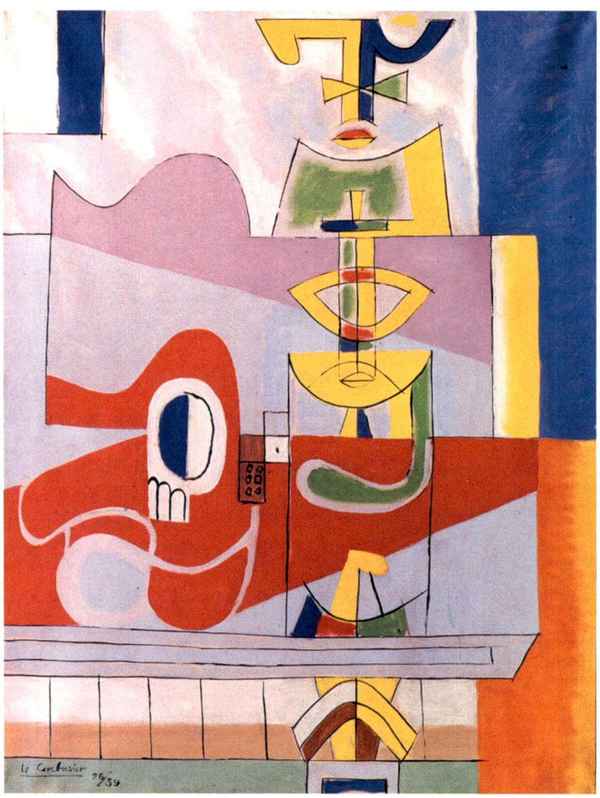

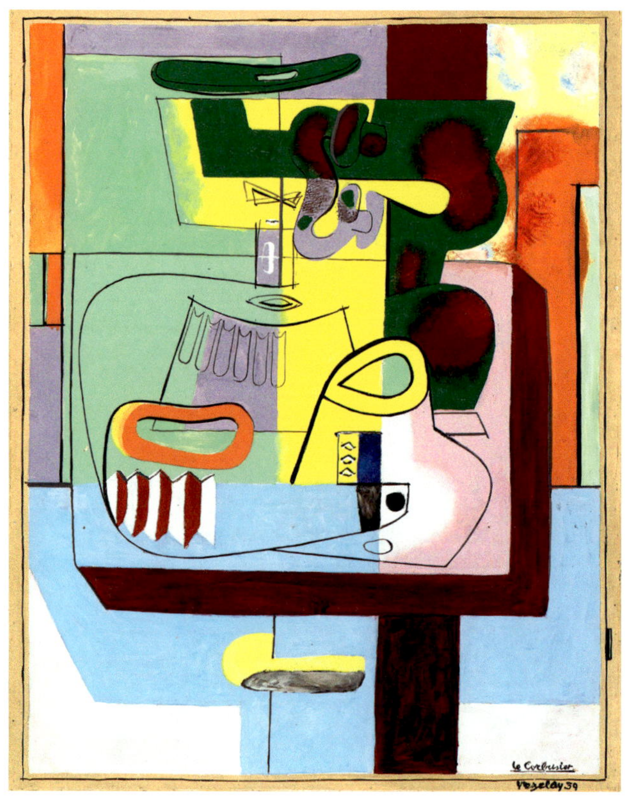

Le Corbusier, preparatory sketch for the still life to the right of the entrance of E1027, 1939, inscribed 'Vézelay 39' |top left|.

Le Corbusier painting the mural next to the door to the guest bedroom (destroyed). Note the terrible scar on his thigh, produced by the boat accident in St Tropez, in August 1938 |top right|.

Le Corbusier, *Totem* (Totem), dated '26-39' |bottom left|.

Le Corbusier, *Nature morte Vézelay* (Still life Vézelay), inscribed 'Vézelay 1939' |bottom right|.

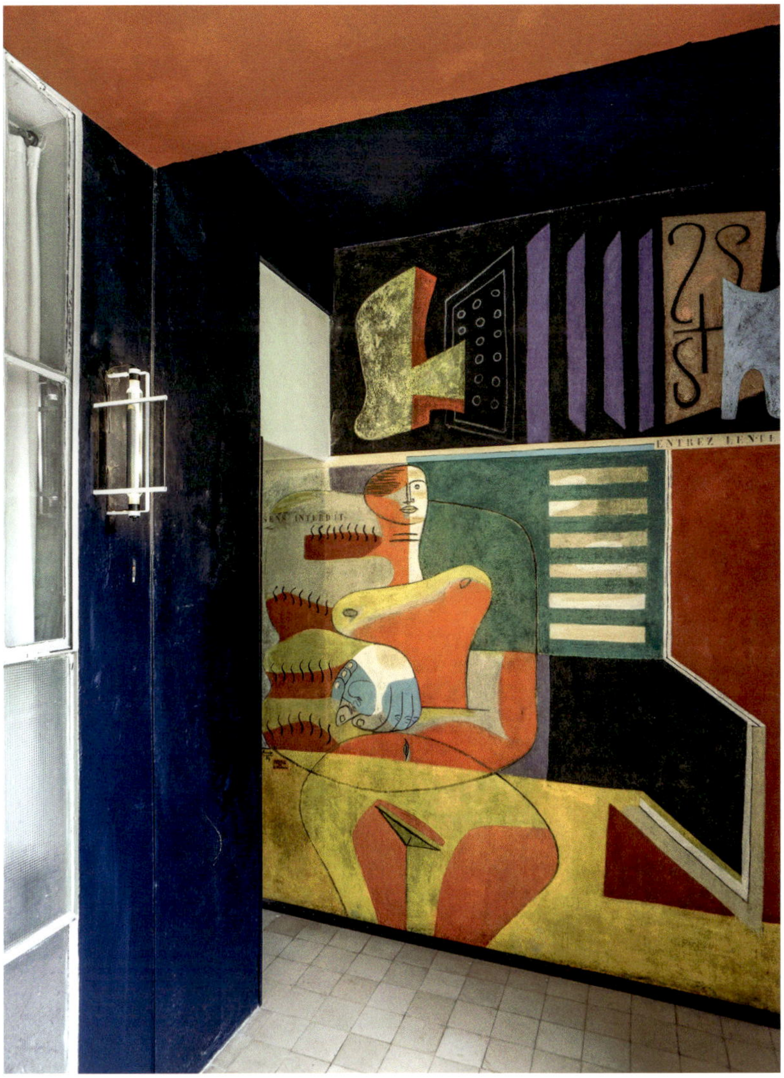

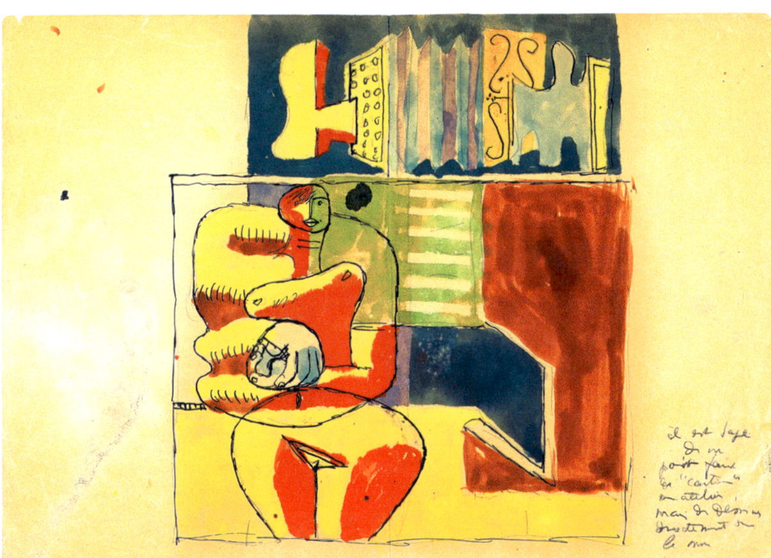

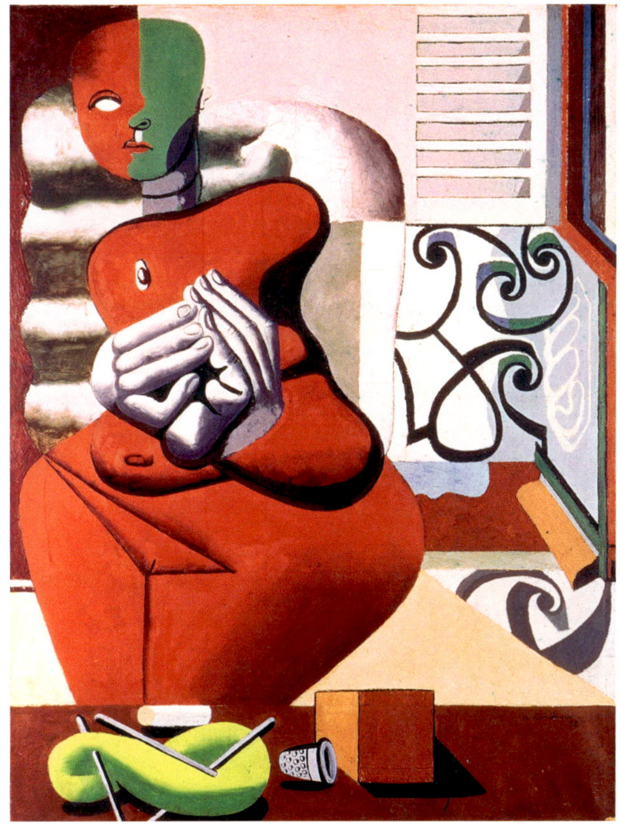

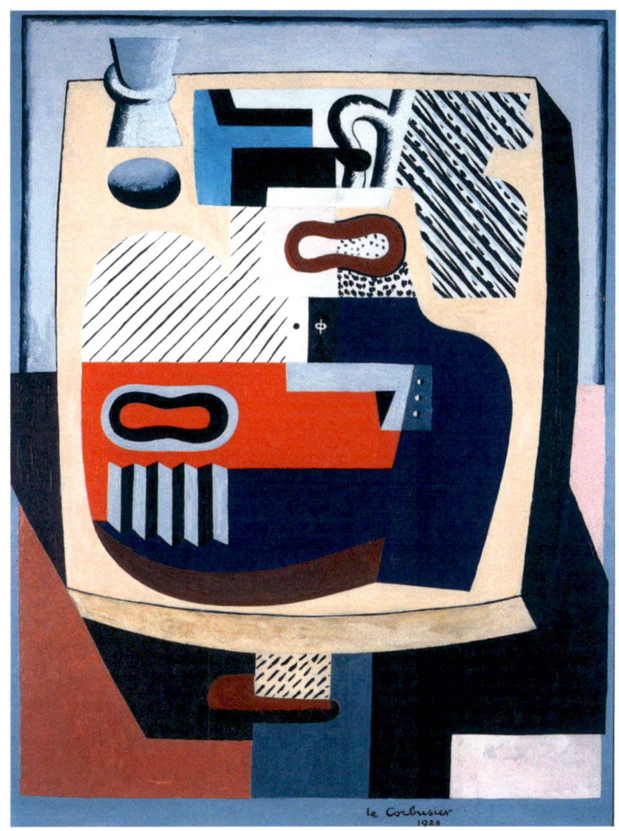

View of the mural in the entrance |top left|.

Le Corbusier, preparatory sketch for the mural in the entrance, 1939 |bottom left|.

Le Corbusier, study for the painting *Femme rouge et pelote verte* (Red woman and green skein of wool), 1932 |top right|.

Le Corbusier, *Nature morte au livre et au coquetier* (Still life with book and egg cup), 1928 |bottom right|.

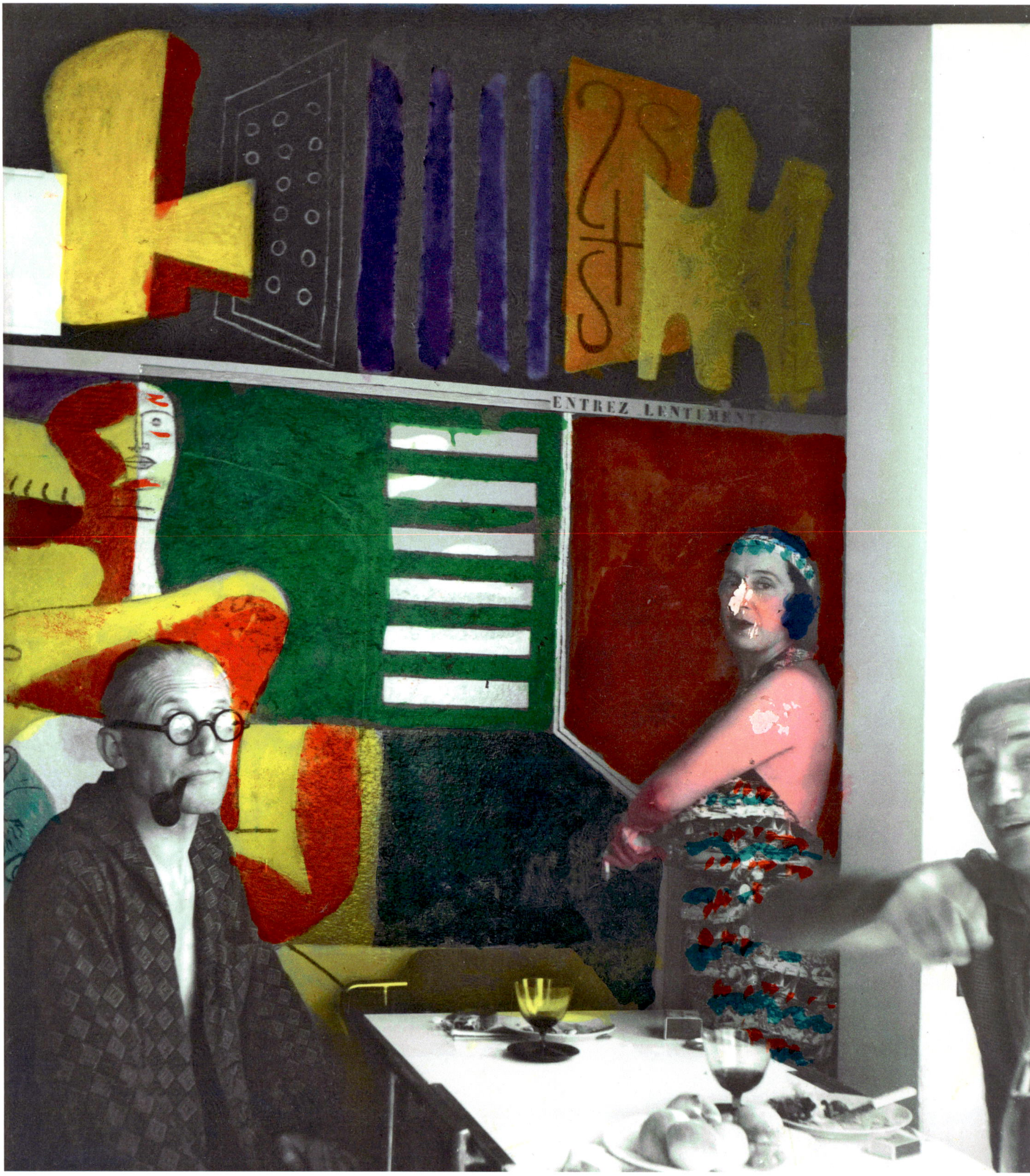

Le Corbusier, Yvonne and Jean Badovici in August 1939, in front of the entrance mural.

Still life at the entrance to the guest room

Once again, Le Corbusier turned to a composition of 1926, *Nature morte à l'accordeon* (Still life with accordion) which had already been reworked in a painting of 1928, *Nature morte au livre et au coquetier* (Still life with book and egg cup) |ill. p. 75 and 118|.[123] The mural is a reversed version of this composition, elongated and truncated to accommodate the narrow wall beside the door. Once again, he worked on this theme at Vézelay after his stay at E1027 producing a canvas labelled *Nature morte Vézelay* (Still life Vézelay, 1939) |ill. p. 74|.[124] He seems to have been sufficiently satisfied by these two still life murals to work them up as paintings for eventual exhibition. They represent a continual process of abstraction of his original Purist paintings. Le Corbusier had himself photographed nude, paint pot in hand, before this mural |ill. p. 74|.[125] Much has been made of this photograph, as if it emphasises Le Corbusier's sexual domination over the house and its architect. More likely, the motif for the photograph was to show off the scar from his terrible accident at St Tropez in August 1938 when his head was split open and his thigh slashed by a motor boat. It was also, as he told his mother, particularly hot.

The mural at the entrance

The brightly coloured mural in the entrance to the house was based on a painting *Femme rouge et pelote verte* (Red woman with green ball of wool) |ill. p. 75| from 1932.[126] The subject of this painting can be firmly identified as Yvonne, who loved to knit and crochet. Their marriage was just two years old. The white shutter and green wrought iron railing suggest a Mediterranean location, but it is also possible that the painting recalls the weeks spent at Le Piquey from 28 July 1932.[127] These details almost disappear in the sketch for the mural and are replaced by a stylised accordion along the top. Yvonne loved to hear the accordion played.

On a sketch for this mural, Le Corbusier wrote in pencil: 'It is wise not to make a "cartoon" in the studio but to draw directly on the wall.'[128] This note is somewhat incongruous, given the closeness of these murals to pre-existing canvases, but it does seem that Le Corbusier drew directly onto the wall, using sketches for general inspiration.

---

123 FLC 328 and 339, respectively.

124 FLC 154.

125 That the photograph was taken in 1939 is confirmed by the fact that the shutter on the left is shown as black, whereas by 1949 it had been repainted white. I am grateful to Renaud Barrès for confirming this observation.

126 FLC 103.

127 In his letter to his mother on 30 July 1932, Le Corbusier says he was drawing constantly (FLC R2(1)175).

128 FLC 4476.

Most of the murals are back to front, compared to the paintings that inspired them, but this sketch is oriented in the same way. He certainly never traced a composition from a projected image, but he did make detailed cartoons for tapestries and for murals such as that at the Centre for Rehabilitation in Rue Le Bua, Paris, that were intended for execution by Raoul Simon.

In the mural, Le Corbusier integrated the inscriptions that Gray had stencilled on the wall: '*Interdit*' (no entry) by the service entrance on the left and '*Entrez lentement*' (enter slowly) by the front door on the right. This last is one of several inscriptions in which Gray appears to encourage the ebullient Badovici to behave in a decorous fashion. It was here, on the north side of the house and next to the kitchen, that Badovici and his guests dined in the summer months. One of the photographs taken by Madeleine Goisot of Badovici, Le Corbusier and Yvonne, was later coloured, perhaps by Yvonne herself.

Le Corbusier later claimed that this was one of the 'unpleasing walls of the house' that he had brightened with his paintings, 'creating space in cramped places'.[129] There is an element of truth to this here, but it is notable that in his rough draft of the description of the house published in *L'Architecture Vivante* in 1929, Badovici's description stressed the importance of the bare wall in the entrance:

> *A large covered space, a kind of atrium, wide and welcoming, not one of those little doors where you enter directly into the living room. Facing you – a key point – is* a bare wall, *this for a certain refinement in conception, suggesting to the visitor a certain resistance. This provides a formally satisfying solution, with the large wall permitting the doors to be hidden: on the right the main entrance, on the left the domestic [entrance].*[130]

It is difficult to understand how, having written this, Badovici could have encouraged Le Corbusier to paint this mural on the wall.

Gray was particularly interested in this idea of 'resistance'.[131] In an unpublished text she wrote of the value of placing a wall to interrupt the circulation on entering an art gallery until a full view of the exhibited objects became visible:

> *Without appearing to offer resistance, the chicane heightens the pleasure of penetration; manages the transition; retains the mystery of the objects to be seen; holds pleasure in check.*[132]

Although this is a striking and in many ways successful mural painting, it is impossible to escape the conclusion that Le Corbusier is placing his personal mark on the house.

---

129 Le Corbusier (1948). *New World of Space*, New York, Reynal & Hitchcock, p. 99.

130 Badovici's manuscript is in the Getty Research Institute archive, 880412, Box 2, Copy 1. For an English transcription and introduction, see J. Badovici and T. Benton, 'Description of E-1027', *W86th*, 28, 1, Spring–Summer 2021, pp. 96–131.

131 Benton, T. (2020). 'Penetrating the Interior: Instinct, Fear and Pleasure', in I. Lehkoživová and J. Ockman (eds.), *Book for Mary: Sixty on Seventy*, Brno, Quatro Print, pp. 28–35.

132 National Museum of Ireland, Dublin, Eileen Gray archive, 2003–044.

The mural in the guest room

This very dominant mural was based on a painting called *Masque et pigne de pin* (Mask and pine cone), 1930. Le Corbusier picked up pine cones in the forests on the sand dunes at the Bassin d'Arcachon, as well as driftwood from the beach and stones and seashells and treasured them as '*objets à réaction poétique*' (objects for poetic stimulation). These objects, which still exist in the collection of the Fondation Le Corbusier, were shown to visitors and journalists as his 'special collection'. Another natural form in this oil painting was a butcher's bone that Le Corbusier included in many of his paintings.[133] He even filmed this bone with his movie camera in June 1936 |ill. p. 80|. In the mural, the pine cone has disappeared and the mask is replaced by a pebble that the artist picked up on the beach nearby. He saw in the form of this pebble, with its white lines, the shape of a head forming the top of a red body that extended behind Eileen Gray's writing desk. This writing desk disappeared and the painting behind it is lost. When the fitment was reconstructed, there was no trace of the painting behind. Some small blurred photographs, taken by Badovici or more probably Madeleine Goisot, show a naked Le Corbusier painting this mural in August 1939 |ill. p. 80|.[134]

The mural in the bar

The second mural in the living room is on the wall facing the sea, in the bar and dining area. Le Corbusier had long been fascinated by proportion in nature and in geometry, particularly after reading Matila Ghyka's books on proportion around 1930.[135] This mural derives from the paintings *Arabesques animées et chien* (Animated arabesques and dog) and *Spirales géométriques animées* (Animated geometric spirals) |ill. p. 84|, both ca 1932, and several sketches associated with it.[136] These compare Dionysian passion, on the left, represented by a woman dancing, and a conch shell incorporating a Pythagorean spiral, on the right. The latter symbolised mathematical and geometrical proportion embedded in natural forms. Le Corbusier associated these with the spiritual world, the sphere of divine proportion. Le Corbusier separated left and right – the Dionysian

---

133 Two pencil drawings follow the layout of the bone in the mural, embedded in an arabesque of swirling lines (FLC 6247 and 6248). The butcher's bone appears in *Sculpture et nu* (Sculpture and nude, FLC 342, 1929), *Composition, violon, os et Saint-Sulpice* (Composition, violin, bone and Saint-Sulpice, FLC 344, 1930), *Nature morte à la racine et au cordage* (Still life with root and yellow rope, FLC 94, 1930), *Femme noire, homme rouge et os* (Black woman, red man and bone, FLC 98, 1931), *Femme grise, homme rouge et os devant une porte* (Grey woman, red man and bone before a door, FLC 8, 1931), among others |ill. p. 28|.

134 FLC L4(10)37.

135 He owned and annotated M. C. Ghyka (1927). *Esthétique des proportions dans la Nature et dans les Arts*, Paris, Gallimard; and M. C. Ghyka and P. Valéry (1931). *Le nombre d'or. Rites et rythmes pythagoriciens dans le développement de la civilisation occidentale précédé d'une lettre de Paul Valéry*, Paris, Gallimard.

136 FLC 105.

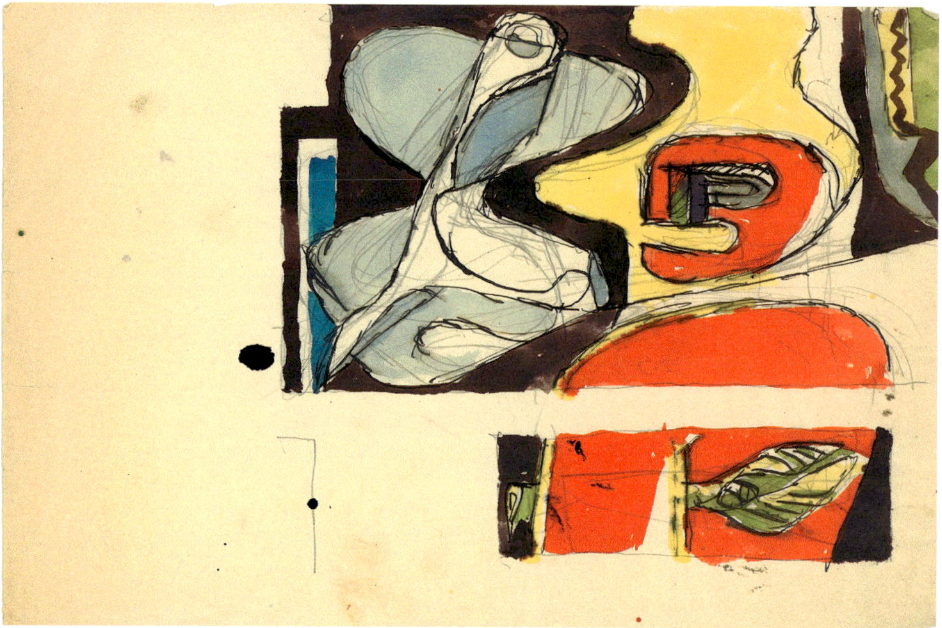

Le Corbusier, preparatory watercolour sketch for the painting in the guest bedroom showing the lower part painted inside Eileen Gray's writing desk.

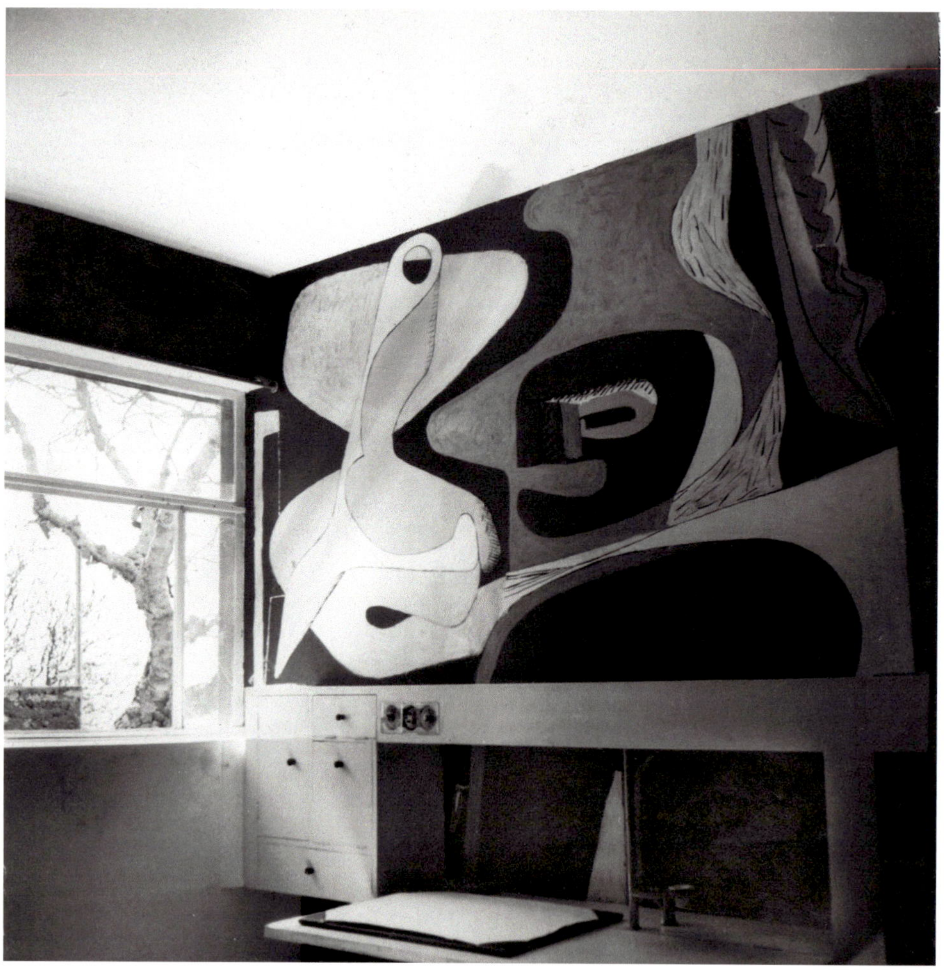

Le Corbusier, *Composition avec figure et os* (Composition with figure and bone), 1938, with the writing desk designed by Gray (1949).

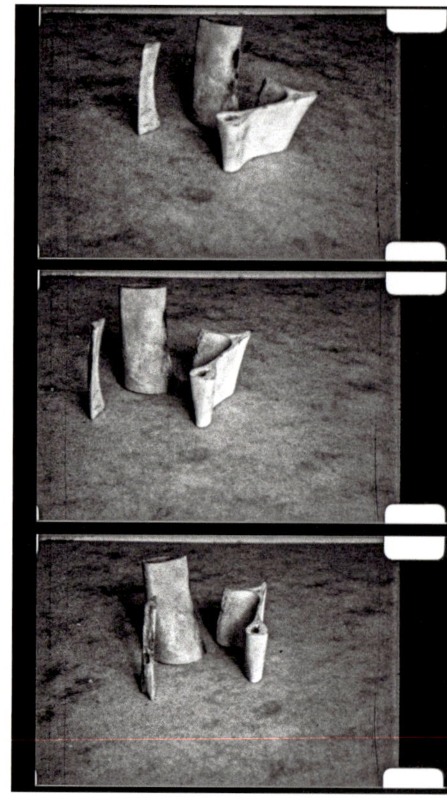

Photographs from a sequence of the butcher's bone filmed by Le Corbusier in 1936.

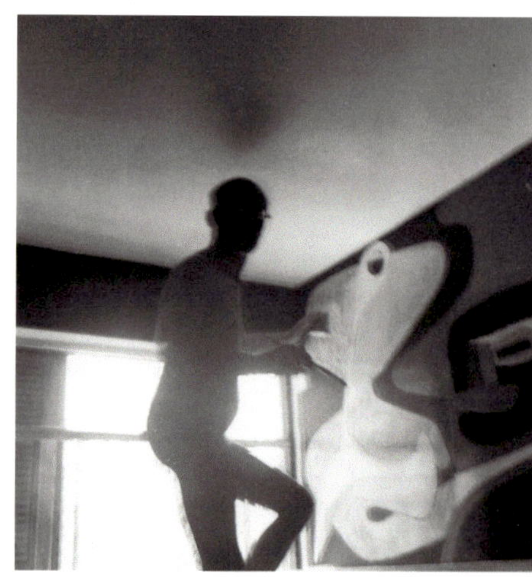

Le Corbusier painting the mural in the guest bedroom, August 1939, photographer probably Madeleine Goisot.

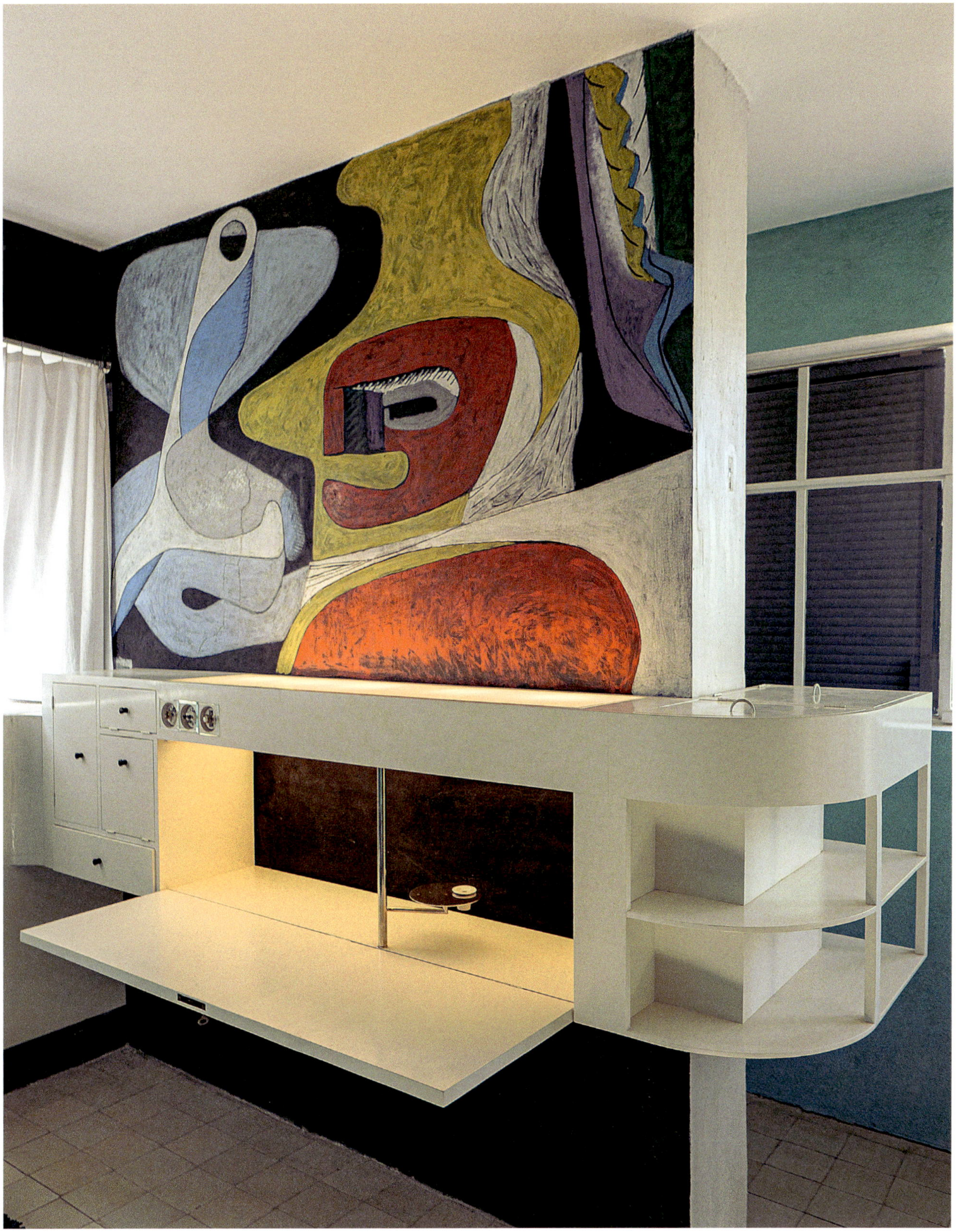

Mural in the guest bed-room after the restoration of Eileen Gray's desk.

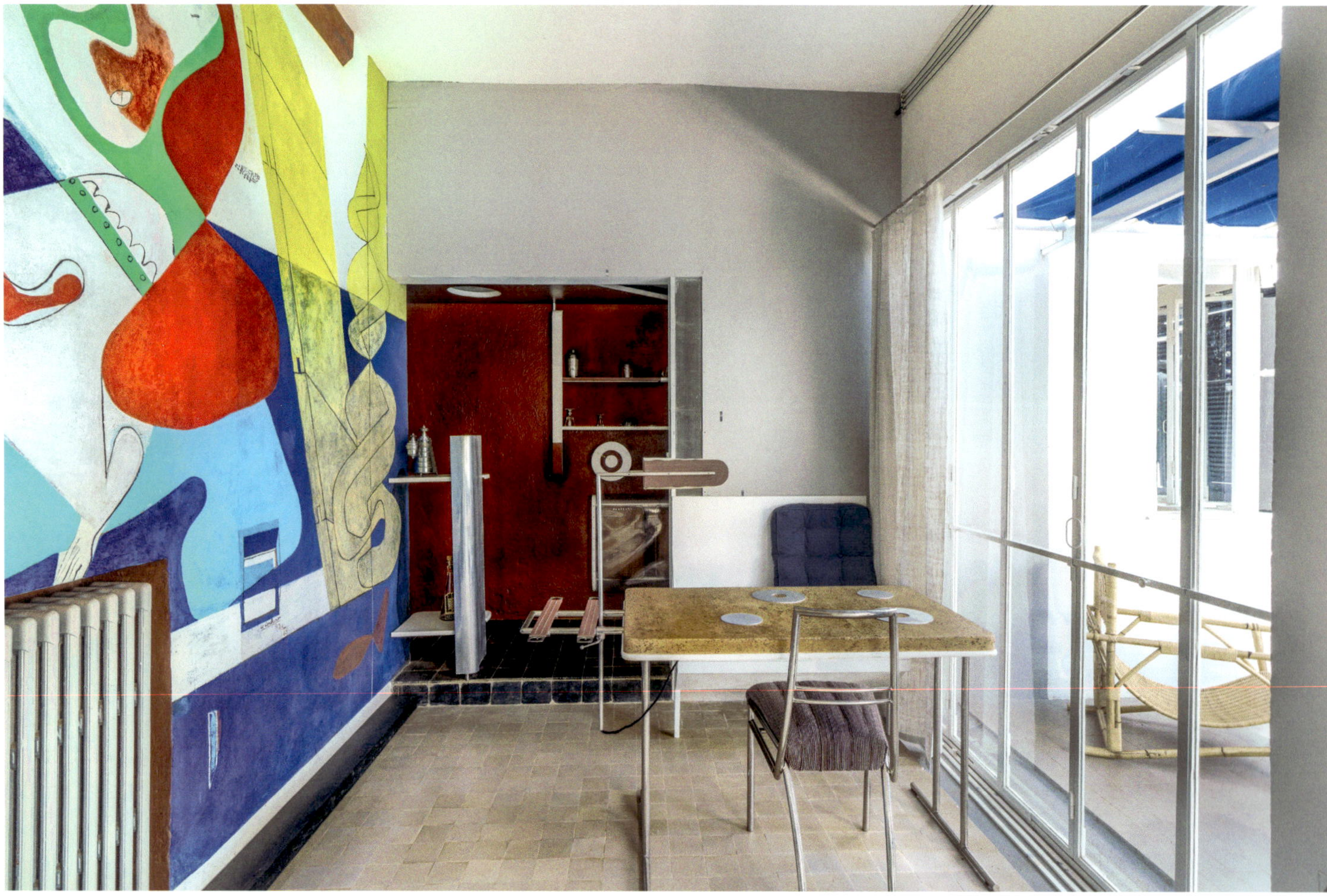

View of the dining area and bar with mural.

and the Pythagorean – by a wooden wall. At Le Piquey, Le Corbusier had sketched some women dancing animatedly to the sound of a gramophone at the 'Baron' cinema run by one of the members of the Vidal family |ill. p. 83|.[137] On 28 August 1932, he wrote:

> *Baron is popular because his 'pickup' is up to date. Waltzes, javas, accordion etc. Le Piquey is having a 'good time': Youth and joy everywhere.*[138]

The figure on the left is clearly derived from a rough drawing in Sketchbook B6. Le Corbusier reproduced the two parts of this painting in his later *Poème de l'angle droit* in the section B2 *Esprit*.[139] In Le Corbusier's later invention of the Modulor (published as a book in 1950), he tried to bring together golden section proportions (the Fibonacci series) with dimensions related to the human figure. In the *Poème*, a lithograph of the Modulor follows, with the twin Fibonacci scale in the middle, flanked by the seashell on the right and the Modulor man on the left.

137 See sketchbooks B6, pp. 399–404 and B8, pp. 520–522, in Le Corbusier et al. (1981). *Le Corbusier Sketchbook*, New York and Cambridge, Mass., Architectural History Foundation and MIT Press.

138 Sketchbook B8, ibid, p. 506.

139 Le Corbusier (1955). *Poème de l'angle droit*, op. cit., folios 52 and 54.

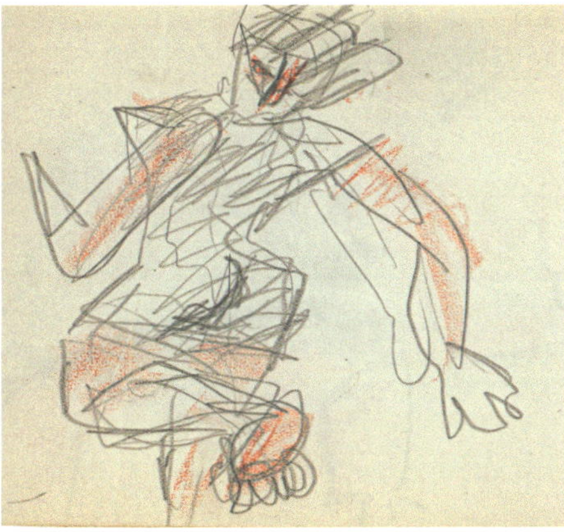

Le Corbusier, sketch of woman dancing at the Baron cinema, Le Piquey, 25 August 1932.

The mural had to accommodate a radiator on the left and was painted around the fixing point for a folding aluminium shelf that created a bar next to the dining area. The theme of physical and spiritual pleasure seems appropriate. As a nod to the immediate context, Le Corbusier picked up the dark blue of Eileen Gray's adjacent screen. He also added a fish at the bottom, perhaps as a reference to the sea or to culinary delights. On a later sketch of this mural, dated 2 September 1949, Le Corbusier wrote: 'For a tapestry by Baudoin; let him come here and make a cartoon.'[140] Le Corbusier was clearly pleased with this painting because he had himself photographed in front of it in 1939 |ill. p. 97|.

Aggression?

On 15 May 1949, Le Corbusier wrote to Badovici asking if he could hire the villa in August to work with Josep Lluís Sert and Paul Lester Wiener on the plans for Bogotá |ill. p. 87|, on their return from the CIAM conference (Congrès Internationaux d'Architecture Moderne) at Bergamo.[141] Following this meeting, Le Corbusier stayed on for fifteen days and restored the surviving murals. Up until this point, Badovici had expressed himself delighted with the murals. For instance, in 1941, after visiting the house to inspect for war damage, he wrote:

> *The 'baraque' is more beautiful than ever, she came through the disaster. Very little damage. All repaired. [...] The 'baraque' is brilliant and the paintings resplendent. [...] Some humble friends who live here told me yesterday: it's funny how the paintings go well with the house and the sea. And they were ecstatic. Hats off to Corbu and a thousand thanks.*[142]

A few days later, he repeated: 'your frescoes are intact and more luminous than ever.'[143] He must have been nervous, however, about having invited Le Corbusier to paint these murals because it seems that Eileen Gray still did not know about them. In January 1942, Yvonne wrote to Le Corbusier from Vézelay, where Le Corbusier had left her during his eighteen months at Vichy:

> *Badovici is completely mad. I put the wind of God up him. I told him that you were perhaps going to St Tropez. I know that he is scared silly that you might meet Gray. I did it on purpose to tease him.*[144]

---

140 FLC 5490. Pierre Baudoin taught at the École nationale d'art décoratif at Aubusson and worked with Le Corbusier on his tapestries.

141 FLC E1(5)68.

142 Letter from Badovici to Le Corbusier, written from E1027 at the end of July 1941 (FLC E1(5)49).

143 Letter from Badovici to Le Corbusier, 2 August 1941 (FLC E1(5)53).

144 Letter from Yvonne to Le Corbusier, 6 January 1942 (FLC R1(12)177).

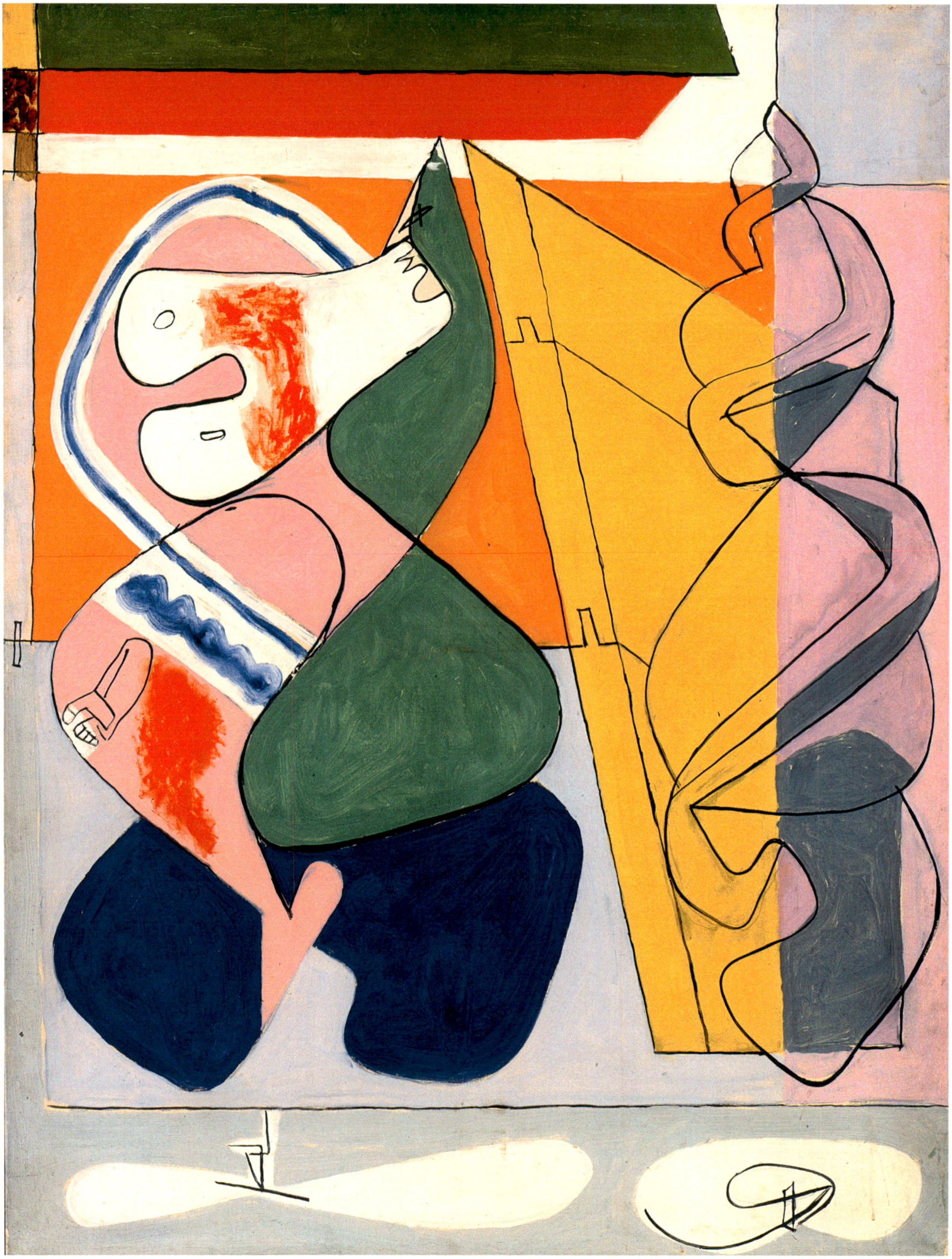

Le Corbusier, *Spirales géométriques animées* (Animated geometric spirals), ca 1932.

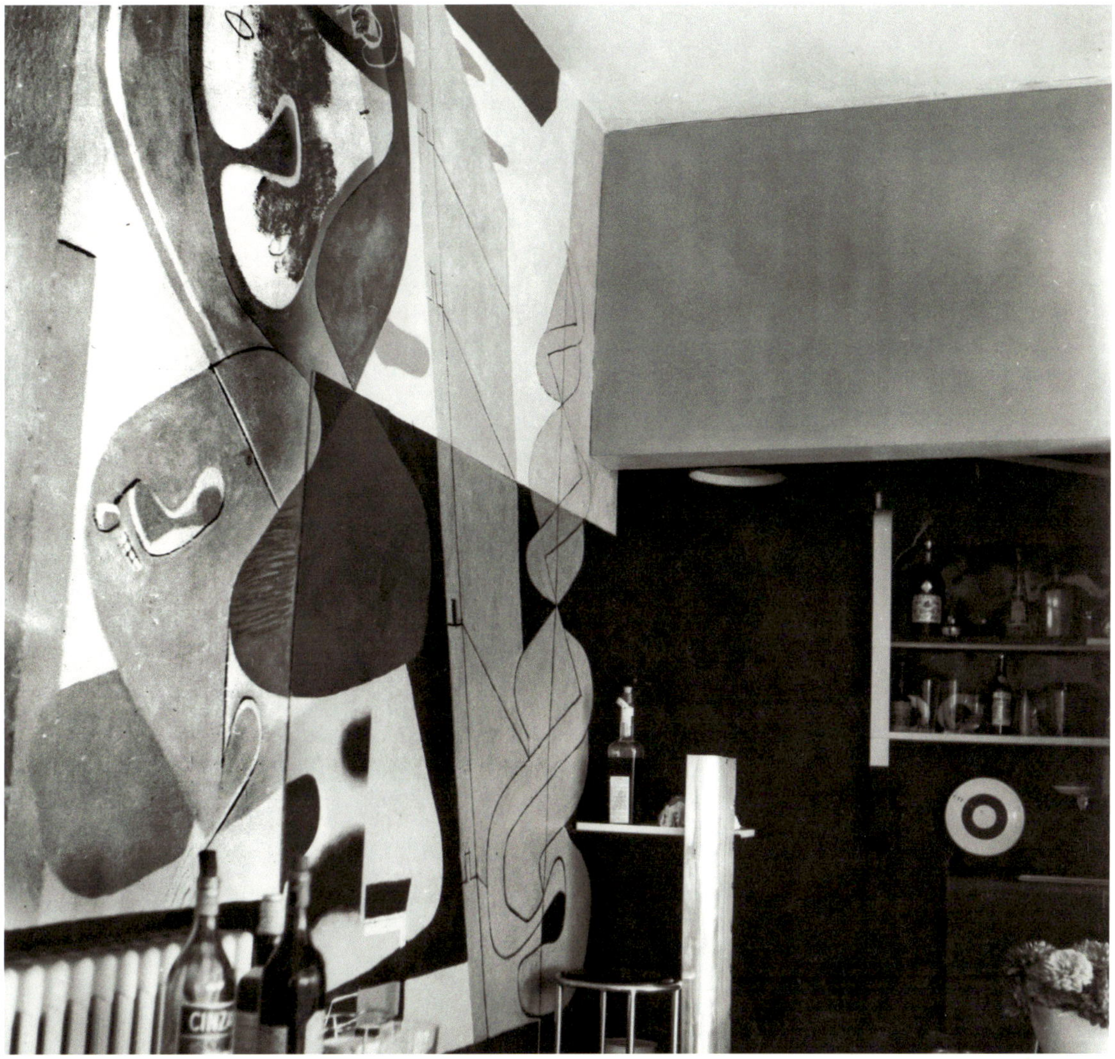

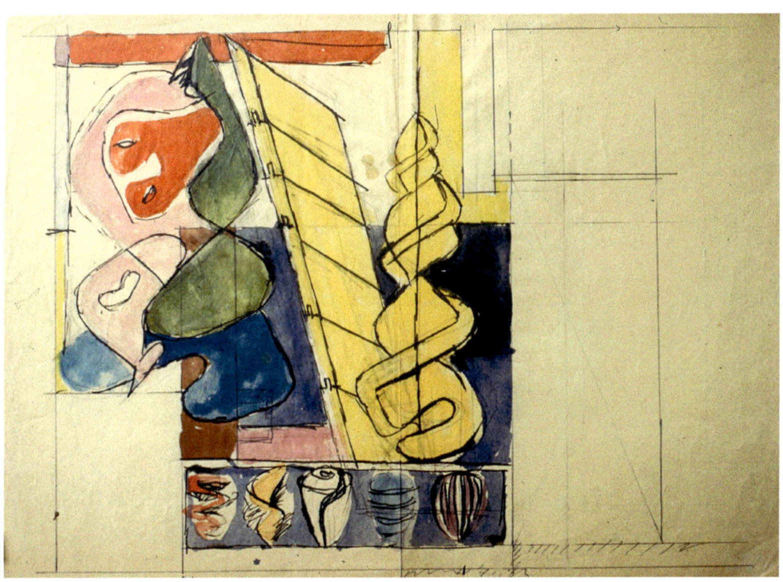

The mural in the bar, August 1939.

Le Corbusier, preparatory sketch for the mural in the bar, showing the cut-out on the left for the radiator.

Whether this is because Gray had found out about the murals or whether Badovici was afraid that Le Corbusier would tell her, is unclear. Badovici was certainly in contact with Gray, because Yvonne complained that he was keeping his cigarette ration for Gray, instead of offering her some.[145]

In 1949, however, the close friendship of Le Corbusier and Badovici came under pressure. Le Corbusier was critical of Badovici's laziness in not completing the paperwork for attending the Bergamo CIAM conference. He was unhappy that Badovici had not arranged for hotels for Sert and Wiener and he criticised him for bringing his new mistress, the eighteen-year-old Mireille Rougeot to the villa while Le Corbusier's distinguished and respectable guests were present with their wives.[146] On 5 September, Le Corbusier wrote an insulting letter to Badovici asking him to pay for the paints he had used in restoring the murals. He also wanted Badovici to have photographs made of the murals, including in his letter precise sketches for each of the ten photographs he wanted.[147] On 2 October, Le Corbusier berated Badovici for his failure to deliver the photographs. He went on:

> *You never thought it worth thanking me [for the paintings], but you drank my champagne instead of offering me some. I specifically asked you, in fair exchange, to have some photographs taken and I drew the compositions I wanted. [...] I am being asked for these photographs for publication. [...] I notice that in your publication of the 'baraque' you found a photographer capable of good work. [added in margin] And I am still waiting, after 14 years, for the three bottles of* gniolle *[rough brandy] which you owe me for the paintings and that I have asked for a hundred times.*[148]

Behind this unpleasant exchange we can detect Le Corbusier's sensitivity about his status as artist. He wanted to be paid, even if it was only in alcohol. The photographer who took the excellent pictures for the publication of E1027 in *L'Architecture Vivante* was Eileen Gray and obviously Badovici never thought to ask her to photograph the paintings.

Then, when Badovici finally found someone to do the job, Le Corbusier told him that his photographer was a 'donkey' and knew nothing about filters to render the colour accurately in black and white.[149] Le Corbusier published photographs of five of his murals in 1946

---

145 Letter from Yvonne to Le Corbusier, 20 December 1941 (FLC R1(12)170).

146 Letters from Le Corbusier to Badovici, 17 June 1949 (FLC E1(5)73) and 8 July 1949 (FLC E1(5)74). Le Corbusier referred to the presence of Mireille Rougeot as a 'coup de bohème' and said that he felt he would have to walk a tightrope negotiating between people of such different characters.

147 Letters from Le Corbusier to Jean Badovici, 5 September 1949 (FLC E1(5)84) and 10 September 1949 (FLC E1(5)85).

148 Letter from Le Corbusier to Jean Badovici 2 October 1949 (FLC E10(5)88).

149 Letter from Le Corbusier to Jean Badovici, 23 August 1950 (FLC E1(5)104). The letter is undated but seems to correspond to a dated envelope (FLC A1(5)105-001) and Badovici's reply on 26 August 1950.

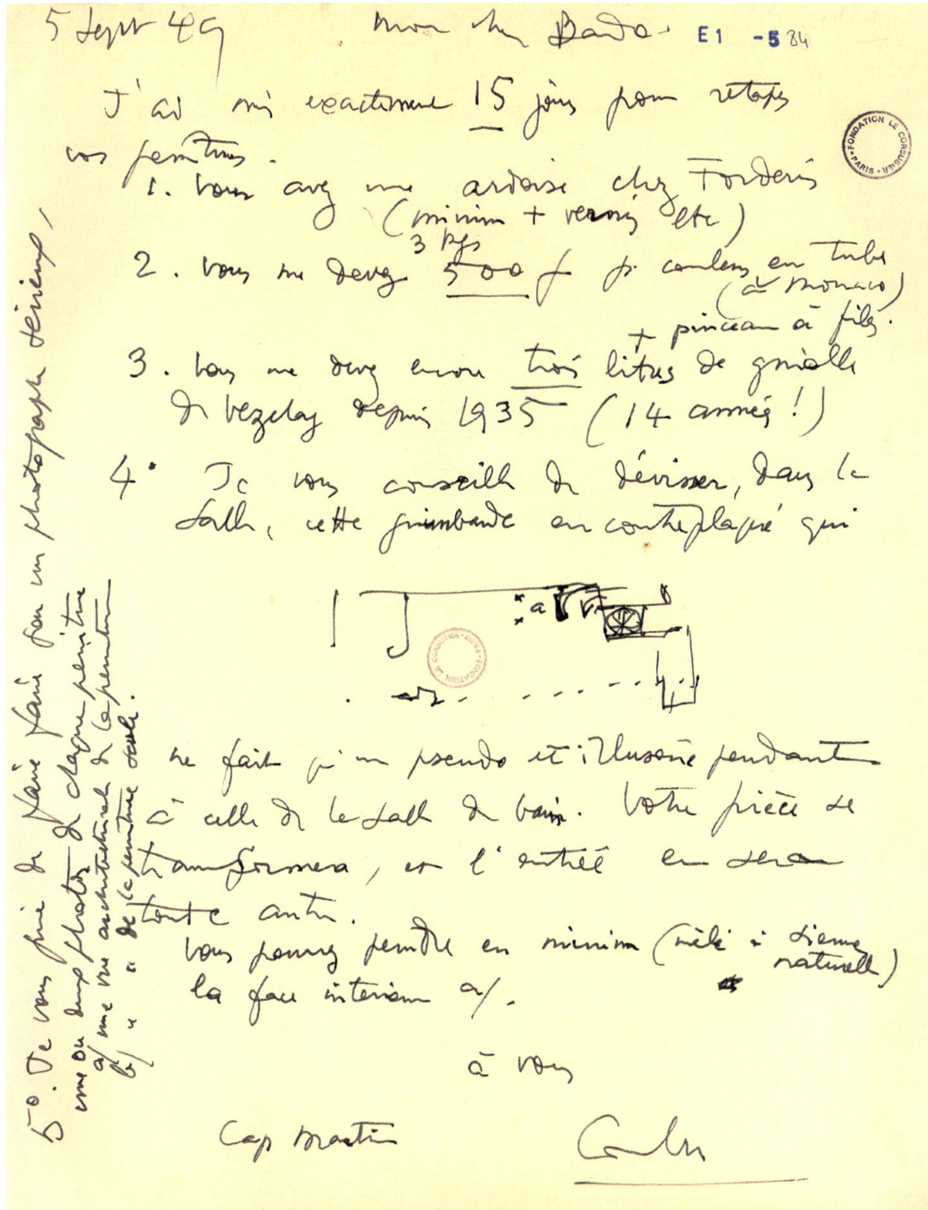

5 Sept 49 mon cher Bado- E1 -5 84

J'ai mis exactement 15 jours pour retaper vos peintures.

1. vous avez une ardoise chez Fonderie (minium + vernis etc)
2. vous me devez 500 f (3 pqs) de couleurs en tubes (à Monaco) + pinceaux à filet.
3. vous me devez encore trois litres de [illegible] de Vezelay depuis 1935 (14 années!)

4° Je vous conseille de dévisser, dans la salle, cette guimbarde en contreplaqué qui

ne fait qu'un pseudo et illusoire pendant à celle de la salle de bain. Votre pièce se transformera, et l'entrée en sera toute autre.

Vous pouvez peindre en minium (mêlé à terre naturelle) la face intérieure a/.

à vous

Cap Martin Corbu

5°. Je vous prie de faire faire par un photographe sérieux [illegible] un ou deux photos de chaque peinture [illegible] d'une vue architecturale de la peinture [illegible]

Letter from Le Corbusier to Jean Badovici, 5 September 1949, after a fortnight restoring his mural paintings. He bills Badovici for his materials, advises him to remove the entrance screen and asks him to have ten photographs made of his mural paintings.

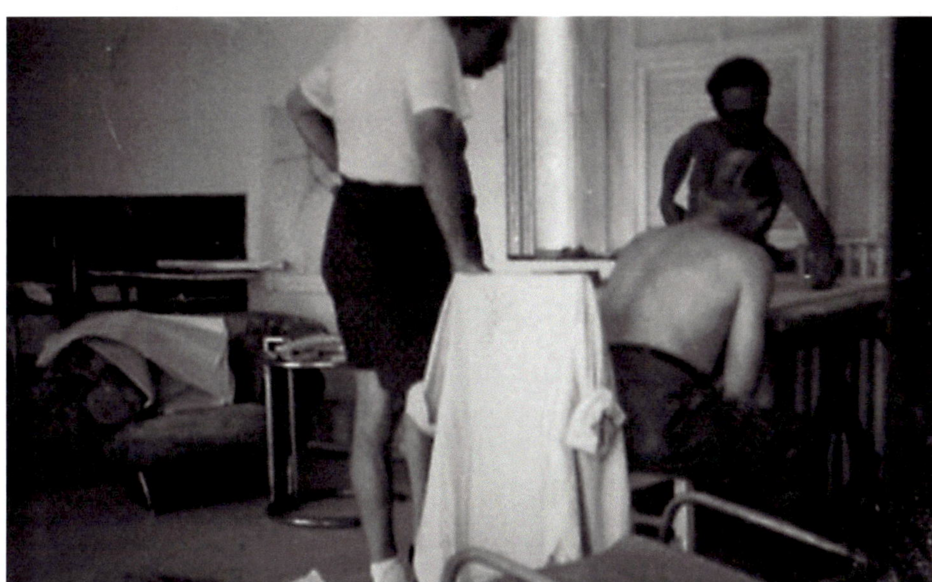

Paul Lester Wiener, Josep Lluís Sert and others working at E1027 on the plans for Bogotá, August 1949.

with a caption claiming 'They are not painted on the best walls of the villa. On the contrary, they burst out from dull, sad walls where nothing is happening.' He also published them in his book *New World of Space* |ill. p. 116|.[150] It is likely that it was only at this point that Gray found out about the murals and was understandably shocked. It was enough to make Badovici finally turn against his friend, complaining of the effect of Le Corbusier's vanity:

> *My 'baraque' has served as a laboratory, sacrificing the profound meaning of an intellectual approach that formally banned painting, being a pure and functional architecture. This is what has been its strength over the years. [...] Unless I see a change of heart on your part I will have to take matters into my own hands and re-establish the original character of the house by the sea.*[151]

It is worth noting that Badovici makes no mention of Eileen Gray in this letter. In fact, he never refers to her in any of his surviving correspondence. With some justice, Badovici reminds Le Corbusier of his unfailing support, publishing seven volumes of *L'Architecture Vivante* dedicated to his work.

In a dreadful, wounding letter, Le Corbusier replied, challenging Badovici to a public debate over the functional purity of E1027 and citing Gray's inscriptions as contrary evidence.[152] He went on: 'I perhaps do not understand completely the deep meaning of your thinking, since although you have lived in Paris for thirty years you have never managed to make what you write understood by others.' He also referred mockingly to Gray's house at 'Castellon' [sic Castellar, i.e. the village where Gray's 'Tempe a Pailla' is located] as 'that submarine of functionalism'.

Le Corbusier understood perfectly what Badovici meant by 'formally banning painting, being a pure and functional architecture' since this had been precisely his own position throughout the 1920s and the first part of the 1930s. He would never have accepted mural paintings in one of his villas of the 1920s. He may have made fun of Gray's inscriptions but we know that he admired E1027. Much later, writing to his associate Willy Boesiger, who was trying to find someone to buy the house after Badovici's death in 1956, Le Corbusier referred to it as 'Badovici's house' (inspired by the house 'Le Lac') built in 1928 with 'great care by Elen (sic) Gray and Bado for their personal use'.[153] It is notable that the only house that Le Corbusier photographed with his cine-camera between 1936 and 1938

150 The paintings were published as follows: Le Corbusier and W. Boesiger (1946). *Le Corbusier Œuvre complète 1938–1946*, Zürich, Artemis, pp. 158–161; Le Corbusier (1948). *New World of Space*, op. cit., p. 90 and pp. 99–102; the article 'Unité' (1948). *L'Architecture d'Aujourd'hui*, no 19, p. 49; Stamo Papadaki and Joseph Hudnut (1948). *Le Corbusier Architect, Painter, Writer*, New York, Macmillan.

151 Letter from Jean Badovici to Le Corbusier, 30 December 1949, manuscript (FLC E1(5)96). There is also a typed version of this letter with some erasures and changes (FLC E1(5)97).

152 Letter from Le Corbusier to Jean Badovici, 1 January 1950 (FLC E1(5)99).

153 Letter from Le Corbusier to Willy Boesiger, 7 August 1958 (FLC E1(5)120).

Spiral staircase with reconstruction of an abstract mural by Eileen Gray.

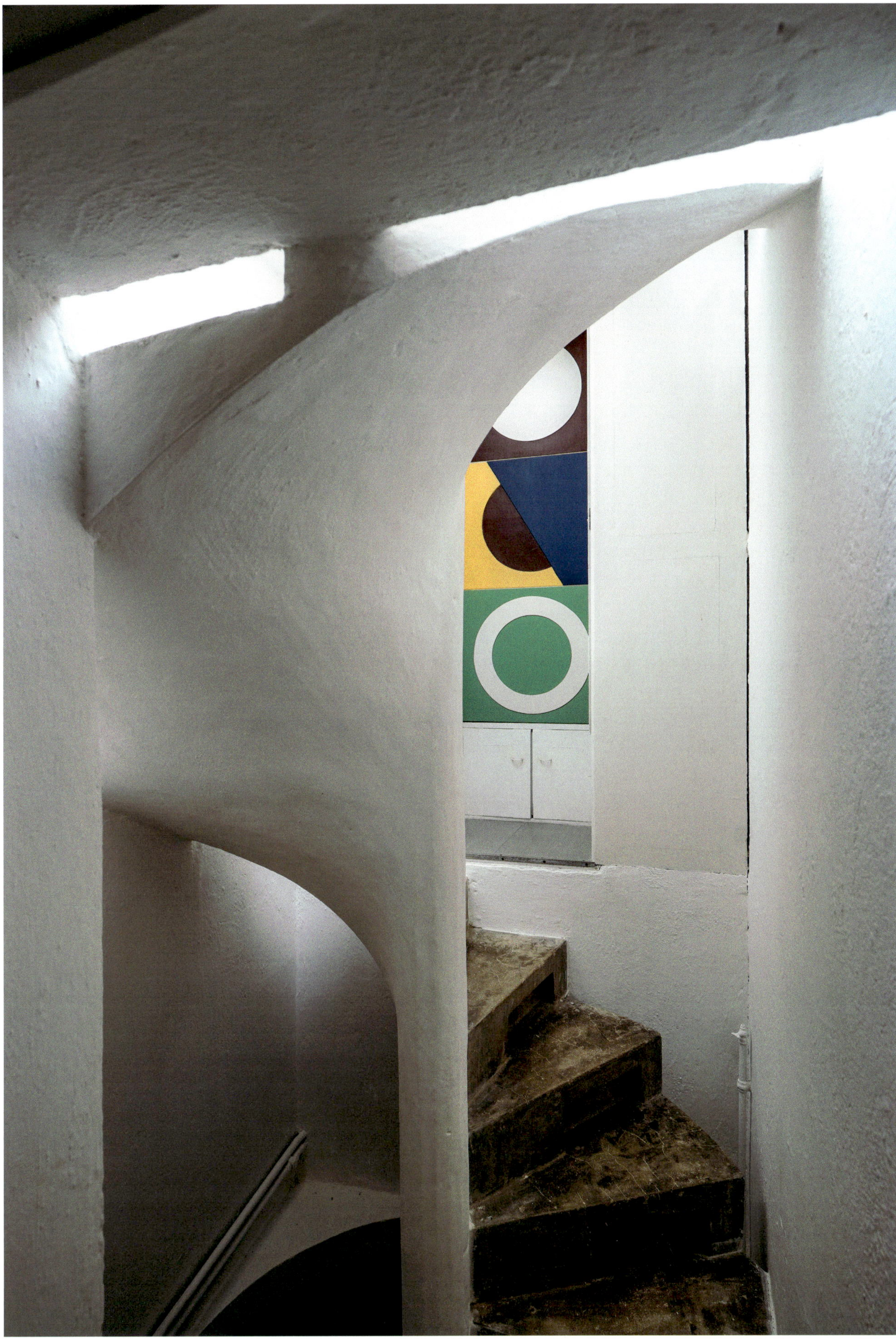

was E1027. But it is also true that Le Corbusier had largely abandoned the Purist style of the 1920s villa in 1929 and was more interested in working with stone, steel and wood. His villa for Madame de Mandrot (1929–1933), not far from Roquebrune, had none of the 'Five Points of the New Architecture'.[154] Nor did his two houses in 1935 'Le Sextant' on the Atlantic coast near Bordeaux and the Weekend house in a suburb of Paris – which were built in rough stone, brick and wood.[155] By 1938, therefore, the pure white style of E1027 was not at the centre of his aesthetic interests.

We may speculate about Eileen Gray's reaction to Le Corbusier's paintings, since the only evidence is second hand and filtered by the views of her biographer Peter Adam or others who met her in the 1960s. She must have been disturbed by the photographs of the murals published by Le Corbusier in 1948 and 1949. It is not the case, however, that she 'formally banned all painting', as Badovici suggests. As discussed earlier, she had tried out a polychromatic treatment of the north wall of the living room and, after abandoning this composition, retained the field of yellow in the large 'marine chart' which she designed. A collage in the V&A Archive records another polychromatic design in black, grey, brown, yellow and blue for the kitchen cupboards.[156] She also allowed herself some discreet abstract compositions. For example, flanking the spiral staircase, she painted the door of a cupboard with a composition of discs in the key colours used in the house |ill. p. 89|. This composition is preserved in an original collage drawing in coloured gouache.[157]

Following this ugly argument, the close relationship between Le Corbusier and Badovici was never really re-established, especially since Badovici had gone to work for Le Corbusier's arch-enemy André Lurcat on the reconstruction of Maubeuge.[158] Le Corbusier does not seem to have had free access to E1027 between 1949 and 1956, the year of Badovici's death. Nevertheless, there is a cheerful photograph of Le Corbusier and Yvonne with Badovici and Mireille Rougeot, taken on the terrace of the Étoile de mer restaurant around 1952.

No doubt Badovici was pleased to have Le Corbusier invest his artistic talent in his two houses and Le Corbusier was happy to be able to express himself. But neither can be exonerated from a seri-

---

154 Benton, T. (1984). 'La villa Mandrot i el lloc de la imaginacio', *Quaderns d'arquitectura i urbanisme*, 163, pp. 36–47, reprinted as T. Benton (2011). 'The Villa de Mandrot and the Place of the Imagination', in Michel Richard (ed.), *Massilia 2011. Annuaire d'Études Corbuséennes*, Marseille, Éditions Imbernon, pp. 92–105.

155 Benton, T. (2010). 'Le Corbusier e il vernacolare: Le Sextant a Les Mathes 1935', in A. Canziani, *Le Case per artisti sull'Isola Comacina*, Como, Nodo Libri, pp. 22–43; and T. Benton (2003). 'The Petite Maison de Weekend and the Parisian Suburbs', in *Le Corbusier & The Architecture of Reinvention*, London, AA Publications, pp. 118–139.

156 V&A Archive, London, AAD 188/31.

157 V&A Archive, London, AAD 188/35.

158 The city of Maubeuge had been heavily bombarded by the German army in 1940, resulting in the destruction of 90 per cent of the city centre. In late 1944, the provisional government of General de Gaulle commissioned André Lurçat as chief architect of the reconstruction.

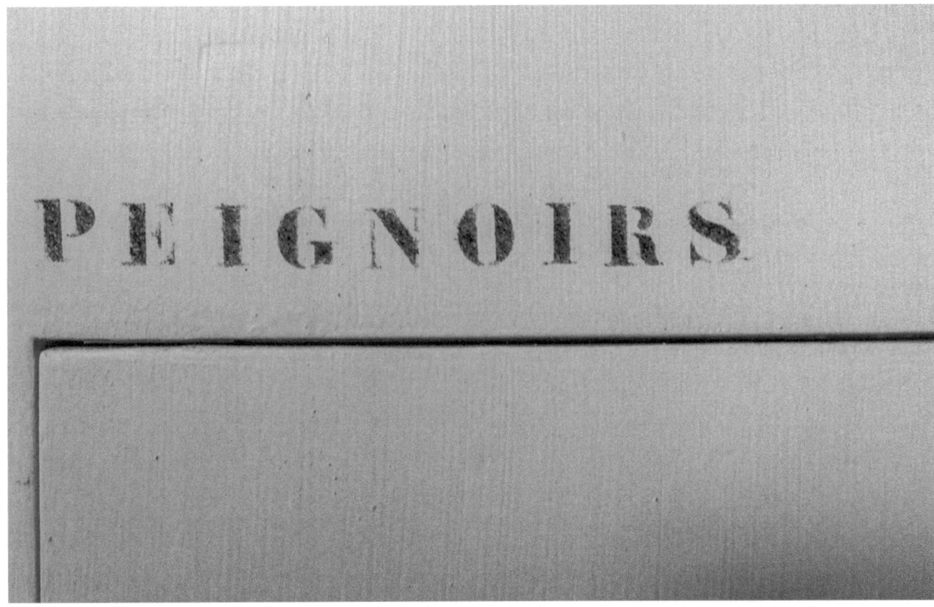

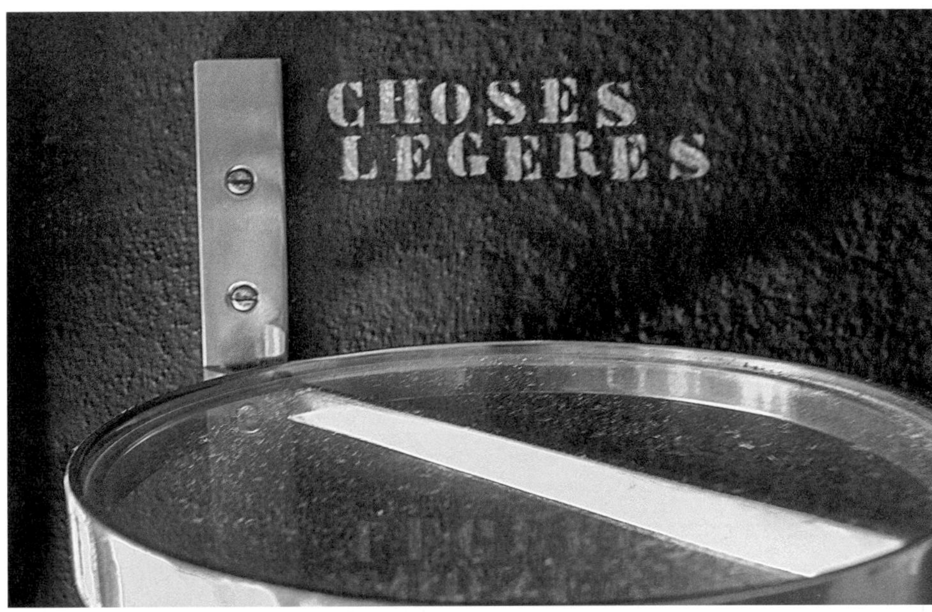

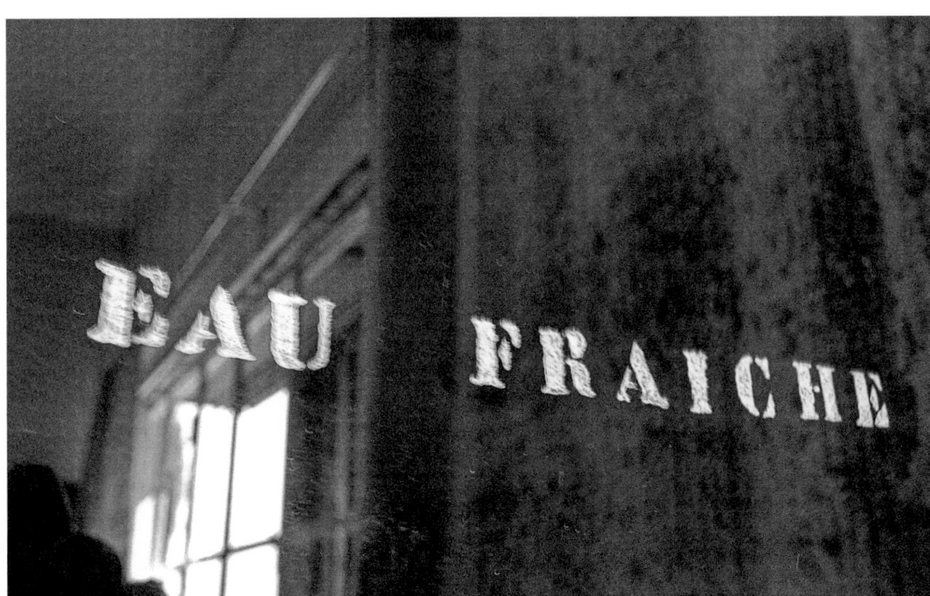

Original stencilled inscription by Eileen Gray '*Peignoirs*' (bathrobes) in the bathroom.

Restored inscription '*Choses légères*' (light objects), based on original photographs, above the wash basin in the master bedroom.

Restored inscription '*Eau fraîche*' (drinking water), based on original photographs, in the master bedroom.

ous mistake in aesthetic decorum. Le Corbusier's radical change of position on the relationship of paintings to architecture seems to have been influenced by Léger, whom he admired, during the conversation recorded by Badovici in his article of March 1937.[159] But there is no evidence to support Beatriz Colomina's argument that the paintings were an attack on Eileen Gray. The fact that Le Corbusier could not spell her name in 1959 proves that he did not know her well and it seems that Badovici did not refer to her much either.

E1027 after Badovici

Badovici had no children and his only heir was his sister Alexandrina who was in a care-home in Budapest. At first, a pastor associated with the religious order that ran the care-home, André Henriot, was in charge of the negotiations. But in 1960, the Romanian Embassy took over and appointed the lawyer Darjou as its representative.[160] Le Corbusier was anxious to preserve his murals and wrote to Willy Boesiger suggesting that the house could become a museum. He claimed that the murals had been widely published:

> *The four big ones have been photographed and printed full size and have toured the world: Musée National d'Art Moderne Paris 1953, travelling exhibition at Boston and the eight great American museums 1948–49 etc.*[161]

He went on to list all the advantages of the house and its site, including the close proximity of Thomas Rebutato's fish restaurant L'Étoile de mer. Boesiger's reply was rather negative so he turned to Heidi Weber[162] for help and it was one of her acquaintances, Marie-Louise Schelbert, who eventually bought the house, on 7 April 1960, at Menton.[163] There are some amusing stories about an auction at which the highest bidder was Aristotle Onassis, only to be prevented by Le Corbusier from buying it. There is no official record of an auction and the story may be apocryphal.[164] Le Corbusier tried

---

159 Badovici, J. (1937). 'Peinture murale ou peinture spatiale', op. cit.
160 Letter from André Henriot to Le Corbusier, 27 April 1960 (FLC E1(5)144).
161 Letter from Le Corbusier to Willy Boesiger, 7 August 1958 (FLC E1(5)119).
162 Heidi Weber was an art collector in Zürich who came to an agreement with Le Corbusier to buy and sell his paintings and furniture through her gallery. A substantial proportion of Le Corbusier's paintings passed through her hands and she published his artwork. See Heidi Weber and Hansjörg Gadient (1988). *Le Corbusier – the Artist: Works from the Heidi Weber Collection*, Zürich and Montreal, Edition Heidi Weber; Heidi Weber, ed. (1988), new exp. ed. 2004. *Le Corbusier: The Graphic Work*, Zürich and Montreal, Edition Heidi Weber. In 1960 she commissioned from Le Corbusier a steel pavilion which was constructed in Zürich to his designs after his death and which now contains a museum and exhibition space. See Catherine Dumont d'Ayot and Tim Benton (2013). *Le Corbusier's Pavilion for Zurich: Model and Prototype of an Ideal Exhibition Space*, Zürich, Institut für Denkmalpflege und Bauforschung and Lars Müller; Arthur Rüegg, ed. (1999). *Le Corbusier – René Burri – Magnum Photos*, Basel, Birkhäuser, pp. 55–67.
163 FLC E1(5)123.
164 Stella, R. (2017). 'Where the Paper Trail Leads', op. cit.

to interest Mrs Schelbert in the house by sending her photographs of his murals.[165]

Mrs Schelbert made various changes to make the house more waterproof and practical, but in general she preserved the building and its furniture. Le Corbusier insisted on the importance of the furniture. On 28 December 1961 he touched up the murals for the last time. In 1978, the local painter Jean Broniarski overpainted the murals with cruder colours which were later removed by the restorer Marie-Odile Hubert.

---

165 Letter from Le Corbusier to Mrs Schelbert, 13 April 1960 (FLC E1(5)143).

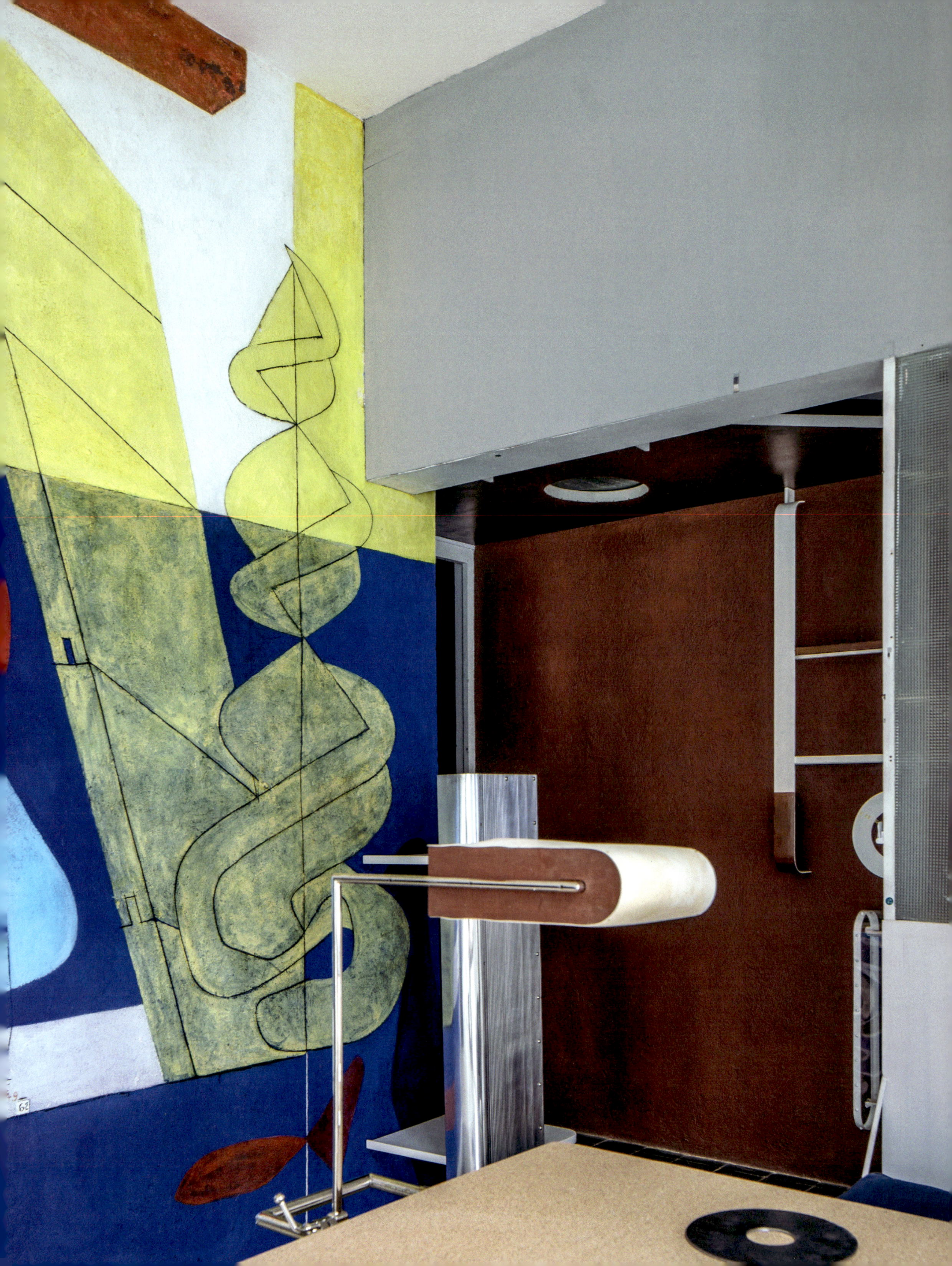

E1027 AS LABORATORY

The American architectural historian Henry-Russell Hitchcock wrote an important piece on 'The Place of Painting and Sculpture in Relation to Modern Architecture' in 1947, the year that CIAM devoted its congress at Hoddesdon to the subject of art. He describes the quandary posed by the insertion of works of autonomous modern art into modern architecture in a pithy couple of sentences:

> *A wall by Mondrian would have been ridiculous in a structure inspired globally by the aesthetic concepts of Mondrian ... Abstract painting, therefore, has remained enclosed in frames as rigidly as any other kind of painting, and draws no real support from the architecture to which it has lent so much strength.*[166]

Reflecting on a lifetime of experimentation as an architect, with the use of colour in buildings and as an artist, Le Corbusier liked to refer to the 'Synthesis of the Arts'. The motivation behind this line of speculation was his strong belief that there must be a relationship between pictorial, sculptural and architectural form. Coming from someone who for long periods painted in the morning and worked on architecture in the afternoon, this line of reasoning seems convincing. The most developed expression of this thought can be found in his book *New World of Space* where he simply juxtaposed examples of his painting and architecture on a sequence of page spreads organised roughly by chronology |ill. p. 116|.[167] But to expand this sentiment into a theory was more difficult. As each of the arts developed their own response to the machinist age, Le Corbusier imagined them coming together. But he had great difficulty picturing how this synthesis might come about, without falling into the trap of the Arts and Crafts or Art Nouveau movements, where architecture, painting and the crafts became submerged in decoration. For this to happen, architects, painters and sculptors would have to have a perfect understanding of each other's medium. For example, consider the painter confronting the wall on which he proposes to paint:

> *The wall has its own laws, its potential, its vitality. A 'wall' (so to speak) is in reality a fragment of a three-dimensional ensemble. We must understand the quality of volumes, their significance, their power, their capacity to compress or expand. And this can only be acquired by visiting built volumes – building sites or studios where plans are drawn up*

View of the dining table and bar (restored) with the mural.

166 Hitchcock, H.-R. (1947). 'The Place of Painting and Sculpture in Relation to Modern Architecture', *The Architect's Yearbook*, pp. 12–13.
167 Le Corbusier (1948). *New World of Space*, op. cit.

> *and where one must learn the technique by which simple drawings are used to create an architectural idea, to express it and eventually build it. I say therefore that men today are up against it and ill equipped for the lack of this understanding.*[168]

The correct approach, then, would be to compose the mural as an empathetic response to the architectural context. It can be argued that this is what Léger tried to do in his murals in the late 1930s – at Vézelay, for example. Le Corbusier himself adopted a different approach. All the mural paintings at E1027 are based on earlier easel paintings, adapted to their situation on the wall in only minimal ways. His later murals in the Étoile de mer restaurant were different. Le Corbusier went on to explain that the problem was that artists were reluctant to try their hand at mural painting. Only by doing so could they learn. Astonishingly, for an architect who was still known for his pure undecorated walls, he went on to say:

> *My humble advice is that all walls should be painted on building sites, never mind where, if only to be covered over later, in order to allow perceptive eyes and sensitive minds to face the tough challenge of architecture.* [169]

Written in the year of his argument with Badovici over the E1027 murals, this statement poses a number of problems. His argument is that only by experimenting in situ can the potential of mural painting in architecture be tested. Paradoxically, the earlier example of the de Stijl-like polychromatic treatment of the north wall of the salon of E1027, tried out and over-painted by Eileen Gray in 1929, would have been a good case in point of Le Corbusier's approach. His own murals, inscribed as national monuments and guaranteed permanent status, run completely counter to his text. Mural painting, like architecture, is a public medium and subject to different rules than easel painting or graphic art. The very forces which stimulated the development of mural painting in the 1930s – the patronage of dictatorships, the promotion of ideologies and commerce, the need to humanise the harshness of stripped classical and modernist interiors, created obstinate difficulties for an art which might truly bring together the aesthetic of modern architecture, painting and sculpture. The informal murals which Le Corbusier painted onto the wall of the Étoile de mer restaurant are a more successful response to the wall and its context. His mural in the Rebutato bedroom also works well, responding to the informality of the situation.

---

168 Le Corbusier, Préface (dated 1949), in A. Fasani (1951). *Éléments de peinture murale, pour une technique rationelle de la peinture*, Paris, Bordas, pp. 1-2. The book is a technical treatise on mural painting, including detailed advice and information on pigments, preparation, and the maintenance of mural paintings in different situations. He also makes frequent references to historic examples of mural art (from Egyptian to Renaissance) and includes sections on colour theory and form. Fasani had developed considerable experience of large-scale mural projects in the 1930s and André Bloc commissioned him to cover the wall of his house at Meudon with an abstract mural.

169 Le Corbusier (1955). *Poème de l'angle droit*, op. cit., p. 2.

Le Corbusier and his mural in the bar, August 1939.

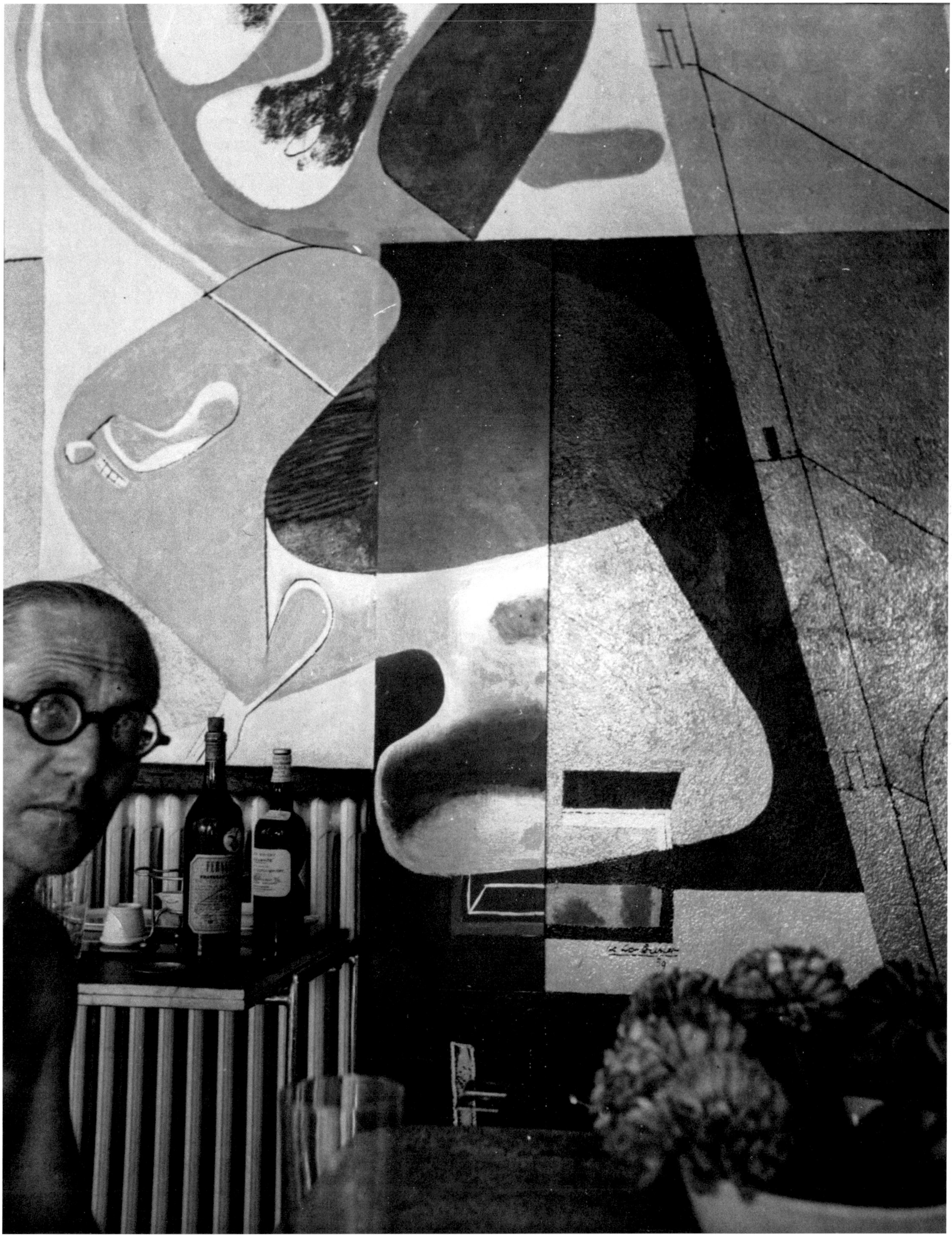

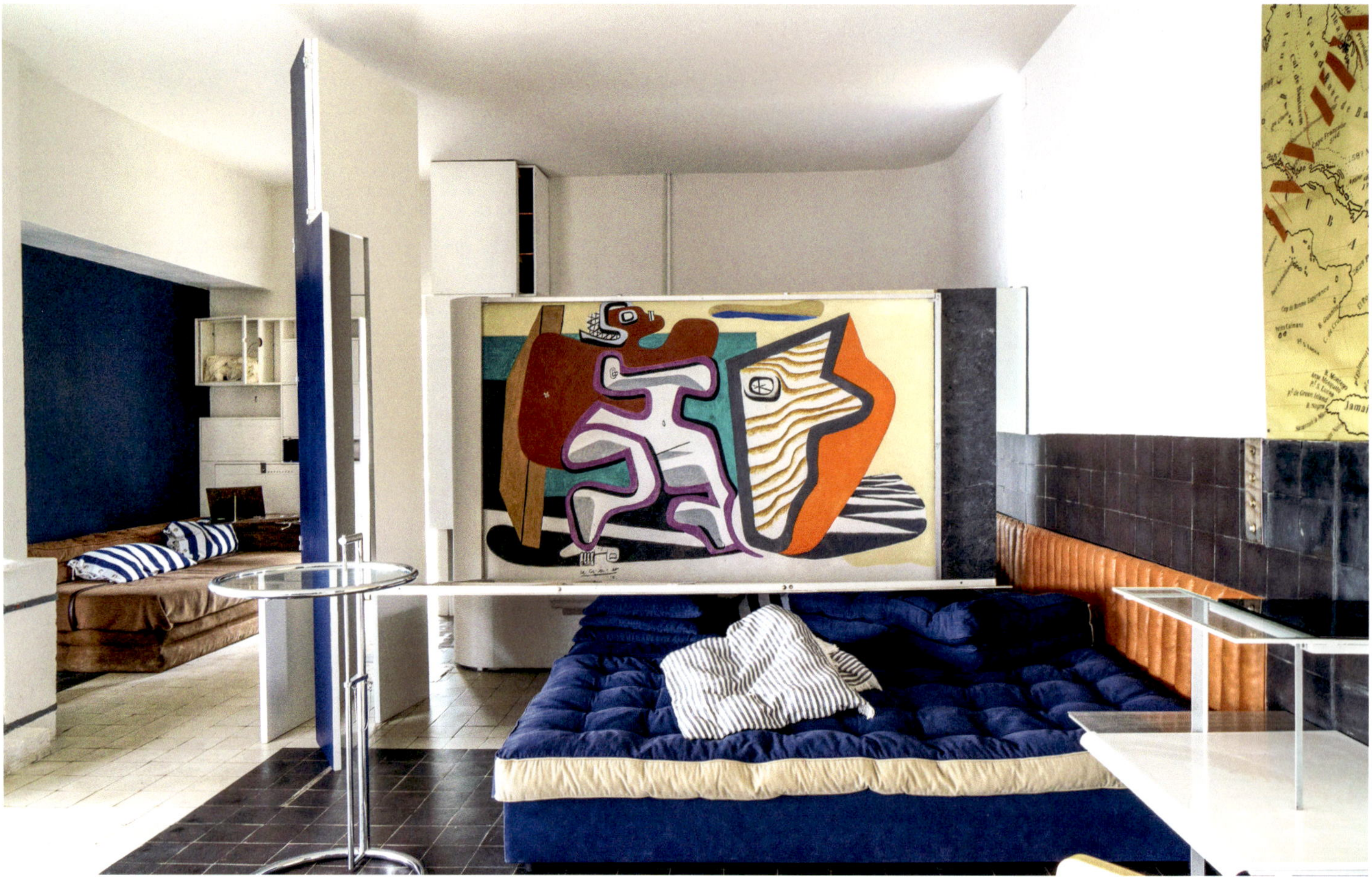

Living room of E1027, showing Le Corbusier's mural (1938) and the hinged panel designed to screen it from public view.

Synthesis of the arts

To try to explain his ideas on the synthesis of the arts, Le Corbusier came up with the idea of 'ineffable space'. His idea was that when all the elements of a space – volumes, sculpture, colour – are perfectly in harmony, a magical transformation takes place which corresponds to the aesthetic moment, when, to use the language of his book *Modulor*, the physical becomes spiritual (or 'divine'). He compared this to the fourth dimension:

> *The fourth dimension is the moment of limitless escape evoked by an exceptionally just consonance of the plastic means employed. [...] Then a boundless depth opens up, effaces the walls, drives away contingent presences,* accomplishes the miracle of ineffable space. *[original italics] [...] Architecture, sculpture, painting: the movement of time and of events now unquestionably leads them towards a synthesis. He who deals with architecture (what we understand as architecture and not that of the academies) must be an impeccable master of plastic form and a live and active connoisseur of the arts.*[170]

170 Le Corbusier, *New World of Space*, op. cit., pp. 8–9.

From 1945 onwards, Le Corbusier began to use colour more and more to modulate the walls, turning also to murals and tapestries. An example of this is his use of large photographic blow-ups of his paintings which he used to cover walls in some of his buildings. For instance, he inserted a large black and white photograph of his *Nature morte au livre et au coquetier* (Still life with book and eggcup) from 1928 in the director's office at the Claude et Duval factory at Saint Dié |ill. p. 118|.[171]

The enamels and stained-glass windows that he composed for the pilgrimage church at Ronchamp and at Chandigarh made a significant contribution to the success of these later works.[172] These were all original compositions made expressly for the site. He also designed a series of very effective tapestries – his so-called 'muralnomads' – which are still produced by Aubusson. A family moving from home to home to home could take their tapestries with them.

Whatever one might think of Le Corbusier's abuse of the 'laboratory' of E1027 in 1938–1939, it formed part of a very rich development in his artistic creativity. Although inappropriate in this context, it did mesh with Eileen Gray's critique of the poverty of functionalist architecture.

---

171 The Claude and Duval hosiery factory was the only industrial building that Le Corbusier designed. The reinforced concrete structure was mounted on stilts, based on the Modulor concept and opened in 1952.

172 See Christian Bjone (2009). 'Minotaur in the Labyrinth and Christ on the Cross', in *Art + Architecture. Strategies in Collaboration*, Basel: Birkhäuser, pp. 61–77; and Flora Samuel and Inge Linder-Gaillard (2020). *Sacred Concrete. The Churches of Le Corbusier* (sec. and revised edition), Basel: Birkhäuser, pp. 84-155.

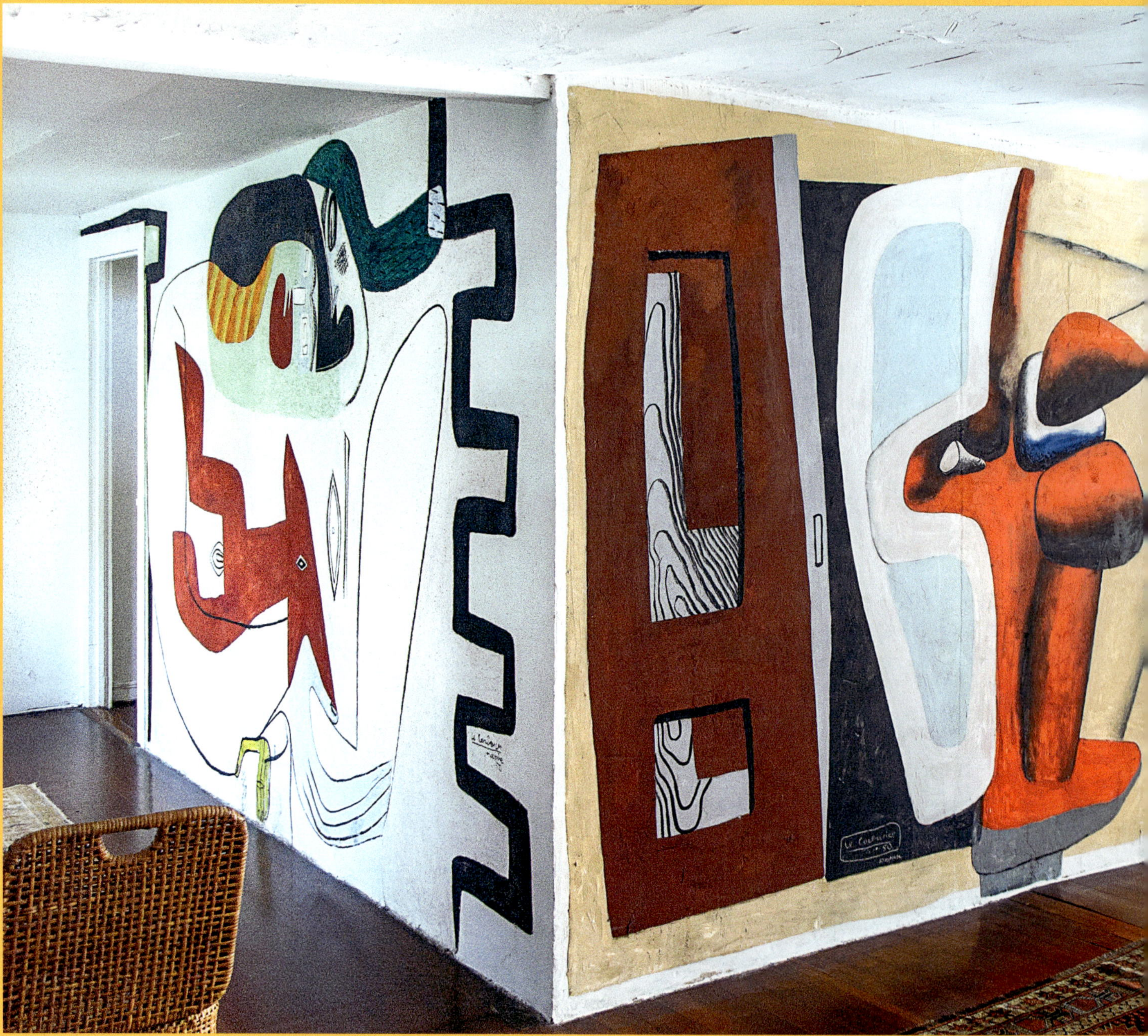

Le Corbusier, two murals in Costantino Nivola's house, Long Island, 1951.

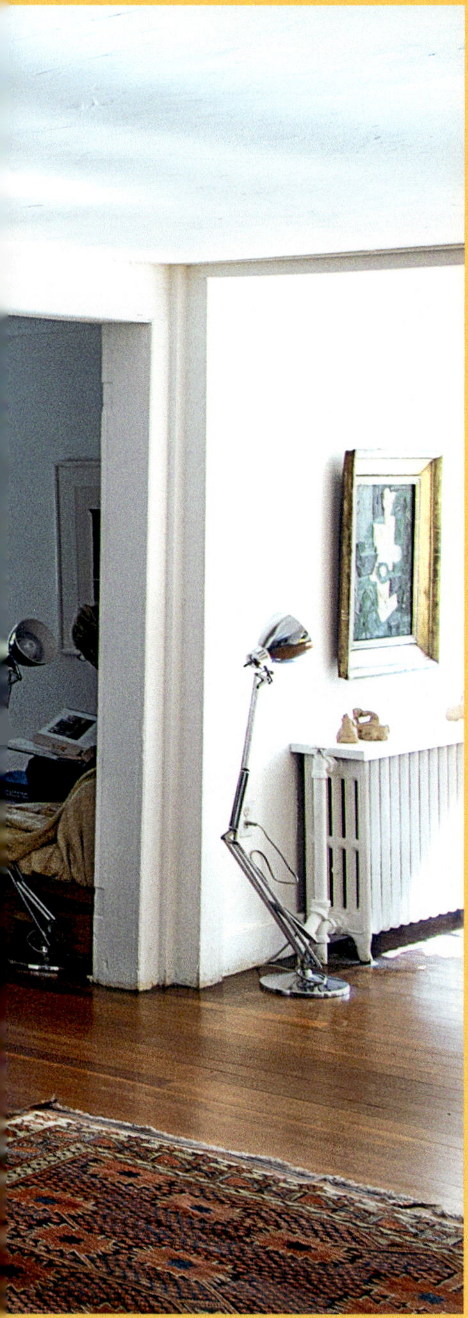

Two murals in Long Island

Le Corbusier painted two murals in the living room of the little house that Costantino Nivola owned on Long Island. The one on the right is a greatly simplified version of *Figure à la porte jaune* (Figure with yellow door), 1938 |ill. p. 66|. It respects the flatness of the wall while introducing a subtle sense of depth. The painting on the left is more abstract and its higher tonality, illuminated by a window to the left, creates an interesting contrast with the other painting. These are a more successful adaptation of painting to architecture than the mural in the salon of E1027.

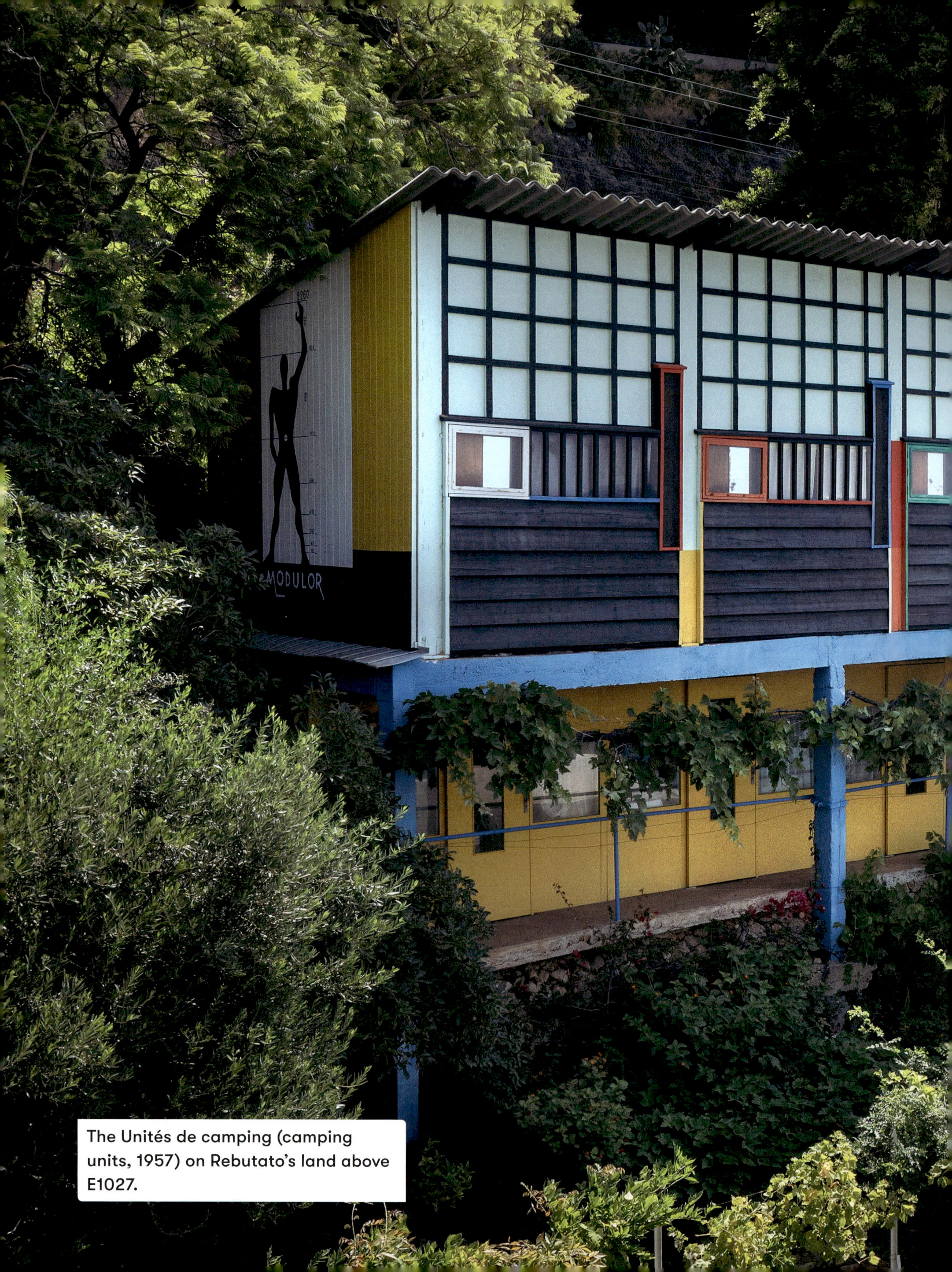

The Unités de camping (camping units, 1957) on Rebutato's land above E1027.

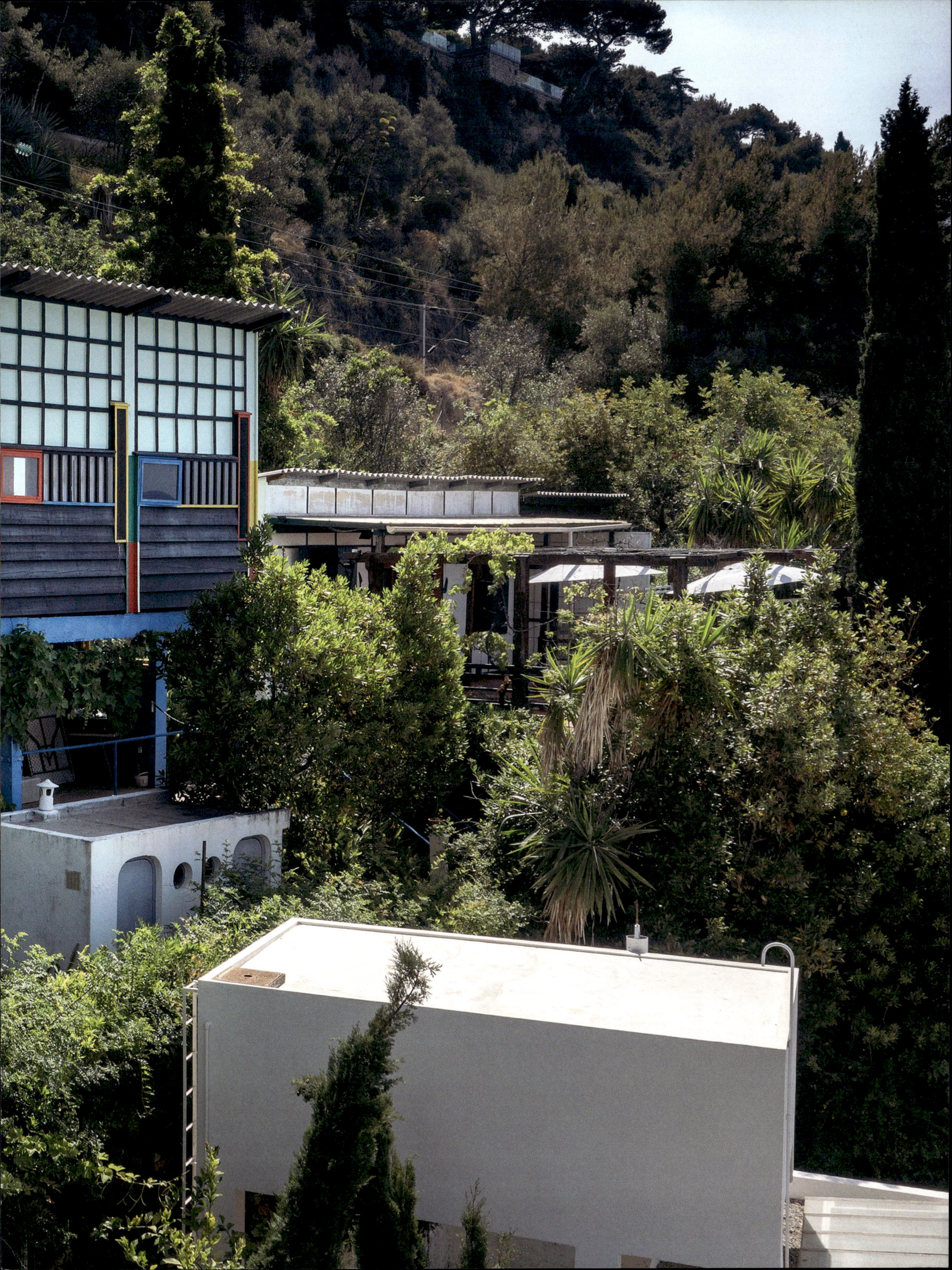

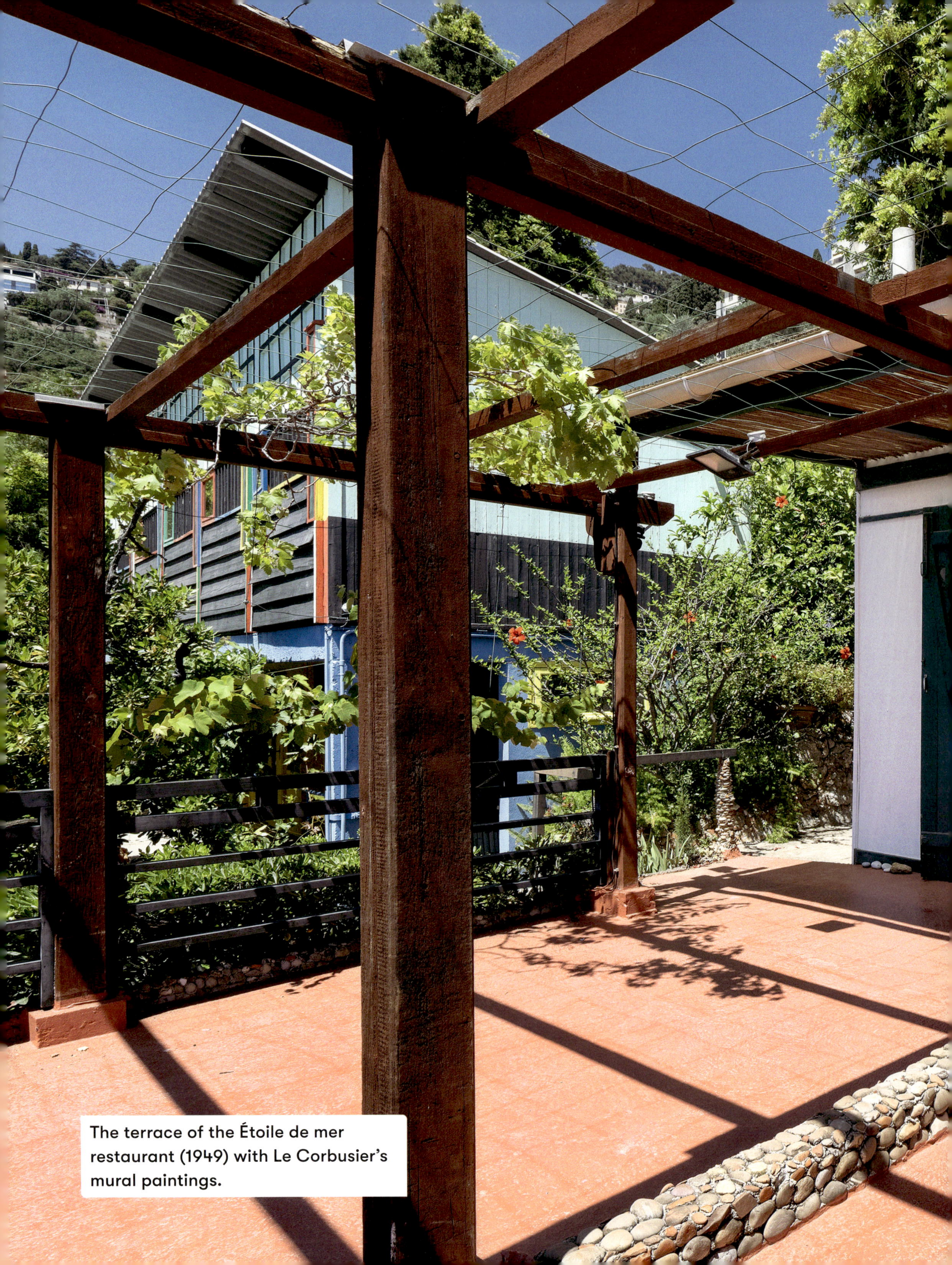

The terrace of the Étoile de mer restaurant (1949) with Le Corbusier's mural paintings.

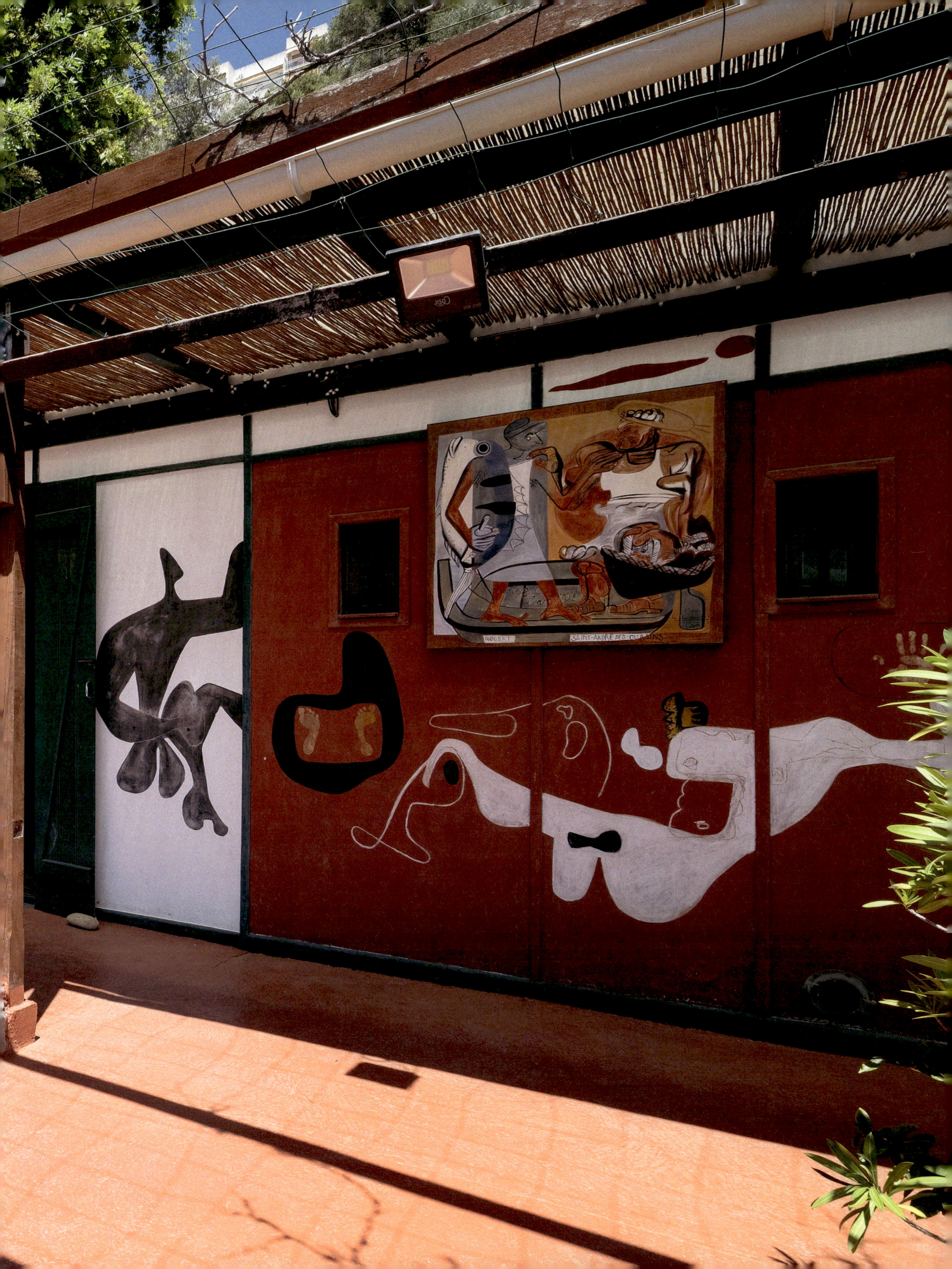
ROBERT
SAINT-ANDRE DES OURSINS

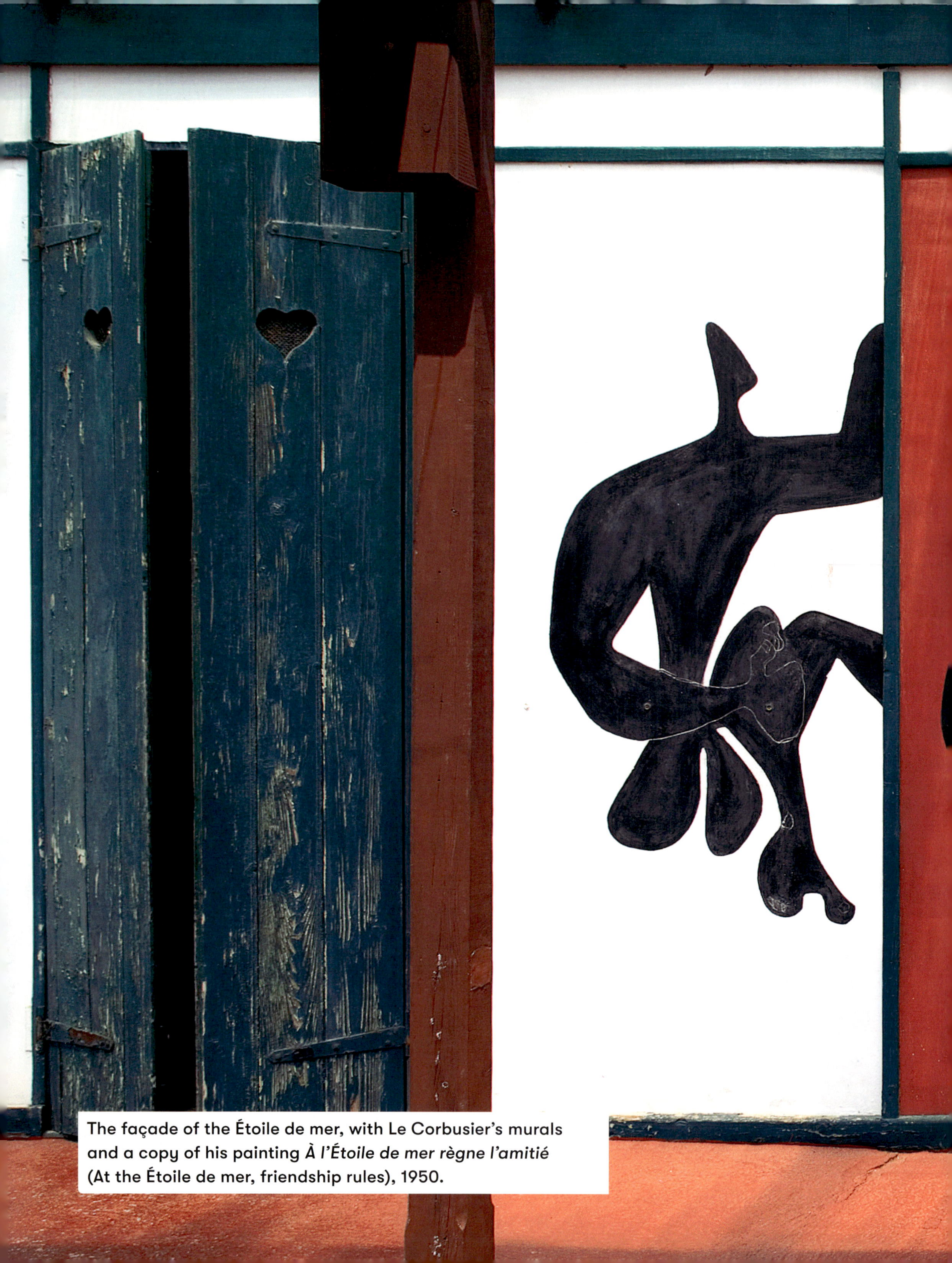

The façade of the Étoile de mer, with Le Corbusier's murals and a copy of his painting *À l'Étoile de mer règne l'amitié* (At the Étoile de mer, friendship rules), 1950.

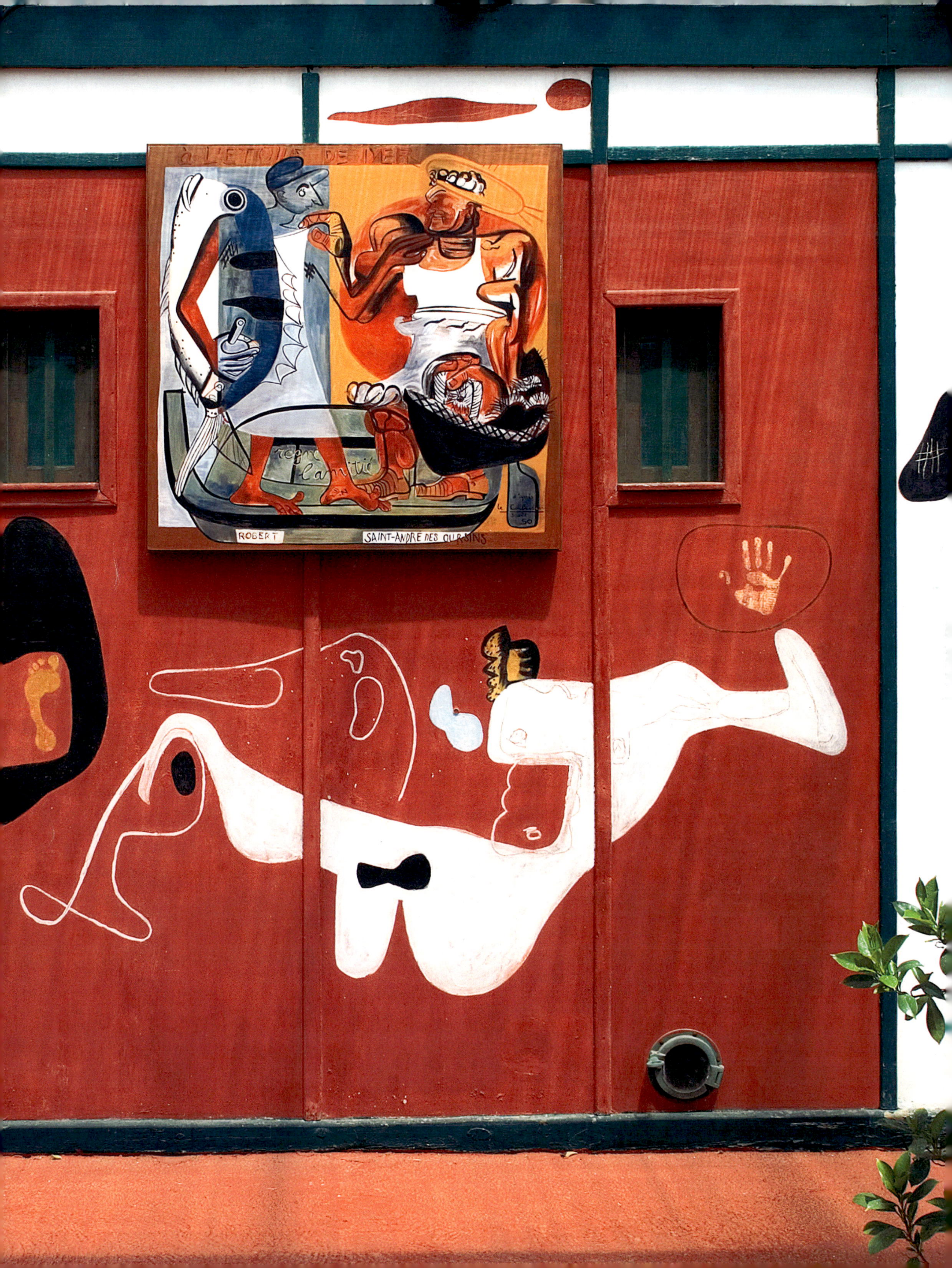
à L'ETOILE DE MER
règne l'amitié
ROBERT
SAINT-ANDRÉ DES OURSINS

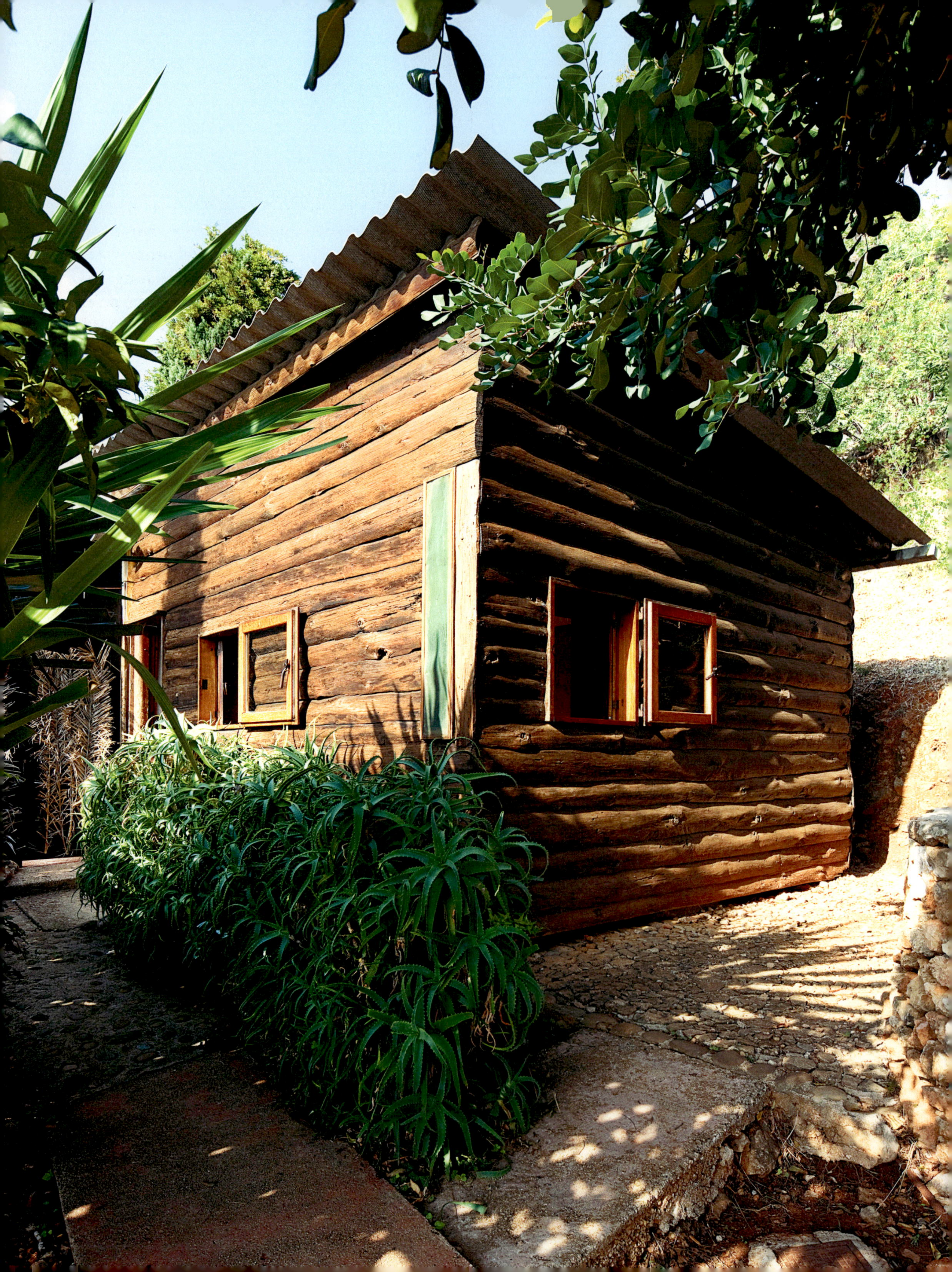

ÉTOILE DE MER AND LE CABANON

In 1949, Le Corbusier met Thomas Rebutato who had just opened a fish restaurant on the site adjacent to E1027. Rebutato was a plumber from Nice who loved fishing and bought the plot with the intention of building a hut where he could sleep and store his gear. But he soon modified his plans and persuaded his wife to drop everything in Nice and set up a snack bar and restaurant with the aim of attracting campers and intercepting the smugglers and coastguard officials that patrolled the *sentier des douaniers* (coastguard path). He even had his architect draw up a plan with altogether eight identical cabins that could accommodate the campers.[173]

This was a happy coincidence because Le Corbusier and his guests Sert and Wiener could eat there regularly while working on the plans for Bogotá. Le Corbusier returned to Roquebrune-Cap-Martin in 1950 and every year thereafter until his death in 1965, sometimes more than once in the year. In the winter of 1951, he sketched the plans for a wooden cabin to be attached to the Étoile de mer restaurant.[174] He described this as a gift for his wife Yvonne. He intended it to be a place for them to sleep and to work if it was wet or too cold to work outdoors. Jacques Michel and André Wogensky worked up the plans in the few next months and Le Corbusier approved them in June 1952, later visiting the Corsican carpenter Charles Barberis in his workshop in Ajaccio, where the prefabricated cabin was assembled for Le Corbusier's inspection.[175] The prefabricated elements were delivered by train and unloaded directly from the track on site. On 5 August 1952 Le Corbusier took possession of his cabanon. The furniture had been carefully designed by Jacques Michel and constructed by Barberis.

Unités de camping

Later on, Le Corbusier wished to provide his friend Thomas Rebutato with some additional income and designed two projects of studio apartments to be located on the rocks below the Étoile de mer

173 Fernand Pietra, site plan date-stamped 18 August 1948, showing the Étoile de mer and seven other identical cabins (FLC 18991). For Pietra's undated plan, elevation and sketch of the Étoile de mer, see FLC 18882.

174 The sketches were published in Le Corbusier (1955). *Le Modulor 2 1955 (la Parole est aux usagers), Suite de Modulor* 1948, pp. 253–254 where they are dated 30 December 1950, but Bruno Chiambretto believes that they date from September. See B. Chiambretto (1987). *Le Corbusier à Cap-Martin*, Marseille, Éditions Parenthèses.

175 Letter from Le Corbusier to Yvonne, from Ajaccio, 18 July 1952 (FLC R1(12)99).

Le Corbusier, cabanon, 1952.

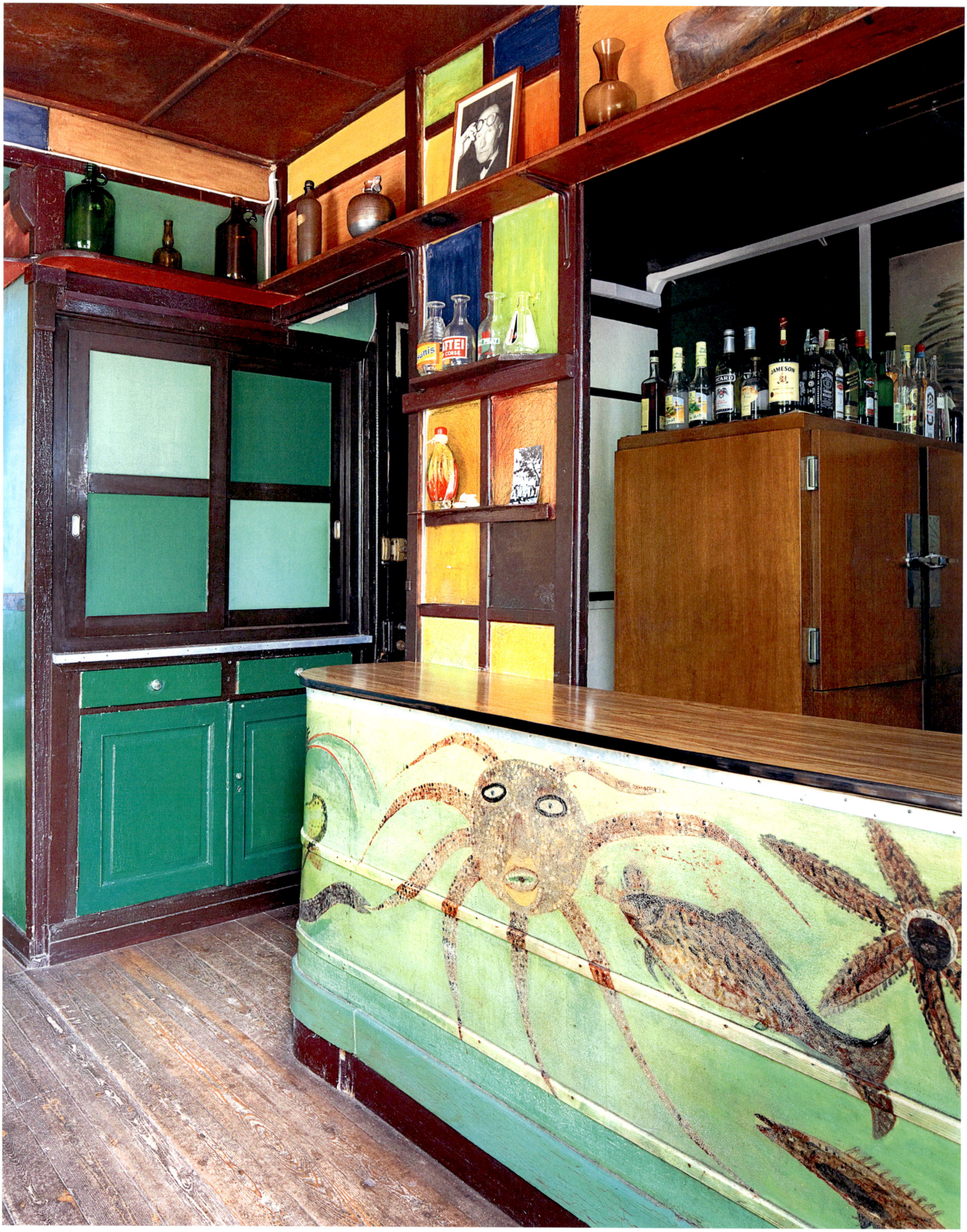
JAMESON

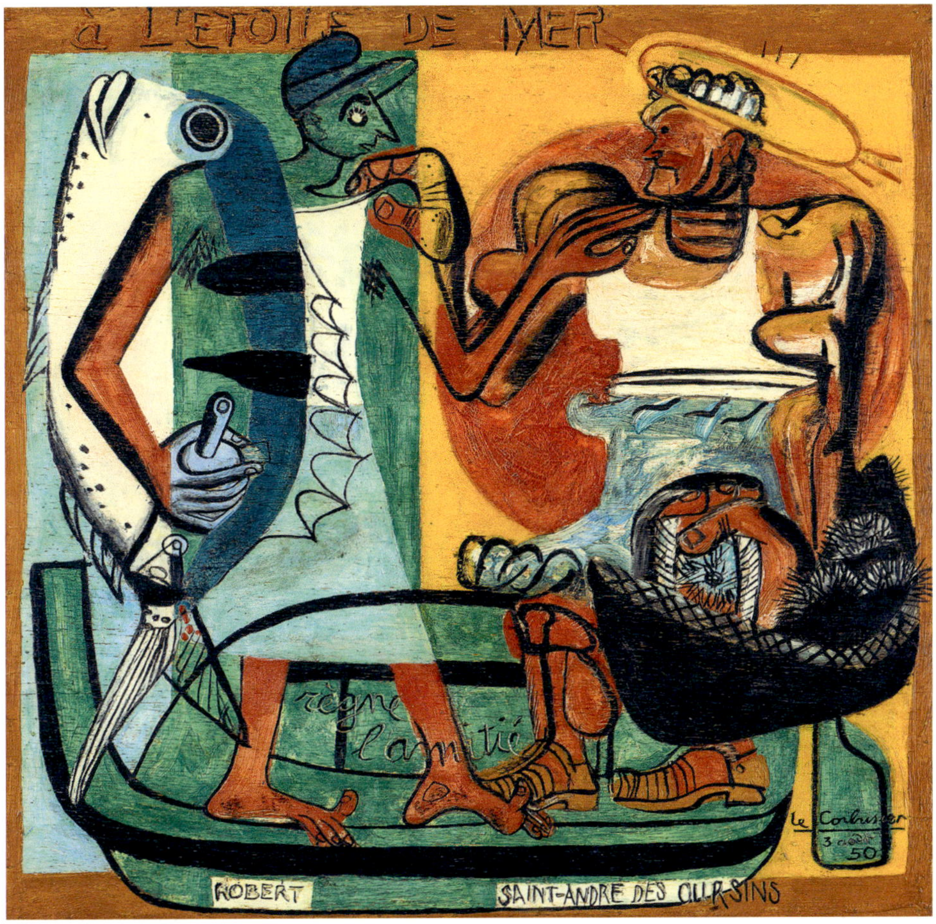

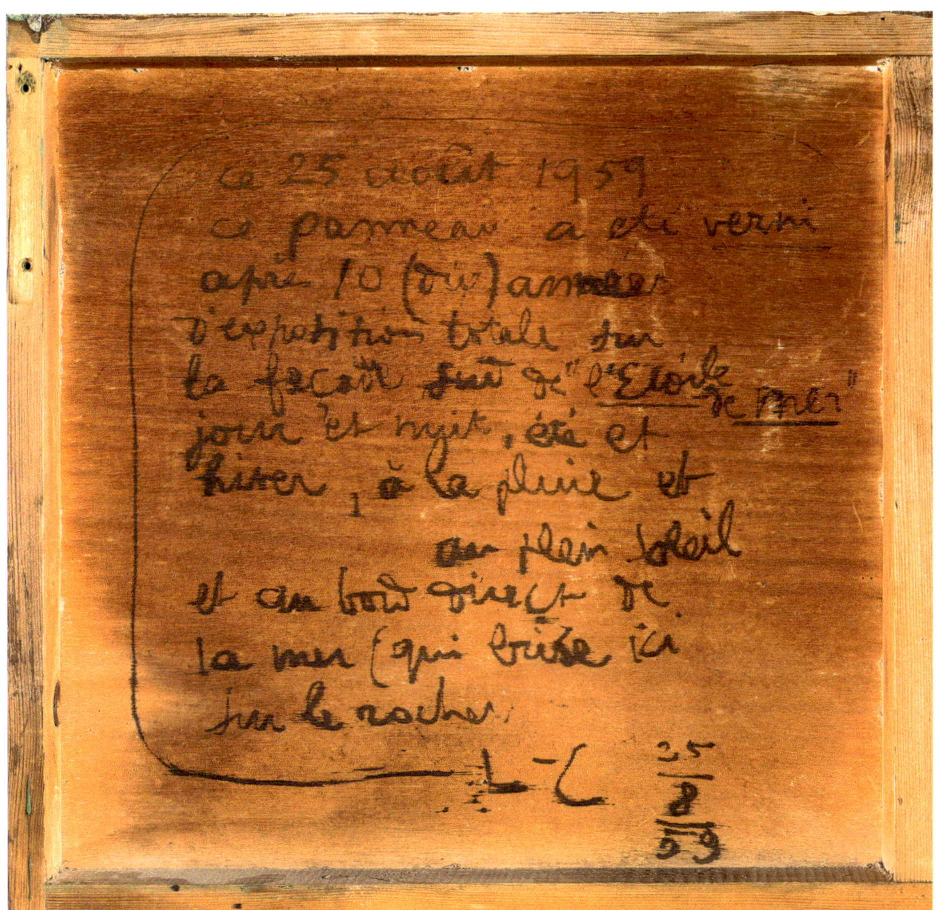

Étoile de mer restaurant with the mural paintings of Thomas Rebutato.

Le Corbusier, *À l'Étoile de mer règne l'amitié* (At the Étoile de mer, friendship rules), 1950.

Back of the painting *À l'Étoile de mer règne l'amitié*. On 25 August 1959, Le Corbusier described how the painting survived ten years of full exposure to the sea air before having to be revarnished.

restaurant (1949–1954). When these proved impractical, he designed five prefabricated wooden cabins to be located on a concrete frame on the terraces overlooking E1027 in 1957, a year after Badovici's death |ill. pp. 102–103|. These were intended for campers and reproduced an idea originally designed for Rebutato by a local architect in 1949.

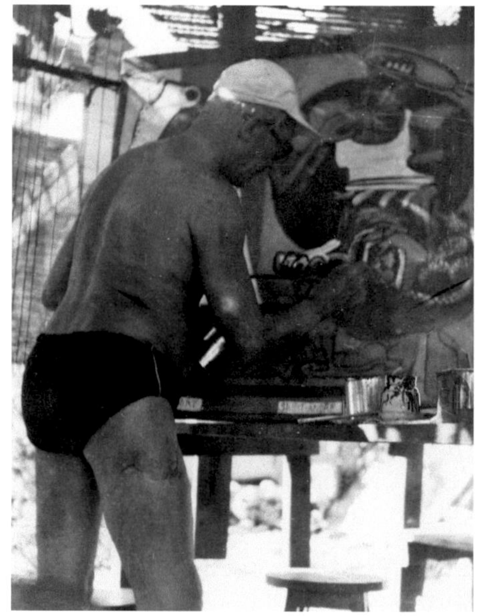

Le Corbusier working on his painting *À l'Étoile de mer règne l'amitié* (At the Étoile de mer, friendship rules) in August 1950.

A 'sign' for the Étoile de mer

As early as 3 August 1950, Le Corbusier painted his first picture on Rebutato's site. He inscribed the back of a photograph of this painting: 'The panel, painted on wood 1.00 x 1.00 m represents 'Roberto' [Thomas Rebutato] and his local buddy "Saint André of the sea urchins"' |ill p. 111|. Thomas Rebutato liked to use the name of his son Robert. He is shown juxtaposed with a giant fish, in reference to his love of fishing, while the other figure has a basket of sea urchins, a favourite of Yvonne's. This painting was hung on the wall of the Étoile de mer in all weathers until it was replaced by a copy.

Le Corbusier later painted the wall of the Étoile de mer with two flattened nudes in the manner of Matisse's cut-outs |ill. pp. 106–107|. These work very well with the panelled construction of the cabin. In the middle, the artist recorded his own foot, and that of Rebutato, in yellow paint on the reddish-brown surface. On the far right, he made an imprint of his hand, no doubt thinking of the 'hands of Fatima' that he had seen on the walls of houses in North Africa as signs of protection. He had even photographed such a hand, impressed into the plaster of a house at Gardhaia in the Mzab.[176]

Le Corbusier encouraged Thomas Rebutato to paint, even paying him, on one occasion, to allow him to avoid having to work over the winter.[177] He insisted Rebutato paint on plywood and not on canvas. Le Corbusier had already shown an interest in the 'primitive' artist André Bauchant, purchasing several of his paintings and had encouraged his cousin Louis Soutter to continue with his densely worked pen drawings, some of them scrawled over illustrations in Le Corbusier's books.[178]

176 FLC film, Sequence 1 06327. Benton, T. (2013). *LC Foto: Le Corbusier: Secret Photographer*, Baden, Lars Müller.

177 Letter from Le Corbusier to Rebutato, 12 December 1958, offering to pay him 250,000 francs as 'an advance' on the paintings he will execute over the winter. Rebutato's rather wild but impressive paintings covered the interior of the Étoile de mer.

178 Le Corbusier, Louis Soutter (2011). *Une maison, un palais: enluminures de Louis Soutter*, with an afterword by Julie Borgeaud, Lyon, Fage.

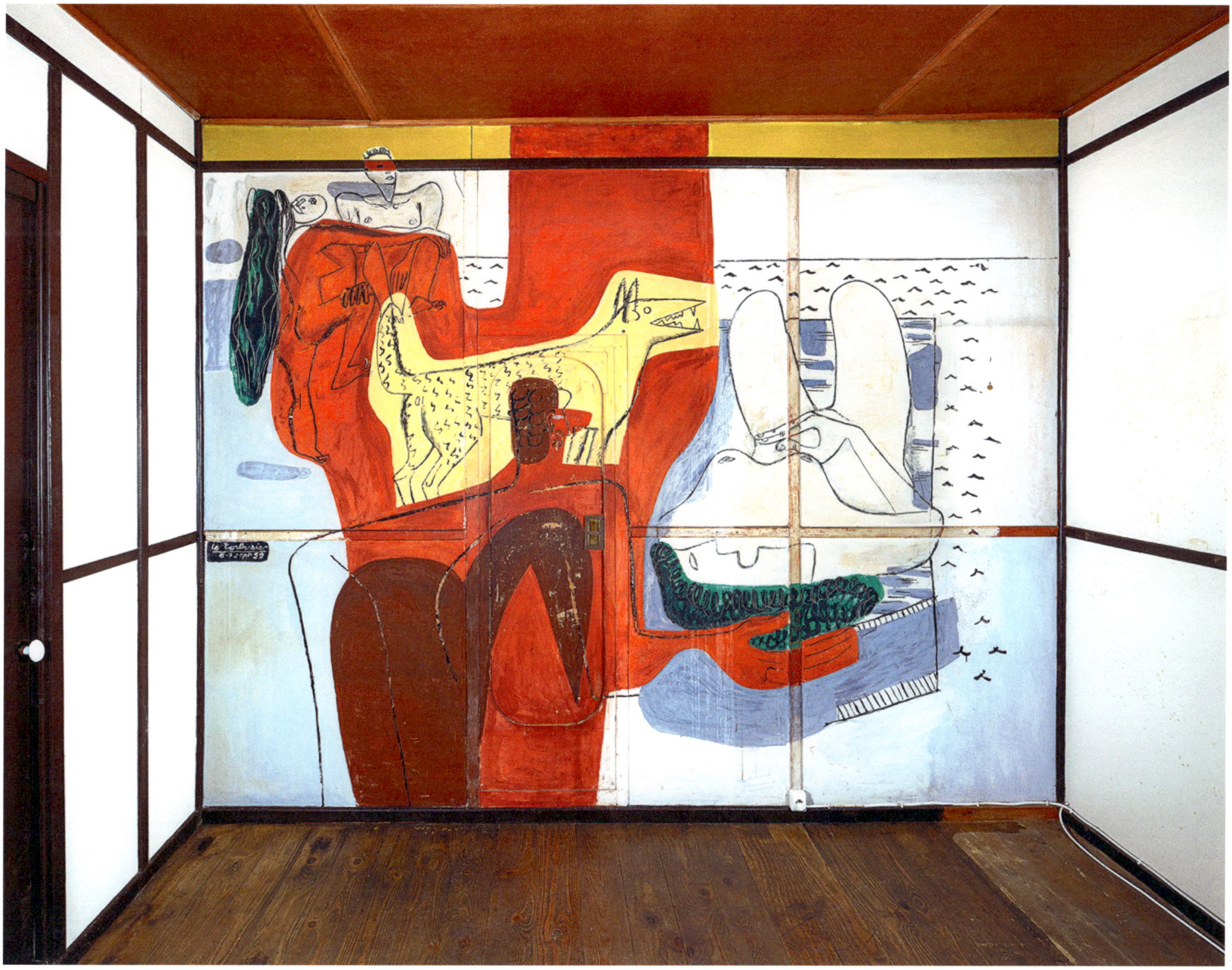

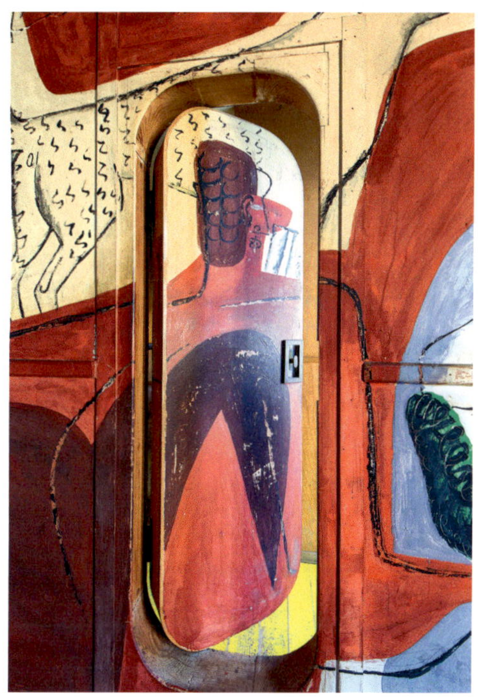

Le Corbusier mural in the Rebutato bedroom of the Étoile de mer restaurant.

Detail of mural in the Rebutato bedroom, showing the door connecting to the cabanon.

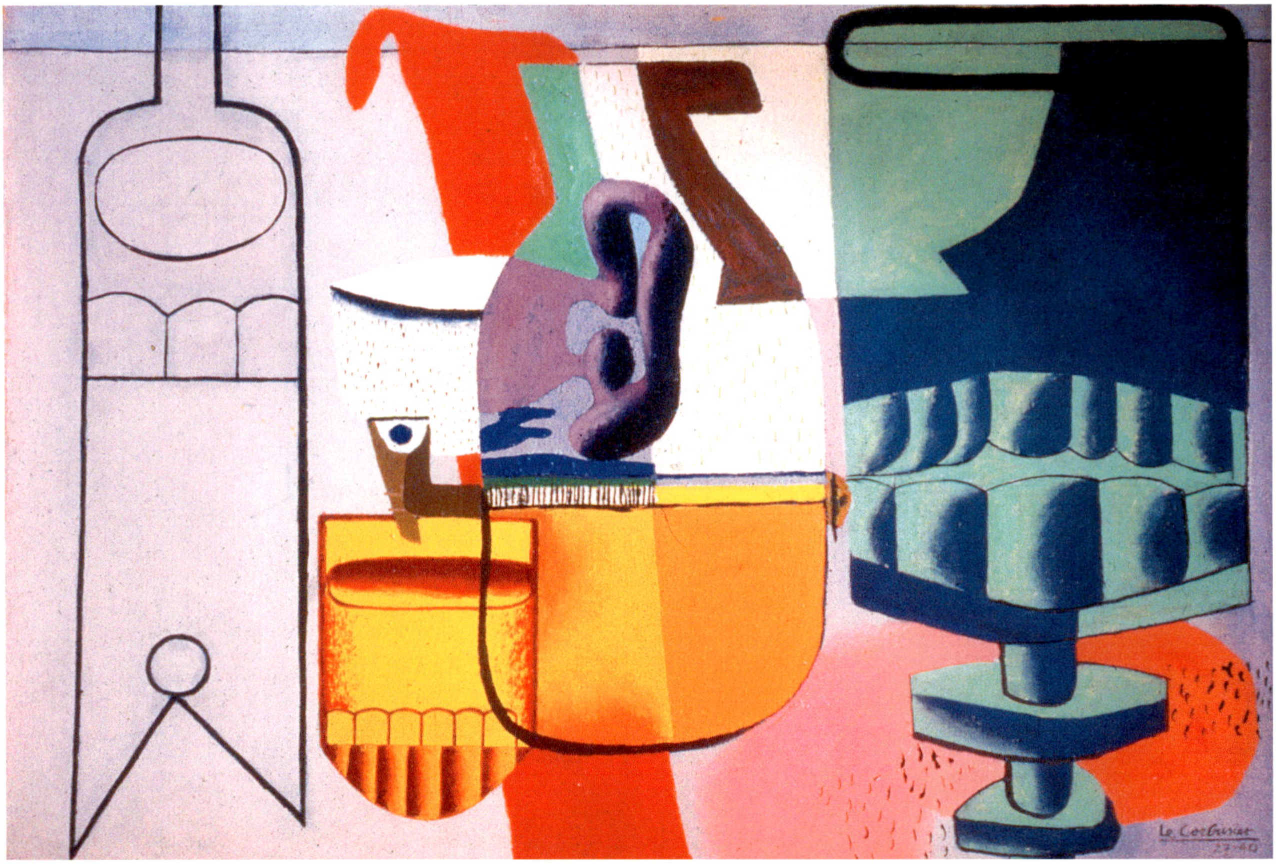

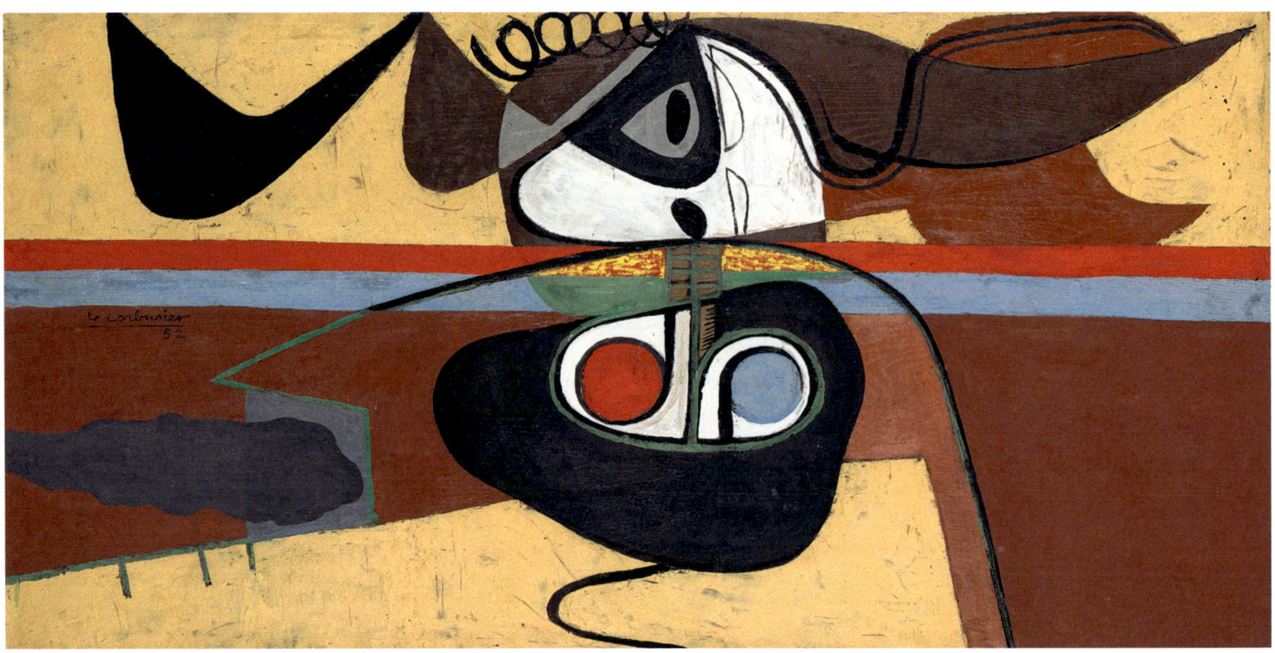

Le Corbusier, *Le grand verre à côtes et l'écharpe rouge* (Large fluted glass and red scarf), 1940.

Le Corbusier, *Taureau I* (Bull 1), 1952.

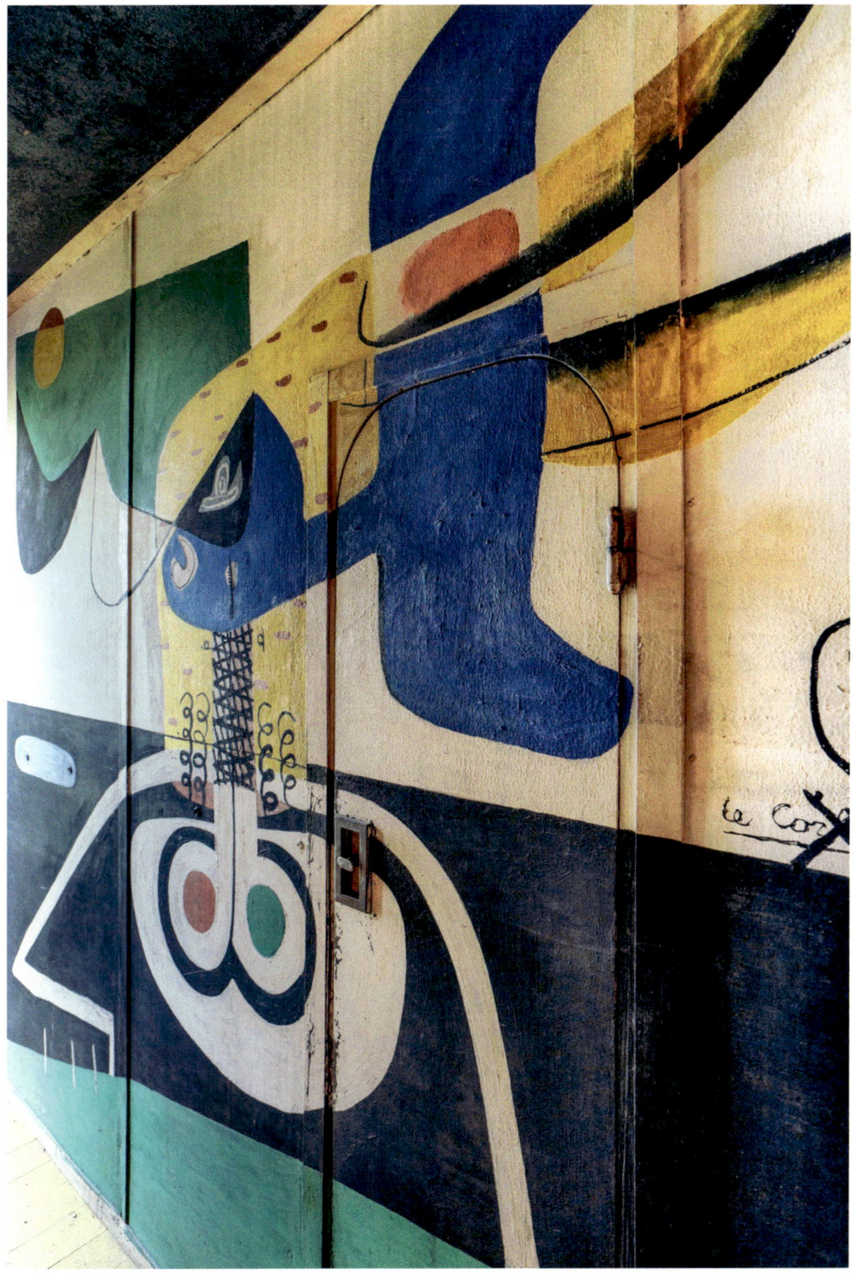

Le Corbusier, mural *Taureau* (Bull) in the entrance corridor of the cabanon.

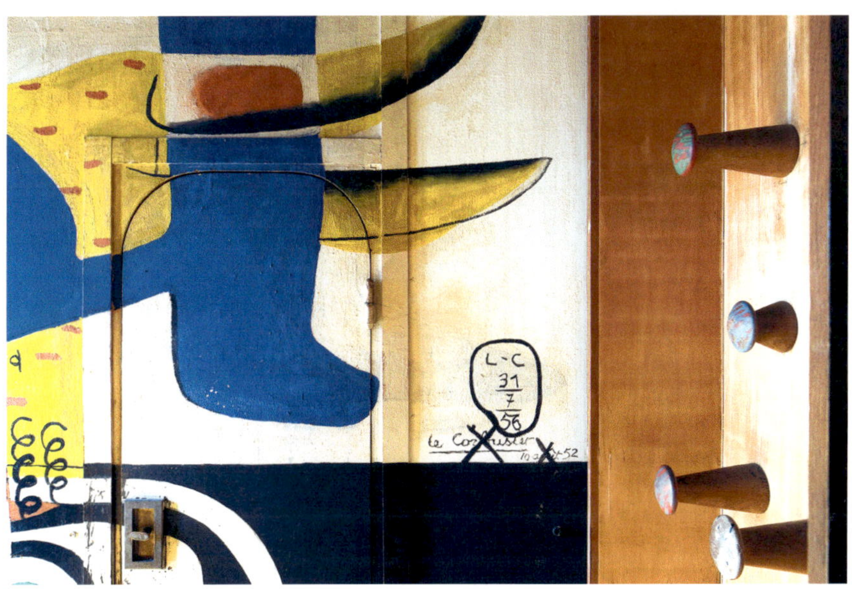

Le Corbusier, detail of the mural in the entrance corridor, with the door to the Rebutatos' bedroom in the Étoile de mer.

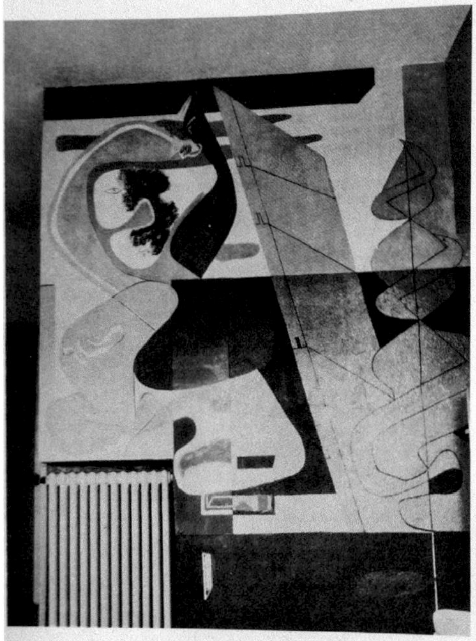

Mural, Badovici house.

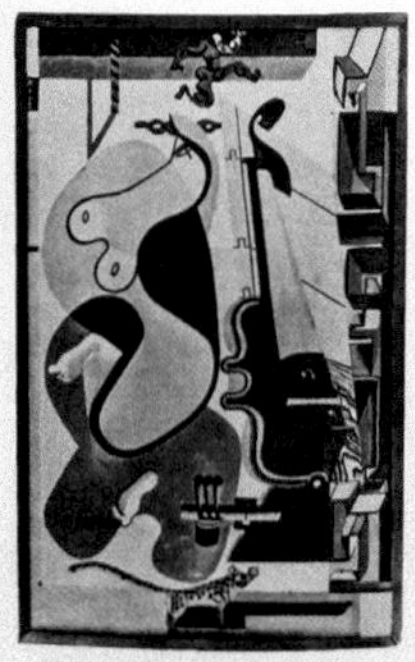

Oil on canvas, 38¼ x 31 inches.
1932.

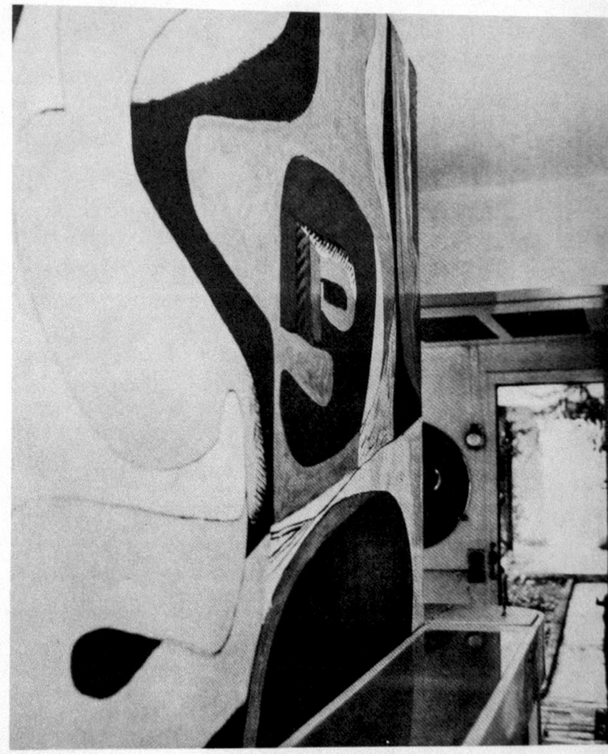

Mural painting, Badovici house.

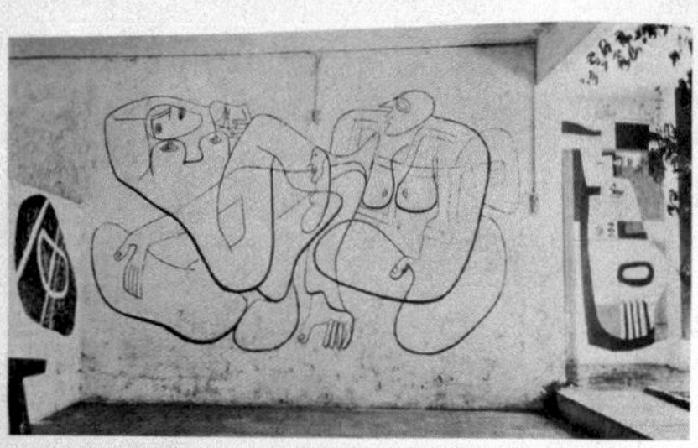

Mural, Badovici house, Cap Martin (Alpes Maritimes). 1938.

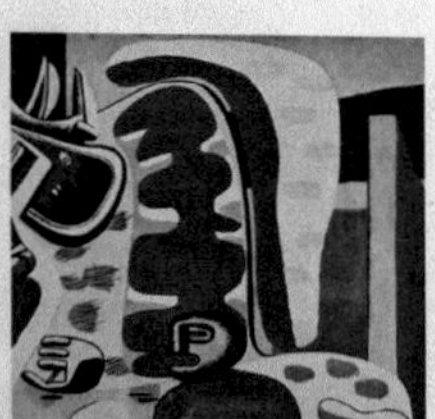

Oil on canvas (detail). 1938.

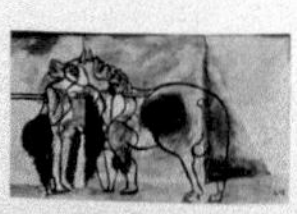

Oil on canvas. 1935-42.

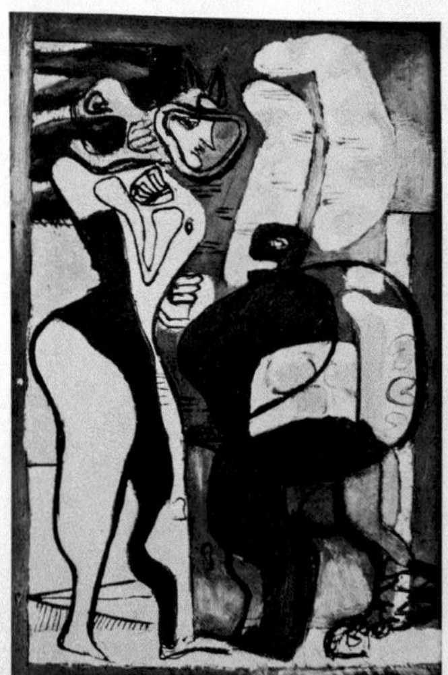

Oil on wood, approximately 14 x 9½ inches. 1935-43.

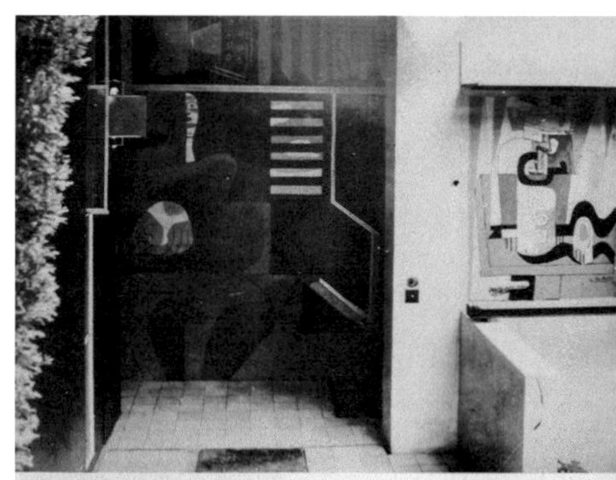

Mural paintings, Badovici house (Alpes Maritimes). 1939.

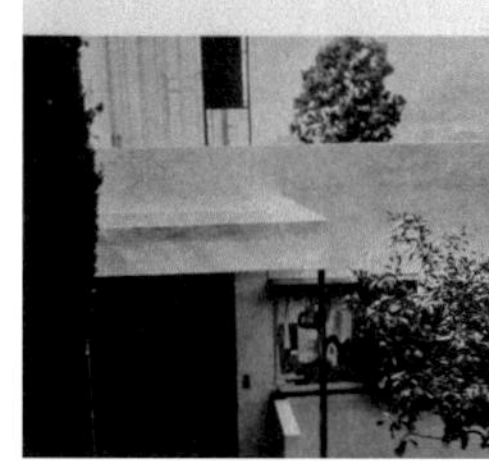

THE mural paintings brightened only the most unpleasing walls of the house. The "good walls" remained white. The paintings created space in cramped places: at the entrance, within the porch, and at the bar.

Paintings in the cabanon

As soon as the cabanon was completed, on 10 August 1952, Le Corbusier painted a mural for the wall of the narrow entrance vestibule |ill. p. 115|. This wall includes a door leading to the Rebutatos' bedroom in the Étoile de mer |ill. p. 122|. This door was indicated on the plans for building permission and allowed Le Corbusiers' to say that his cabanon was simply an extension to the restaurant.[179] But it also gave him access to the restaurant when it rained. On the wall of the Rebutatos' bedroom, Le Corbusier painted a mural representing the two Rebutato children, Robert and Monique, and Thomas' wife Marguerite and their dog |ill. p. 113|. Thomas is represented in outline, his hand cradling Marguerite's hair. This painting, dated 6 and 7 September 1952, is an original composition and works well in the cramped space. Both the dog and figure of Marguerite appear in the *Poème de l'angle droit* opposite a text celebrating the cosmic forces of nature:

The sun and earth dance
the dance of the four seasons
the dance of the year
the dance of the twenty-four hour day
the high and low points of the solstices
the plane of the equinoxes.[180]

Le Corbusier clearly associated the simple life by the sea, governed by what he called cosmic forces, with the Rebutato family.
The mural in the corridor of the cabanon is a more ambitious work and full of meaning for Le Corbusier. It comes at the beginning of a series on the theme of the bull which occupied him to the end of his life. The origins of this series are complex, from both an iconographic and symbolic point of view.[181] The specific origins of the *Taureau* paintings were explained by Le Corbusier in the *Poème de l'angle droit* and in correspondence with the British Museum curator Ronald Alley in May and June 1958.[182] Le Corbusier explained that while at Ozon in the French Pyrenees, he had sketched the oxen passing his window, as well as roots and pebbles:

> *The elements of a vision coalesce. The key was a piece of dead wood and a pebble, both of them picked up on a sunken road in the Pyrenees. Some oxen passed by my window*

Pages from Le Corbusier, *New World of Space*, 1948. Shown are the mural in the bar |top left|, in the guest room |top right|, the 'sgrafitte' under the pilotis |bottom left| and the mural in the entrance and to the right of the entrance |bottom right|.

---

179 FLC 24334, published in B. Chiambretto (1987). *Le Corbusier à Cap-Martin*, op. cit., p. 50.

180 Le Corbusier (1955). *Poème de l'angle droit*, op. cit., p. 66. A preparatory sketch for this mural shows the Étoile de mer in the background (FLC 0061).

181 For a close study of this iconographical theme, see J. Coll (1995). 'Le Corbusier Taureaux: An Analysis of the Thinking Process in the Last Series of Corbusier's Plastic Work', *Art History*, 18(4), pp. 537–567.

182 Le Corbusier (1955). *Poème de l'angle droit*, op. cit., pp. 75–76; and *Le Corbusier (1955). Le Modulor 2 1955 (la Parole est aux usagers), Suite de Modulor 1948*. For the correspondence with Alley: FLC C2(11)21. On one sheet, Le Corbusier lists 28 works associated with the *Taureau* series.

> *every day. By dint of being drawn and redrawn, the ox, the root and pebble became a bull.*[183]

In the *Poème* Le Corbusier went on to immediately associate the theme with the memory of his beloved dog Pinceau, who had to be put down when he became dangerous. The mural in the cabanon is one of the first of the *Taureau* series.

Another source for the *Taureau* series is a still life *Le grand verre à côtes et l'écharpe rouge* (Large fluted glass and red scarf), dated by Le Corbusier '27–40' |ill. p. 114|, which, turned on its side, suggested the form of a bull.[184] The bottle in the still life, turned round, becomes the head of a woman and a fish while the handle of a teacup turns into the bull's muzzle. In April 1952, on his return from India, Le Corbusier made a quick sketch on a piece of plywood which he called *Taureau I* (Bull I) |ill. p. 114|.[185] The mural in the cabanon derives directly from this sketch.

Although most of the *Taureau* paintings have a vertical format, the mural is almost square. Le Corbusier signed and dated the painting 10 August 1952 but then replaced it with the date '31 7 56'. It is difficult to know whether this represented a simple restoration of the painting or a reworking of it. It would be surprising if the existing composition dated from 1956, since all the later versions of the *Taureau* series introduced new elements into the composition.

Le Corbusier later noted that the *Taureau* series related directly to his wife Yvonne, whose health was deteriorating in 1952 and who passed away in December 1957:

> *These 'Taureaux' = total and intimate confession Corbu-Yvonne: my wife, present, ill, dying, dead = Taureaux!! Incitements! From whom? Subconscious acts! Yes. Divinations, from the bottom of the heart and soul. Yes.*[186]

Inside the cabanon, Le Corbusier pinned up a set of watercolours associated with Yvonne |ill. p. 121|. The painting on the left represents two heads, the top one referring to Yvonne's astrological sign, the Capricorn, while the bottom one represents her as the crescent moon. The second painting, showing a woman with a unicorn's head (again, the Capricorn), resembles the motif at the right end of his mural in the Swiss Pavilion which was accompanied by a text from Mallarmé: 'Keep my wing in your hand' |ill. p. 46|.[187] From 1946, Le Corbusier had frequently returned to this motif of hand and wing, often citing Mallarmé and occasionally naming Yvonne. In the *Poème de l'angle droit* the motif of the hand and the unicorn-headed Yvonne is also accompanied by the silhouette of the tree in the yard of the Vidal

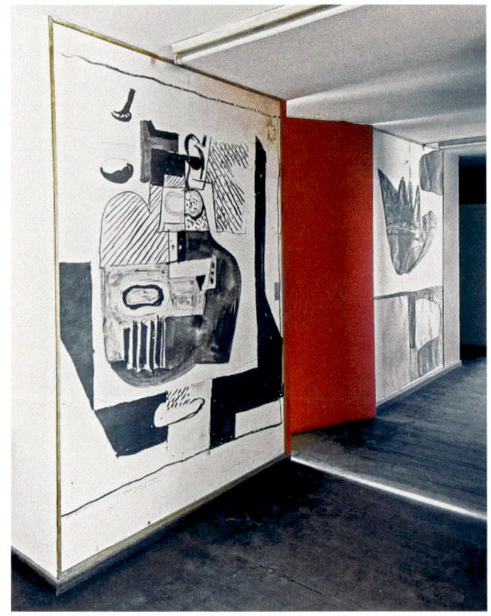

Le Corbusier, photographic enlargement of *Nature morte au livre et au coquetier* (Still life with book and egg cup), 1928, Claude and Duval factory, St Dié, 1948–1952.

183 Le Corbusier (1955). *Poème de l'angle droit*, op. cit., pp. 75–76.
184 FLC 226.
185 Written on the back of this painting: 'begun at 13h, finished 15 1/2h'.
186 Sketchbook R63 (1961–1963), cited in J.-P. Jornod and N. Jornod (2005). *Le Corbusier: L'œuvre peint*, op. cit., p. 878.
187 Liniger, J. (1998). *Le Corbusier – Le mural de la Fondation Suisse – Paris 1948*, Paris, Édition Fondation Suisse.

family at Le Piquey as part of the section *C4 Chair* (flesh).[188] The third painting derives from the series of seven paintings representing a woman with a candle that he executed between 1947 and 1948. A lithograph similar to this painting introduces the 'E4 Characters' section of the *Poème*.[189] The fourth painting is a loose transcription of the left-hand figure in his painting *Trois musiciens* (Three musicians), 1936, a tribute to Yvonne's love of music. Finally, the fifth painting represents an embracing couple, certainly a reference to himself and Yvonne.

On the folding shutters he paints two nudes. The first is a version of his painting *Femme à la poitrine nue* (Bare breasted woman) of 1939 which in turn refers to a series of paintings from 1936 based on tourist postcards he collected of nude Arab women.[190] The other shutter is loosely based on the left part of *Femme et cheval* (Woman with horse), a tapestry cartoon from 1930.[191] These rather crude paintings, which can only be seen at night, when the shutters are closed, are intended to be viewed under weak electric light.

---

188 Le Corbusier (1955). *Poème de l'angle droit*, op. cit., p. 86. The unicorn-headed Yvonne appears in other pages of the *poème* and especially on folio 111 coming just before the section 'Fusion' that marks the passage from the sensual to the spiritual worlds.

189 Le Corbusier (1955). *Poème de l'angle droit*, op. cit., p. 131.

190 FLC 225 (1939). Of the earlier paintings, see *Deux femmes à la balustrade* (Two women at a balustrade, FLC 220, 1936), *Deux femmes fantasques* (Two fantastical women, FLC 221, 1937) and *Deux femmes et mains* (Two women and hands, FLC 47, 1937).

191 FLC 114.

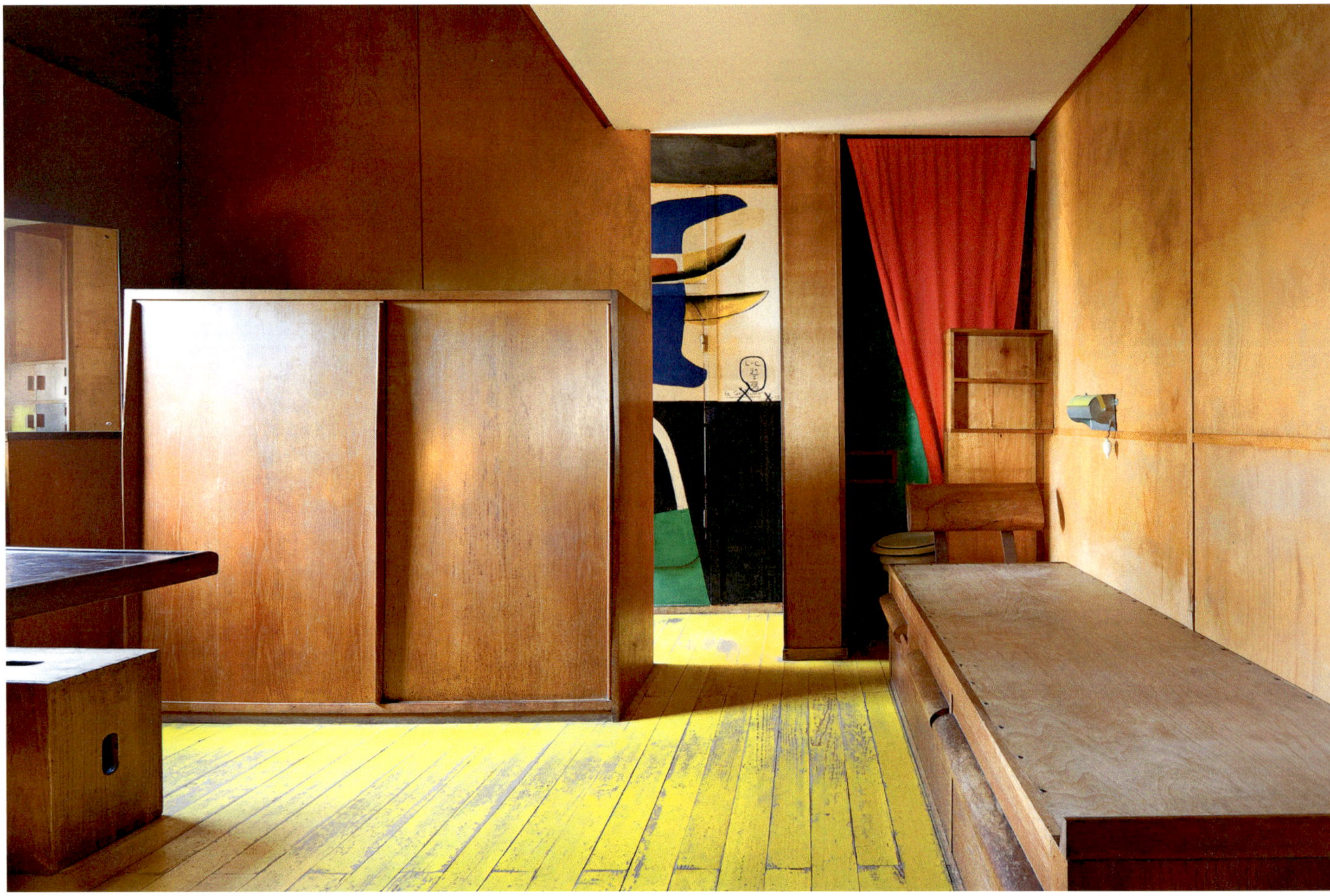

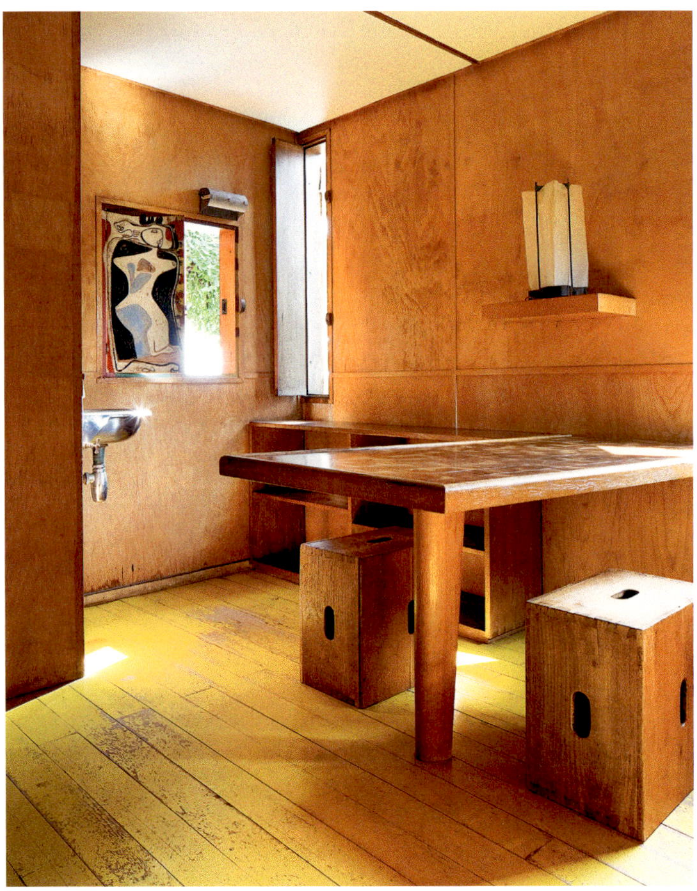

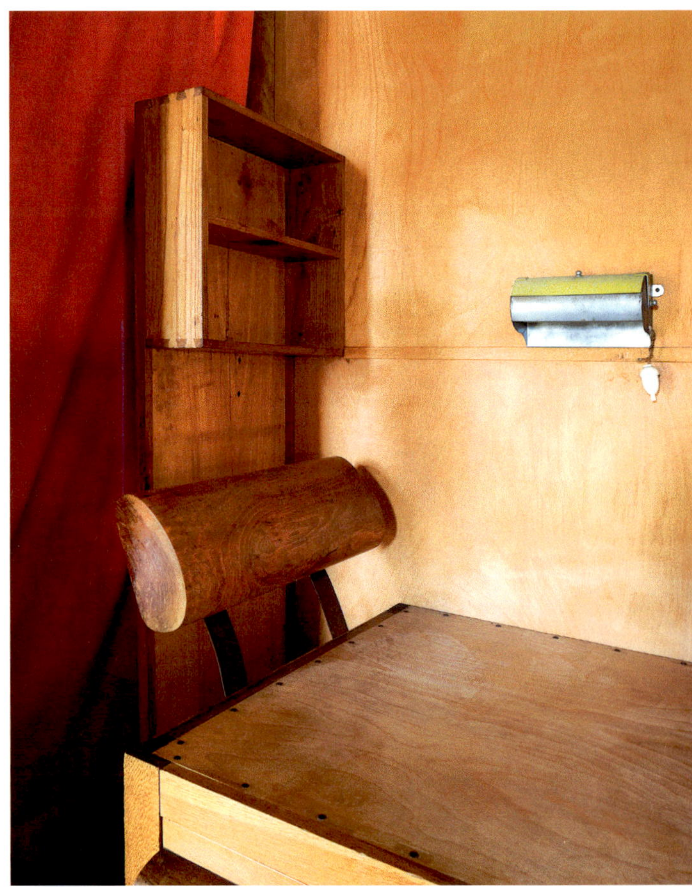

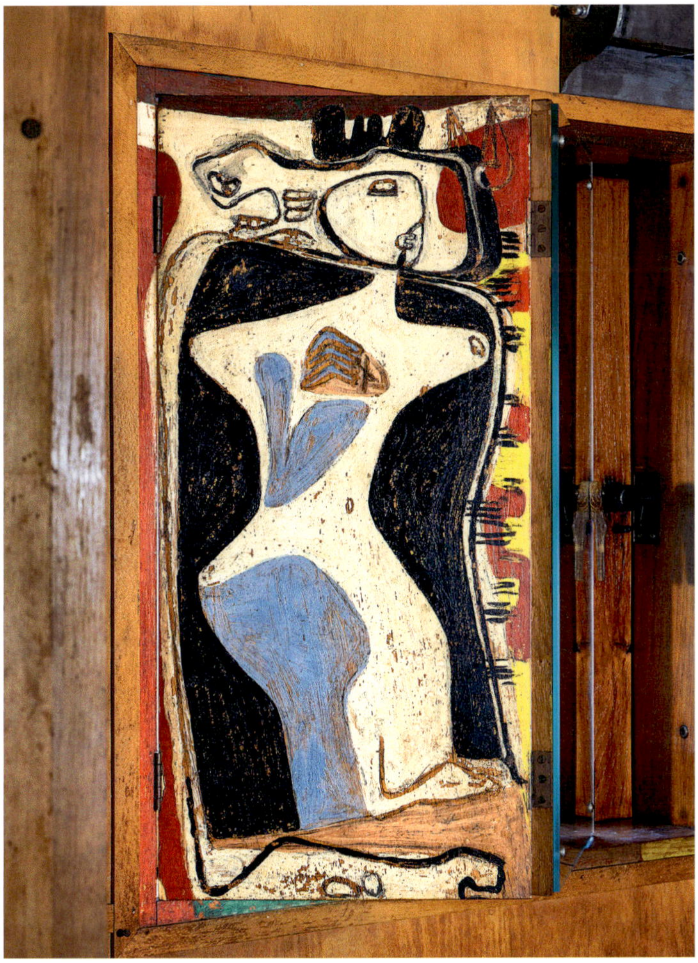

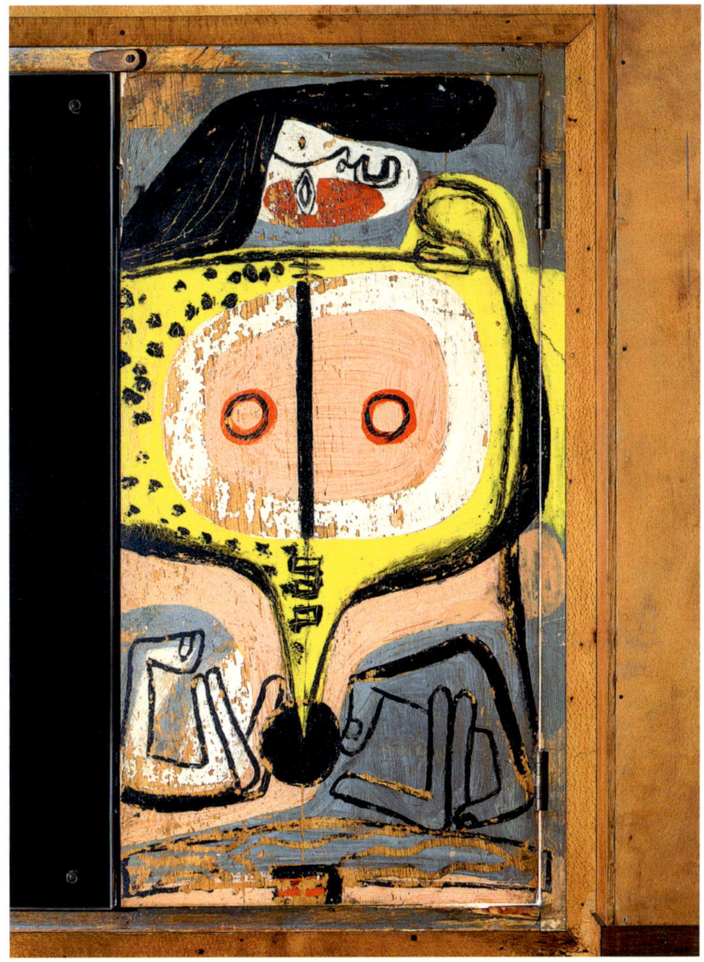

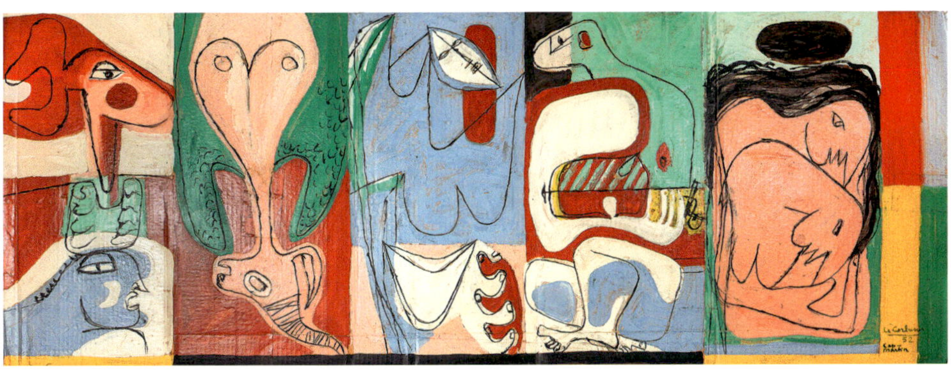

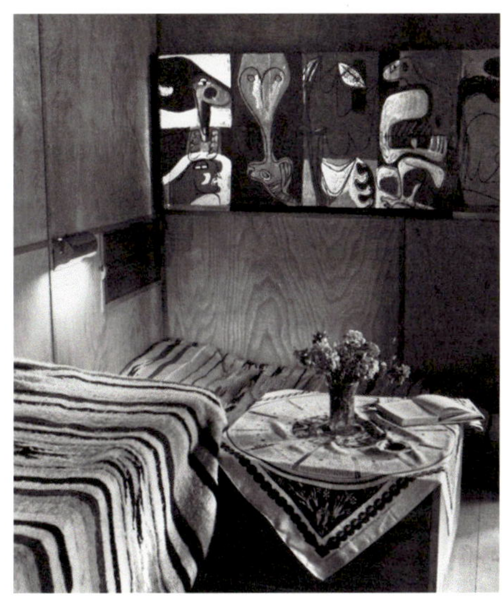

S. 120

|top| Le Corbusier, cabanon, with Yvonne's bed on the right, 1952.

|bottom left| Le Corbusier, cabanon, 1952. The furniture was designed by Jacques Michel and constructed by Charles Barberis who also manufactured the prefabricated elements of the cabanon.

|bottom right| Le Corbusier, cabanon, 1952. The red curtain hides a WC.

S. 121

|top left and right| Le Corbusier, paintings on the window shutters of the cabanon.

|centre left| Le Corbusier, the five compositions on the interior wall of the cabanon.

|bottom right| Le Corbusier, the five compositions on the interior wall of the cabanon, above Le Corbusier's bed.

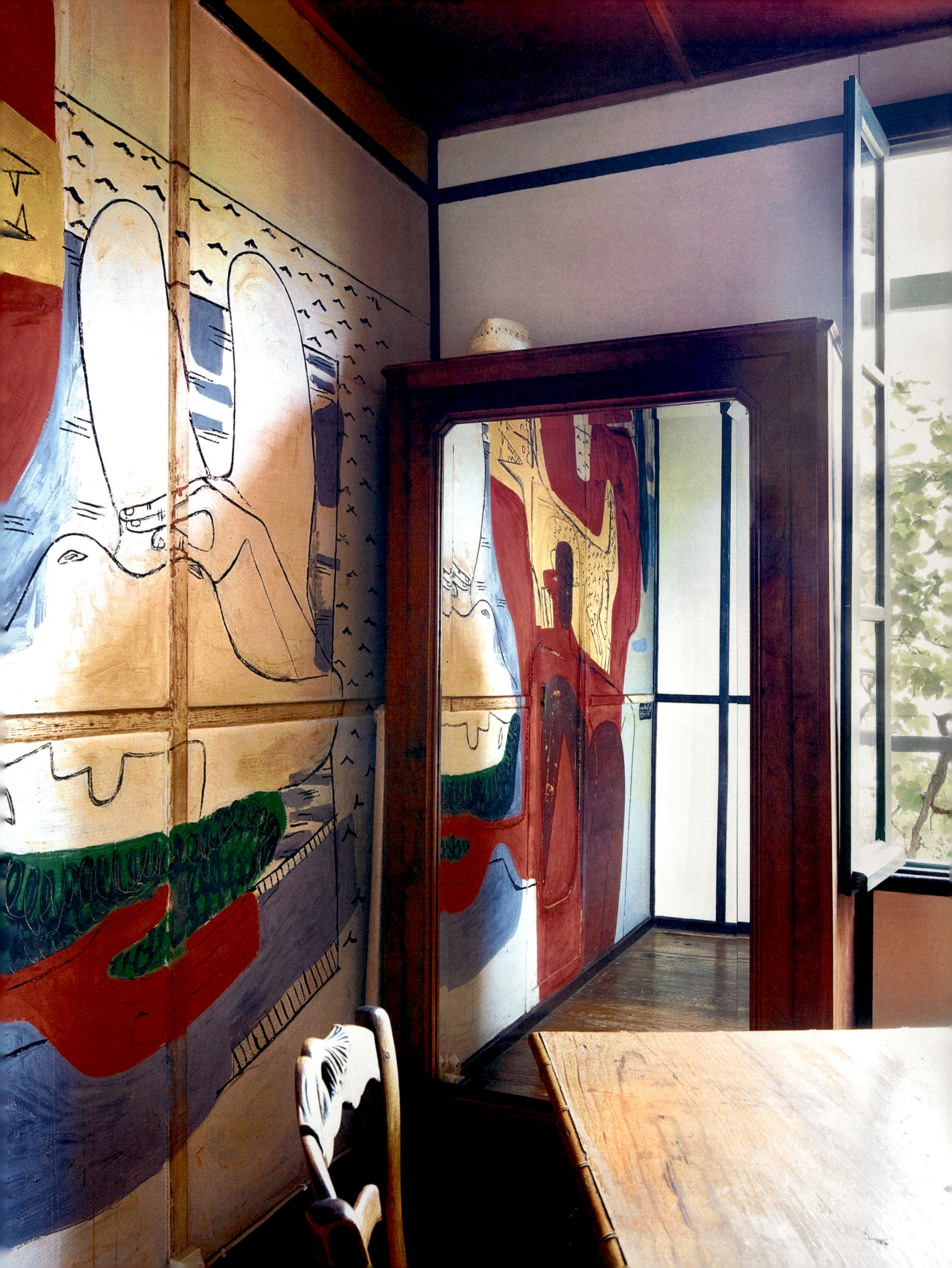

POSTSCRIPT

MAGDA REBUTATO

Robert Rebutato was a friend, disciple and admirer of Le Corbusier. He was very happy, in 2015, to pay tribute to Le Corbusier's talent as a visual artist, by encouraging the publication of this book by Tim Benton. Having succeeded Robert as President of the Association Eileen Gray. Étoile de mer. Le Corbusier in 2016, after his death, I very much appreciate the great artistic and scholarly quality of the research accomplished by our friend Tim, enhanced by the work of the photographer Manuel Bougot. It brings to the fore the heritage treasures of Cap-Martin and is the culmination of an adventure that has lasted more than twenty years – an era of hard work to preserve a major site of twentieth-century architecture, which is now fully restored.

Robert Rebutato was one of the pillars of this adventure, and thanks to his charisma and determination, he was able to bring together an enthusiastic community within our association. With the reprint of the original French edition in 2021 and with this first English edition, we are continuing Robert's commitment to promote a scientific and cultural programme designed to enhance the Cap Moderne, in which Le Corbusier's work occupies a major place.

Paris and Roquebrune-Cap-Martin,
April 1923

The Rebutatos' bedroom at the Étoile de mer with Le Corbusier's painting.

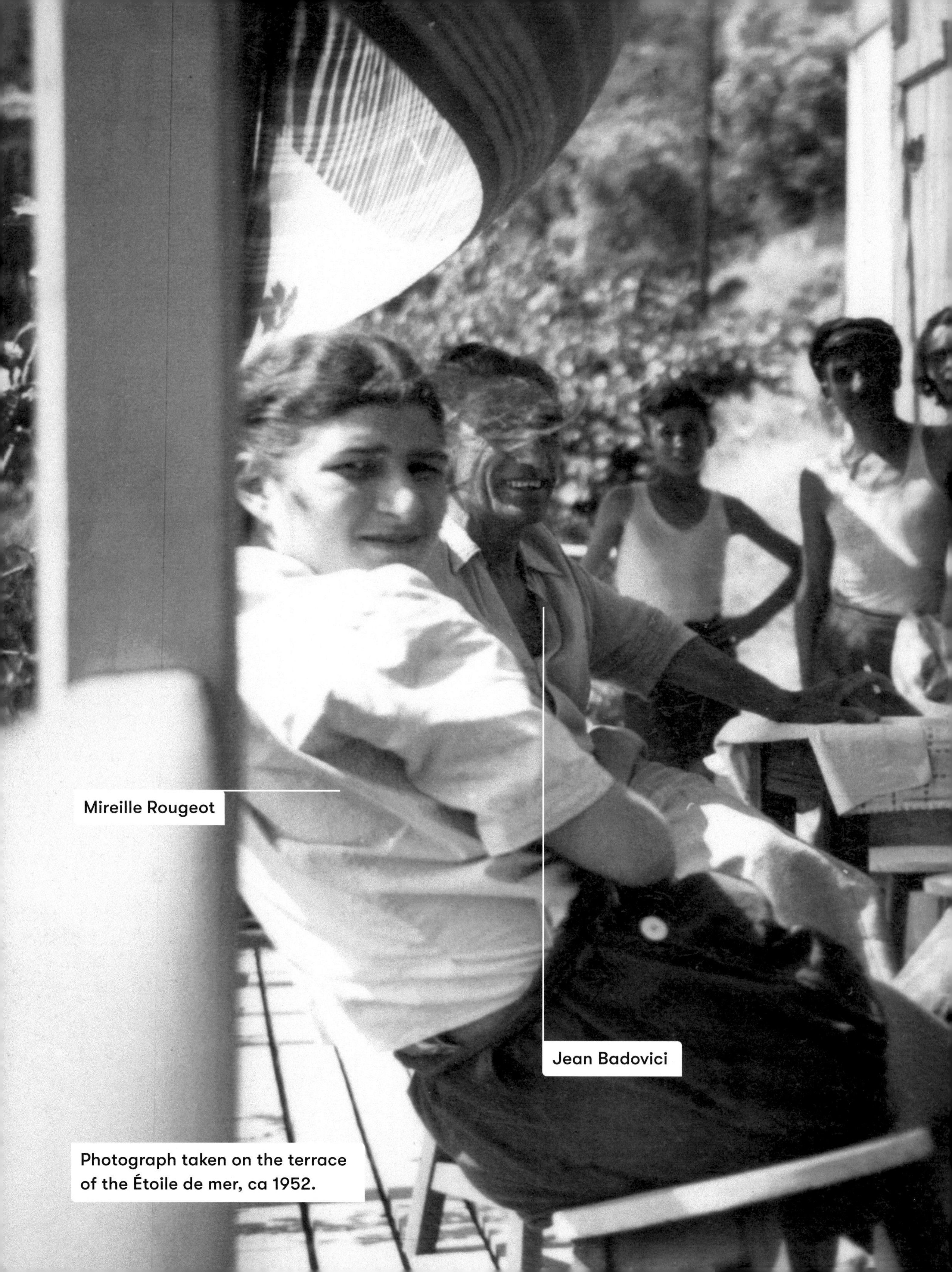

Photograph taken on the terrace of the Étoile de mer, ca 1952.

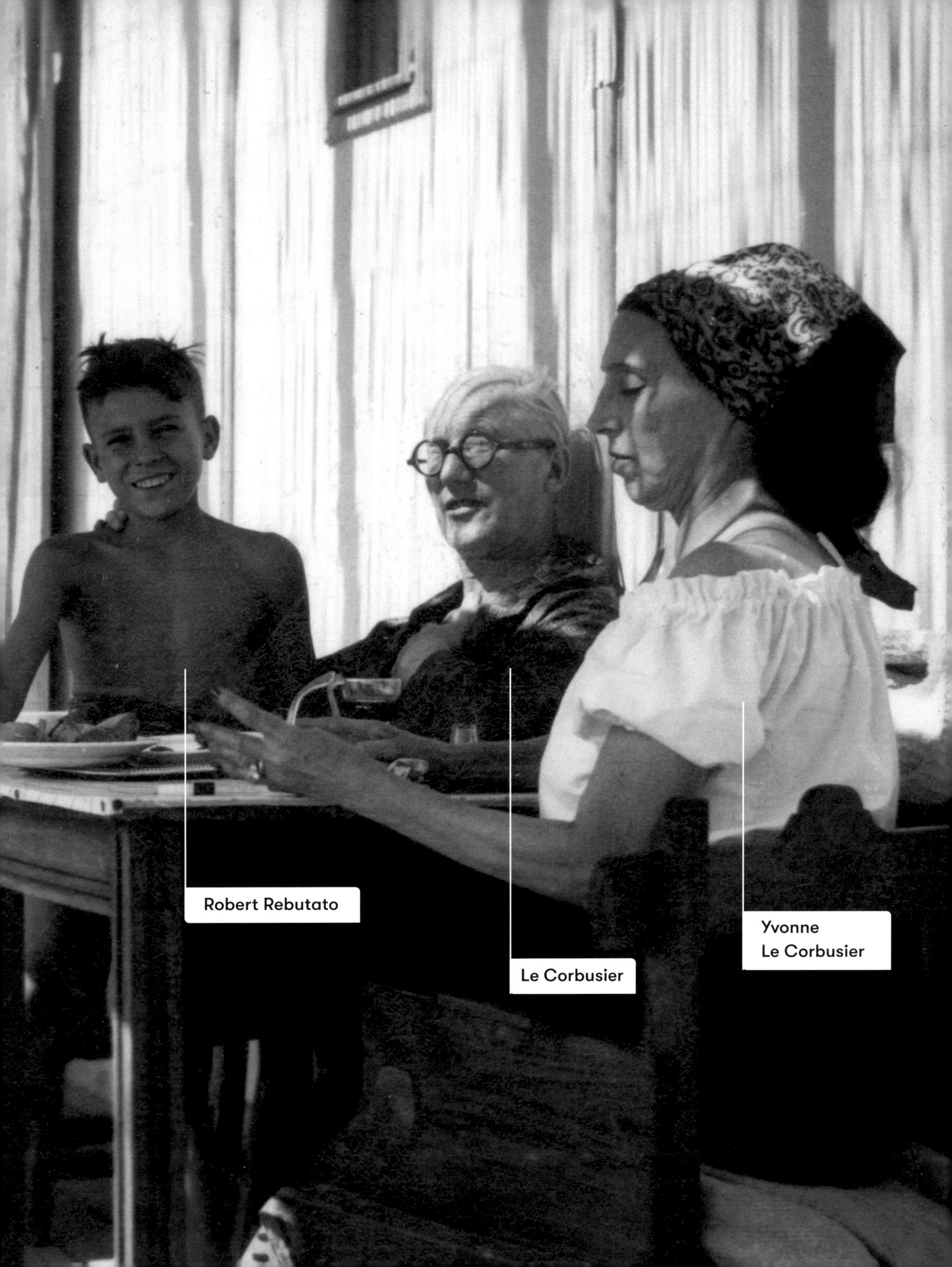
Robert Rebutato
Le Corbusier
Yvonne
Le Corbusier

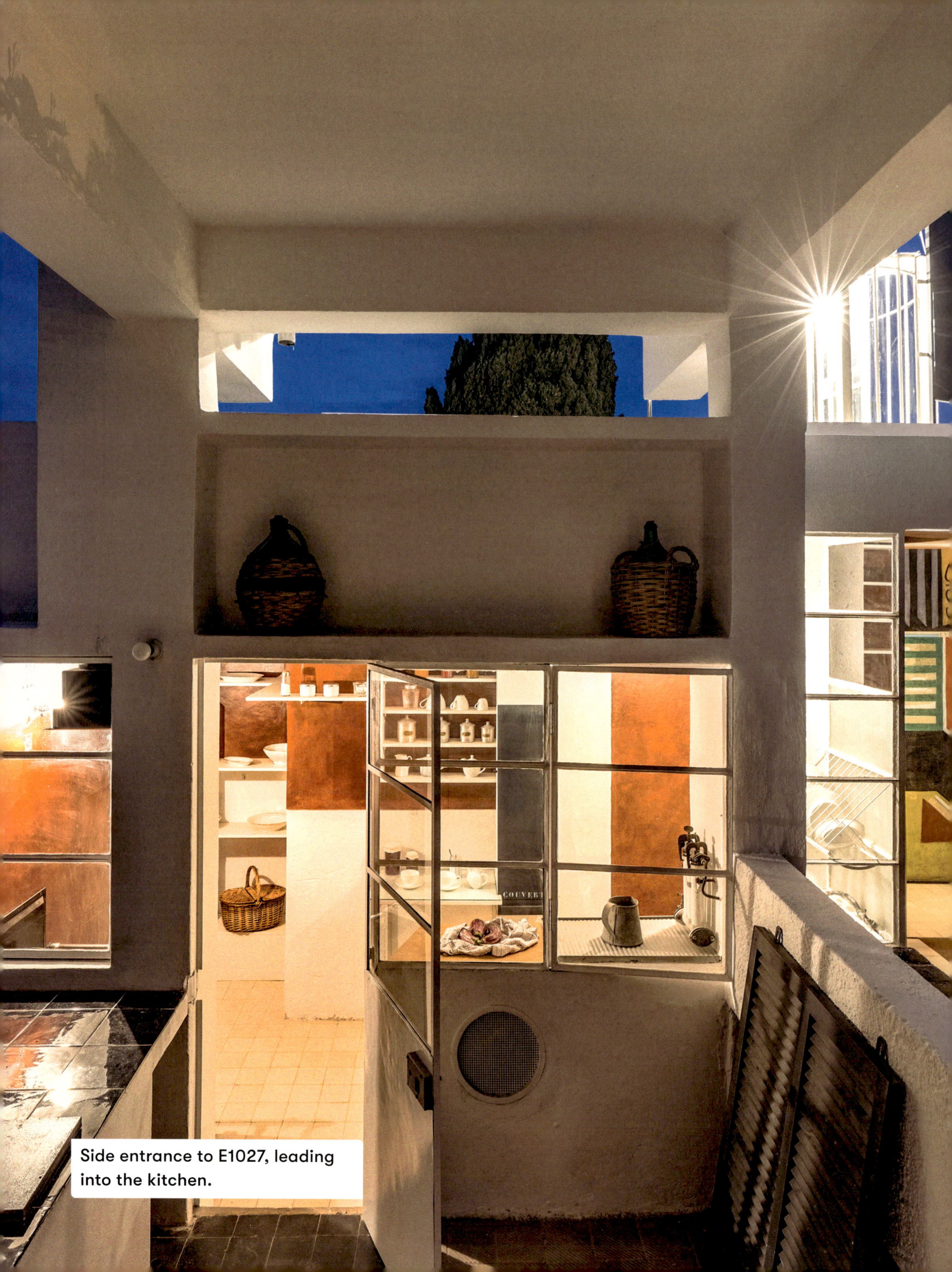

Side entrance to E1027, leading into the kitchen.

AUTHORS

TIM BENTON is Professor Emeritus of Art History at the Open University, London, and an internationally renowned scholar in the history of modern architecture. He has participated in several exhibitions including *Modernism: Designing a New World 1914–1939* (Victoria & Albert Museum, 2006). An expert on Le Corbusier, he is the author of numerous articles and books on the architect and his work. His seminal book *The Villas of Le Corbusier, 1920–1930* was first published in 1987 by Yale University Press and has since been republished several times (by Birkhäuser in 2007) and translated into several languages. His work *The Rhetoric of Modernism – Le Corbusier as Lecturer* (Birkhäuser, 2009) studied Le Corbusier's lasting academic influence. With Éditions du patrimoine, he published *Cap Moderne. Eileen Gray and Le Corbusier. Modernism by the Sea* (2022) and he contributed to the anthology *E1027. Restoring a House by the Sea* (2022). His publication *LC Foto: Le Corbusier: Secret Photographer* (Lars Müller, 2013) provided new evidence about Le Corbusier's photographic œuvre. Tim Benton advised the Cap Moderne Association on the restoration and management of the Eileen Gray, Étoile de mer and Le Corbusier site in Roquebrune-Cap-Martin.

MANUEL BOUGOT is a photographer based in Paris. Trained in New York and then at the École Nationale Superieure Louis-Lumière, he has had a long-standing career in architectural and artistic photography. Besides fine arts and interiors, his interest lies in observing nature but also exploring urban space. Manuel Bougot focuses his attention on the way that humans interact with their environment. Manuel Bougot's photographs – which have been exhibited in Arles, New Delhi, Chicago, Cardiff, Brussels and New York – document the complex and subtle relationships that inhabitants form with their living space. With Éditions du patrimoine, he published *Voyage à Chandigarh* (2019) and took all of the photographs for *Cap Moderne. Eileen Gray and Le Corbusier. Modernism by the Sea* and the volume *E1027. Restoring a House by the Sea* (2022), edited by Jean-Louis Cohen. Other publications he has contributed to include *Le Corbusier. Cinq unités d'habitation* (2022), *Jean Prouvé. Cinq maisons sur mesure* (2020), *Art Nouveau. Cinq villas et hôtels particuliers* (2022), published by Éditions Le Moniteur.

ANTOINE PICON is a prize-winning author of books and articles on modern architecture, urbanism, and design. Professor at the Harvard Graduate School of Design since 2002 he is also President of the Fondation Le Corbusier and has worked to develop an understanding of Le Corbusier's work across the globe. His numerous publications include the groundbreaking work *Digital Culture in Architecture. An Introduction for the Design Professions* (Birkhäuser, 2010), as well as his recent book *The Materiality of Architecture* (University of Minnesota, 2020).

MAGDA REBUTATO is a corporate lawyer and married Robert Rebutato in 1961, at the Étoile de mer restaurant. Le Corbusier was present and made the speech of honour. With Robert, she set up the Association Eileen Gray. Étoile de mer. Le Corbusier in 2000 with the aim of preserving the site and encouraging a better understanding of the architecture and design. Following Robert's death in 2016, she has continued to preside over the association, as well as serving as the vice-president of the Cap Moderne Association.

LE CORBUSIER, EILEEN GRAY, JEAN BADOVICI

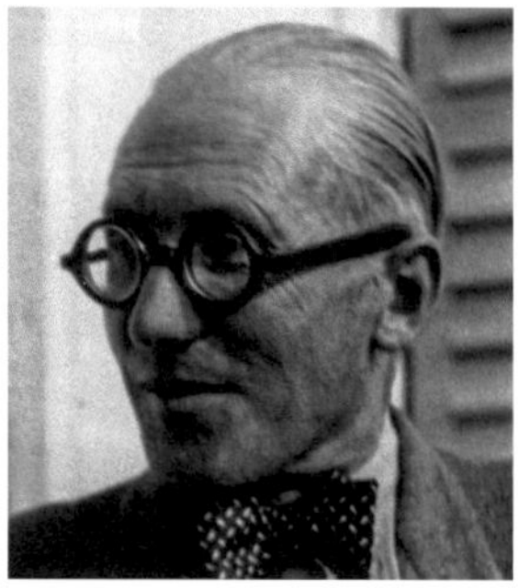

LE CORBUSIER (1887–1965)

Le Corbusier was born Charles-Édouard Jeanneret in the watchmaking town of La Chaux-de-Fonds in the Swiss Jura. He trained as an artist decorator in the local art school and in 1907 began ten years of travel to Italy, Paris, Germany, the Balkans, Istanbul and Athens. In 1917 he moved definitively to Paris and, with his friend Amédée Ozenfant, launched an art movement – Purism – and edited a magazine, *L'Esprit Nouveau* (1920–1925). He also adopted the *nom de plume* Le Corbusier. His articles in this journal were subsequently published in five books (1923–1925), among them *Vers une Architecture* (1927 published in English as *Towards a New Architecture*), arguably his most influential book, and established his reputation as a leading exponent of modern architecture. He had designed four houses and a cinema in La Chaux-de-Fonds in various styles, but in Paris he developed a Modernist idiom, in association with his cousin Pierre Jeanneret, characterised by the use of reinforced concrete to separate structure from enclosure, lifting his houses off the ground on thin concrete struts *(pilotis)* and employing windows that went from wall to wall. In 1929 he abandoned this style and began to use natural materials – stone, brick and wood – and more organic forms. After the Second World War, this emphasis on the organic developed further, with the rough concrete forms usually described as Brutalist. While Le Corbusier's œuvre as a painter is not as well-known as his architecture, it was nevertheless a pursuit of great concern and ambition for him. After exhibiting his Purist paintings with Ozenfant in the early 1920s, Le Corbusier did not exhibit again until 1938, but he continued to paint every day and considered this activity essential. Jean Badovici began publishing Le Corbusier's work in his journal *L'Architecture Vivante*. The two men became close friends in 1928 and spent several vacations together.

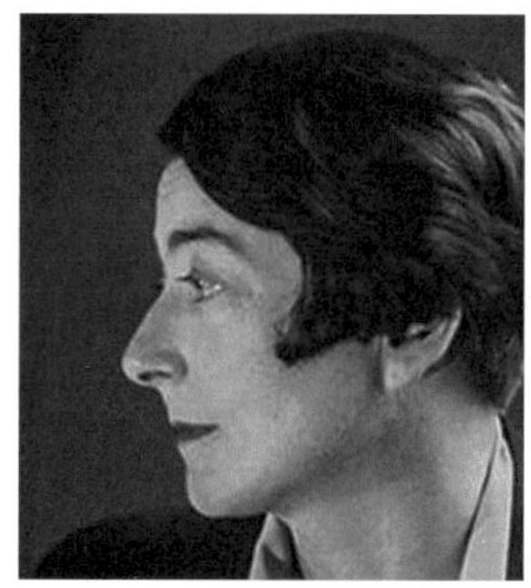

EILEEN GRAY (1878–1976)

Kathleen Eileen Moray Smith was born in Enniscorthy, Ireland; she later changed her name to Eileen Gray in 1895 when her mouther claimed the right to adopt the name of a Scottish noble ancestor. She studied at the Slade School of Art in London and at the ateliers Colarossi and Julian in Paris (1902–1905) before settling permanently in Paris in 1907 when she purchased the apartment where she lived until her death. She had already begun studying the techniques of Japanese lacquer in London and quickly established a reputation in Paris with increasingly ambitious work in lacquer. In 1910, she opened a rug-making workshop with her friend Evelyn Wyld and a lacquer workshop with a Japanese lacquer artist Sougawara. After purchasing one of her lacquer screens, the couturier Jacques Doucet began collecting her furniture in 1914. Three years later, she designed the apartment for Juliette Lévy, with extensive use of lacquer. In 1922, she opened a gallery, which she called Jean Désert, where she sold her rugs and furniture until 1930. At this time, she lived a glamorous life in the circle of Parisian Sapphic Modernism. Probably in 1924, she met the Romanian architect Jean Badovici who opened her eyes to modern architecture. This began a close friendship that lasted during his lifetime, despite his affairs with other women. Together they visited many of the key buildings in Europe. She designed a modern house for him (unbuilt) and, together they designed and built the house by the sea – E1027 – at Roquebrune-Cap-Martin (1927–1929) to which Badovici held the deed. For the house, she also designed the table E1027, today an icon of modern furniture design. It is not clear how long Gray may have lived in E1027, if at all, since Badovici met his new mistress, Madeleine Goisot, in 1930. At the same time, she bought land in Castellar near Menton on which she refurbished a house for herself, called 'Tempe a Pailla' (1927–1934). She also redesigned the bedroom in her apartment and an apartment for Badovici in Paris. After the completion of this work, Gray continued to develop architectural projects but nothing was completed until she adapted a little stone house near St Tropez, which she called Lou Perou (1954–1965). The renewal of interest in Art Deco design led to the re-discovery of Gray in the 1970s and her pieces began to circulate at very high prices in the auction houses. She was appointed Royal Designer for Industry in 1972 and elected honorary member of the Royal Institute of Architects of Ireland in the following year. An exhibition of her work was held by the RIBA in London in 1973.

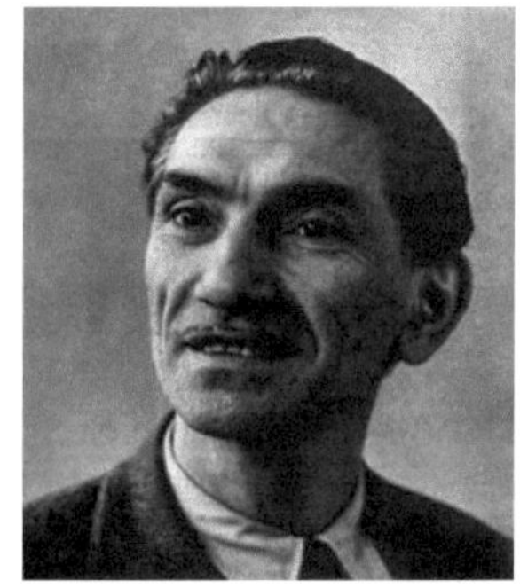

JEAN BADOVICI (1893–1956)

Jean Badovici was born in Bucharest, Romania, and moved to Paris for good in 1915. He studied architecture at the École des Beaux Arts and at the École Spéciale d'architecture, where he emerged top of his class in 1919. He began to edit books on Art Deco subjects for the publisher Albert Morancé who set him up with a journal of his own, called *L'Architecture Vivante*, in 1923. Badovici was a resourceful editor, writing numerous articles and illustrating the avant-garde work of the Russian Constructivists, the de Stijl architects in Holland and the functionalists in Germany. In 1929, he brought out a special edition of his journal on the villa E1027. He also began to be increasingly obsessed with Le Corbusier's work and was able eventually to publish seven volumes dedicated to the work of Le Corbusier and Pierre Jeanneret. Beginning in 1927, he reconstructed a stone house in Vézelay in Burgundy for his neigh-bour and friend, the artist Georges Renaudin. He bought several houses in Vézelay and converted one of them for his own use (1928–1929). Le Corbusier praised this house in his book *La Ville Radieuse* (1935). He also joined up three houses which he intended for visiting friends and artists. After the demise of *L'Architecture Vivante*, Badovici spent much of his time in Vézelay and Roquebrune-Cap-Martin. After the war he worked on the reconstruction of Maubeuge and Bavay, under the direction of André Lurçat, but his health was deteriorating and he died in 1956 in the hospital at Monaco, with Eileen Gray at his bedside.

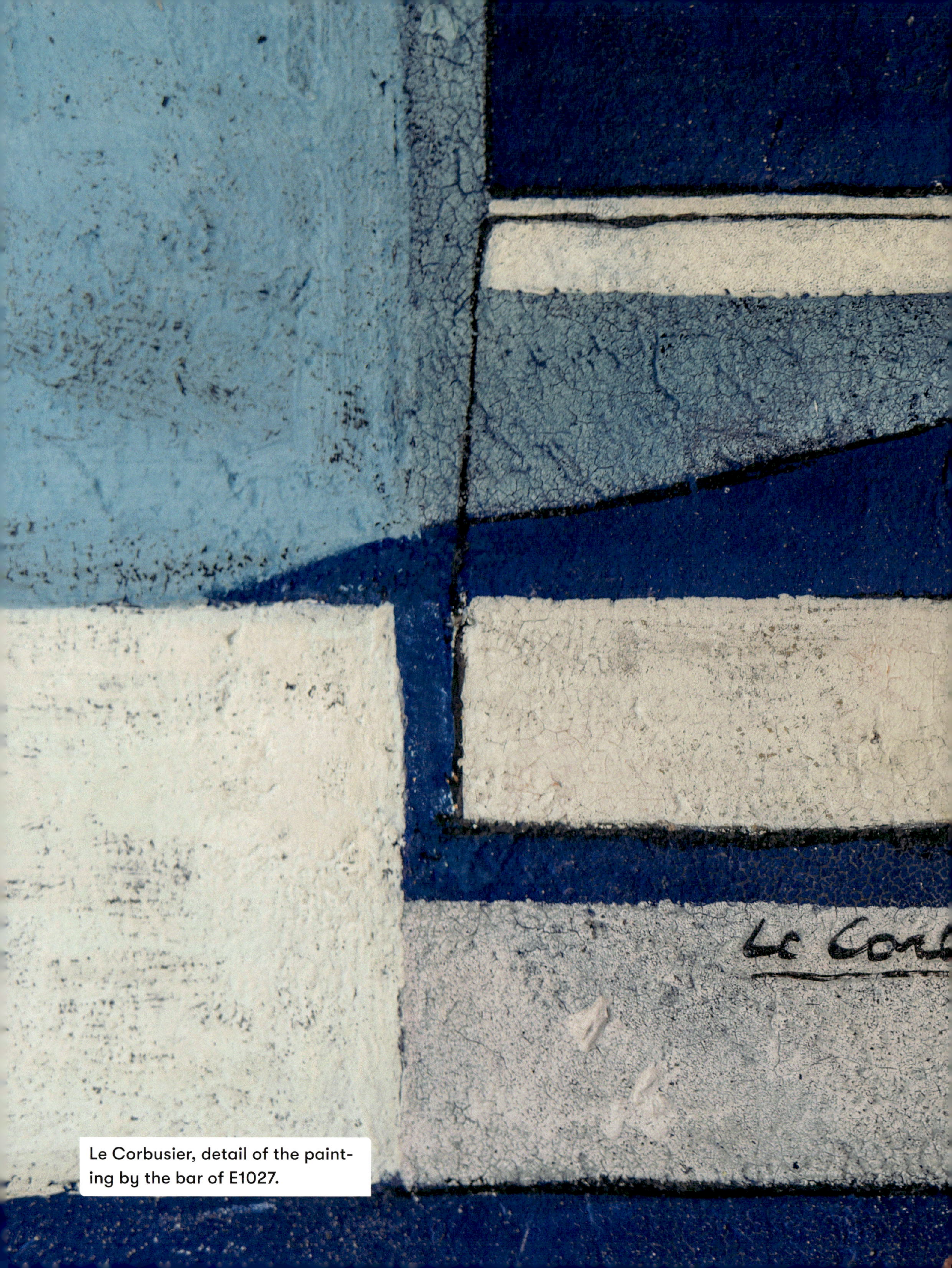

Le Corbusier, detail of the painting by the bar of E1027.

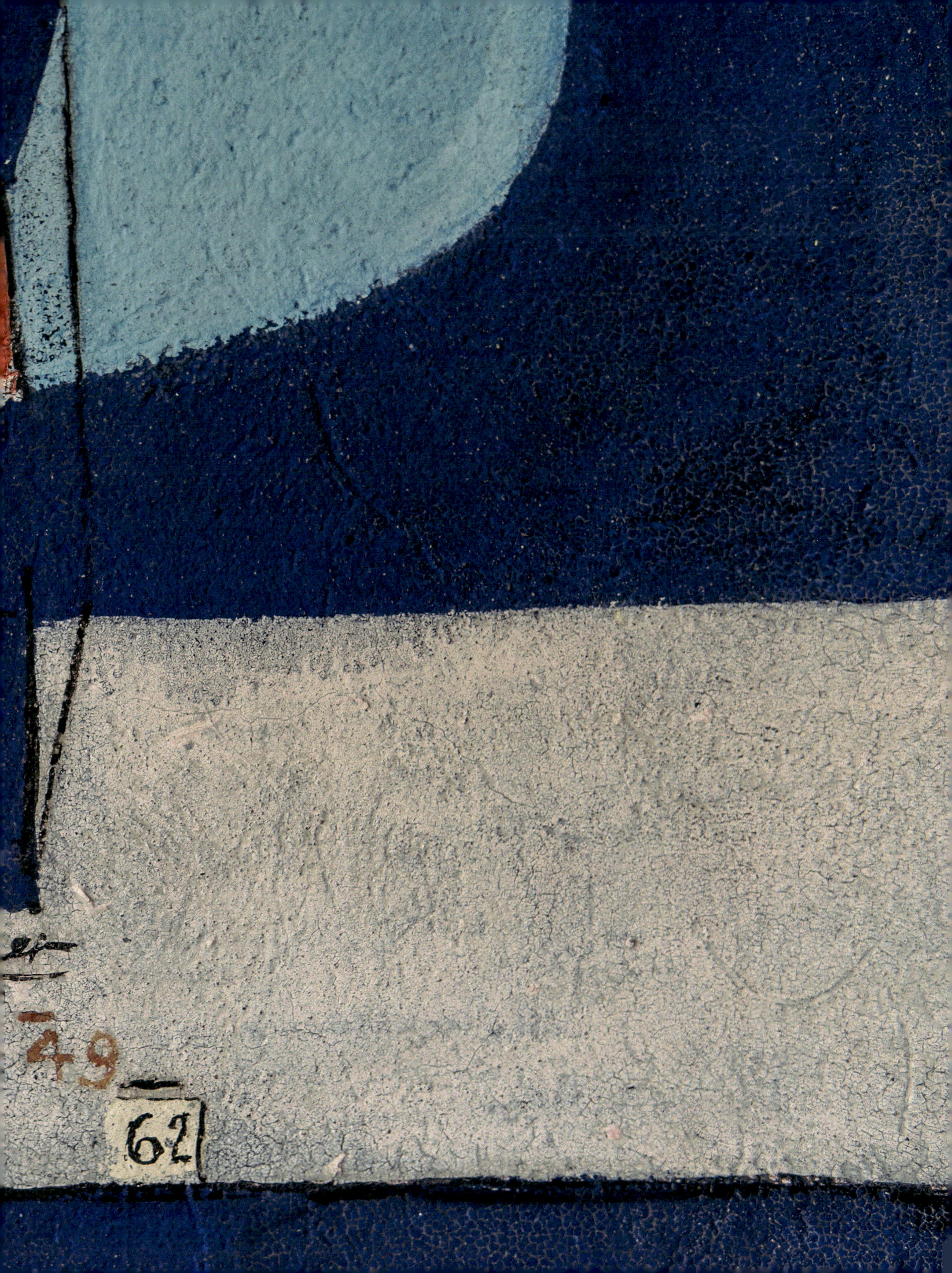
49
62

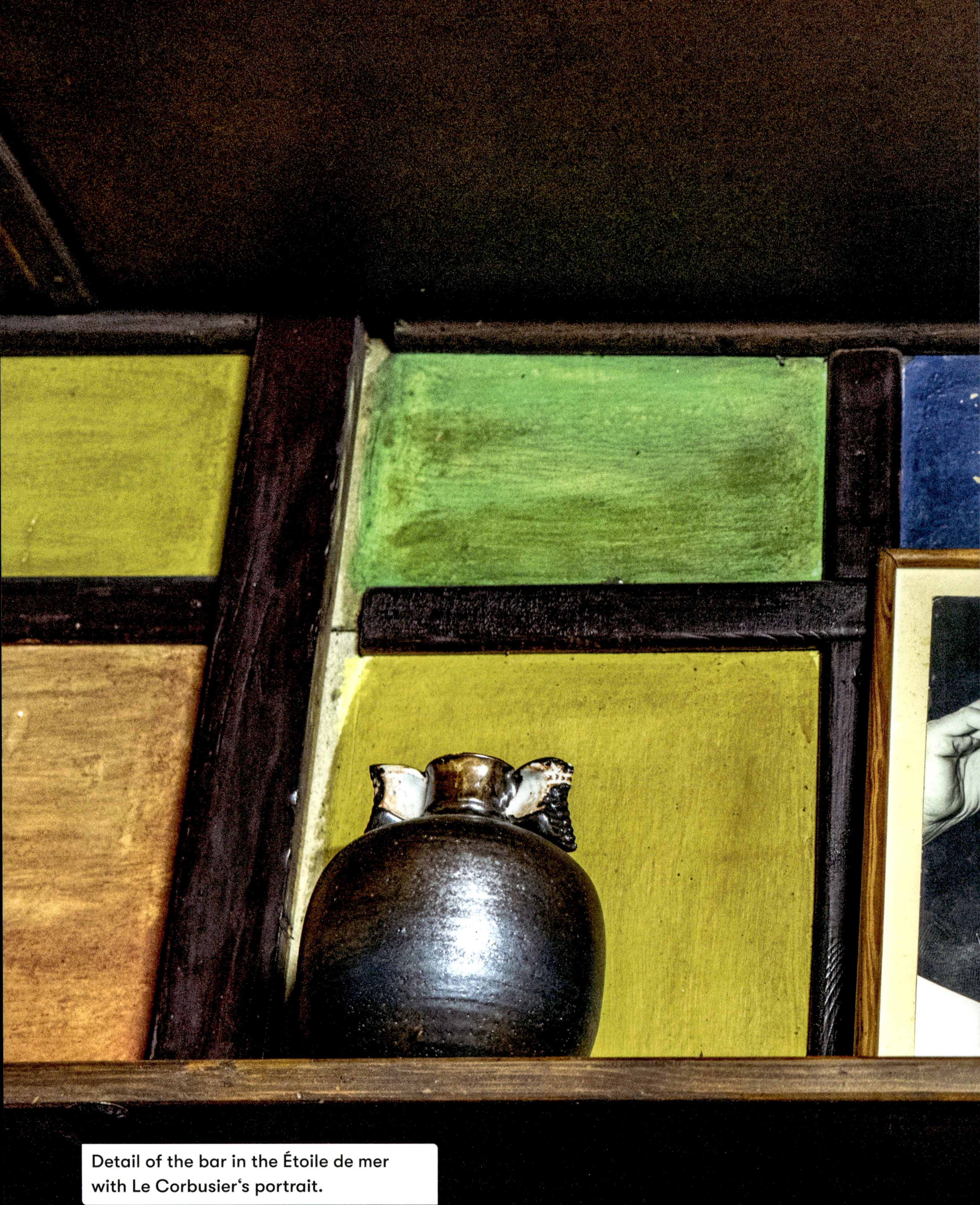

Detail of the bar in the Étoile de mer with Le Corbusier‘s portrait.

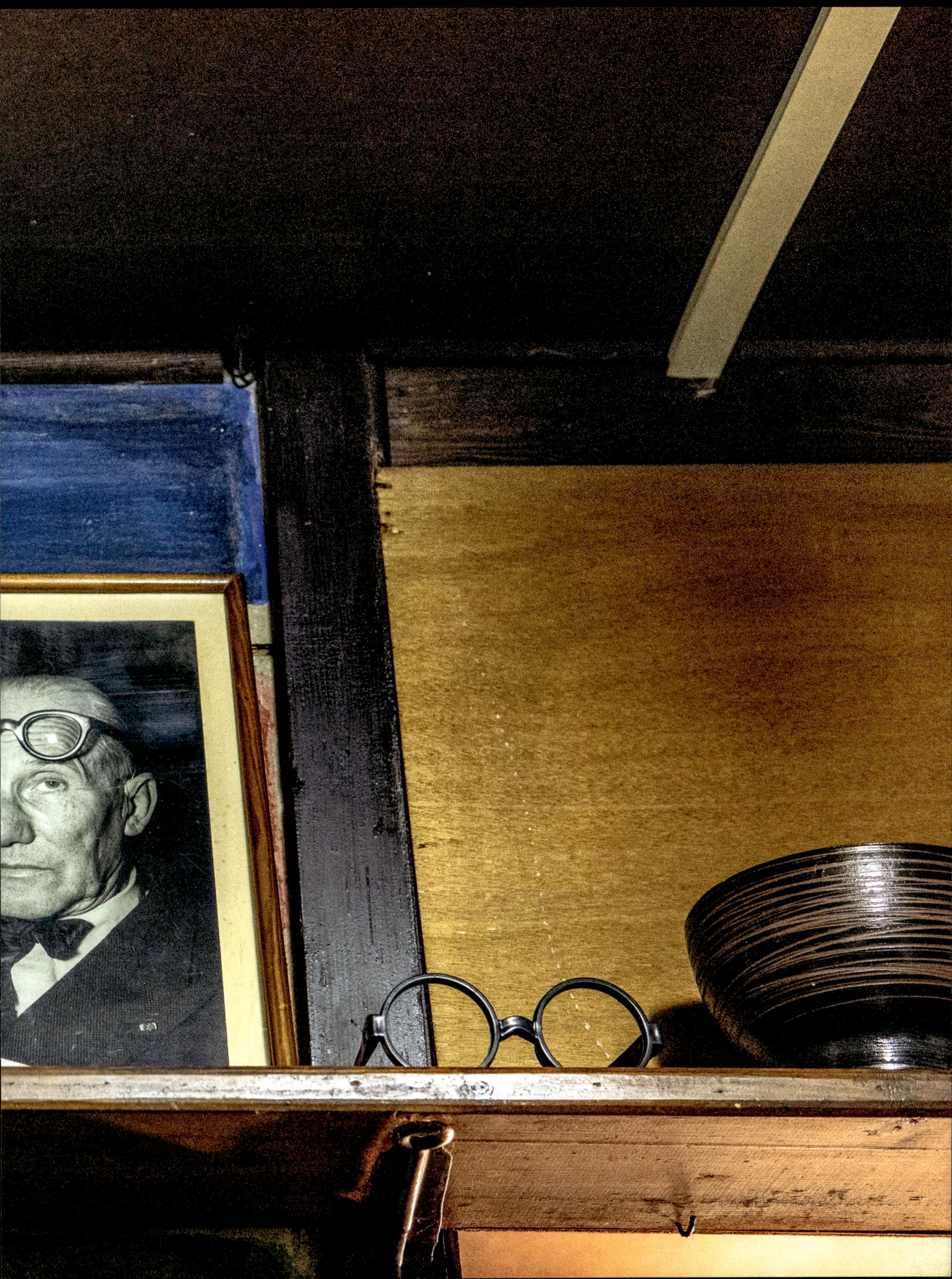

INDEX

ILLUSTRATION CREDITS

Cover photographs: Manuel Bougot

pp. 6–7, 8, 10–11 Manuel Bougot
pp. 12–13, 14–15, 16–17, 18–19, 20, 23 Tim Benton
p. 24 FLC 15243
p. 27 *Étreinte II* (FLC 375)
p. 28 left *Femme grise, homme rouge et os devant une porte* (FLC 8)
p. 28 right *Le déjeuner près du phare* (FLC 77)
p. 30 left FLC, Séquence 1 06885
p. 30 right FLC, Séquence 1 2044
p. 33 Tim Benton
p. 34 top From: Louis Chéronnet, 'La Publicité moderne la gloire du panneau', *L'Art vivant*, no 40, 15 August 1926
p. 34 bottom ©Mouron Cassandre/ www.cassandre.fr
p. 36 Fernand Léger/VG Bildkunst
p. 37 FLC
p. 39 © Centraal Museum, Utrecht/ Ernst Moritz/Pictoright
p. 41 Vilmos Huszár/VG Bildkunst. From: *L'Architecture Vivante*, Autumn–Winter 1924
p. 42 From: *L'Architecture Vivante,* Autumn–Winter 1929
p. 43 FLC 08309
p. 44 Manuel Bougot
p. 45 top Tim Benton
p. 45 bottom From: *L'Architecture Vivante,* Autumn–Winter 1929
p. 46 top Tim Benton
p. 46 bottom FLC/Marius Gravot/VG Bildkunst
p. 49 top FLC 12
p. 49 bottom MNAM-CCI (Musée National d'Art Moderne, Centre Georges Pompidou; donation by Sonia Delaunay and Charles Delaunay)
p. 50 left and top right From: Jean Badovici, 'Peinture murale ou peinture spatiale', *L'Architecture d'Aujourd'hui*, March 1937
p. 50 bottom right FLC, Séquences 02823–02825
p. 52 top Musée Christian Zervos, Vézelay (photo Tim Benton)
p. 52 bottom Private collector
p. 55 left FLC
p. 55 right, p. 57 From: Jean Badovici, 'Peinture murale ou peinture spatiale', *L'Architecture d'aujourd'hui*, March 1937.
p. 58 FLC 4579
p. 60 FLC
p. 61 Musée Christian Zervos, Vézelay
p. 62, 64 left Tim Benton
p. 64 left NMIEG (National Museum of Ireland, Eileen Gray archive)
p. 65 Marc Brugier
p. 66 top *Figure à la porte jaune* (FLC 365)
p. 66 bottom left Sketch for *Arbre, nu et cordage* (FLC 3425)
p. 66 bottom right Sketch for *Figure devant une porte blanche* (FLC 3422)
p. 68 left Private collector
p. 68 right FLC, Séquence 31819
p. 69 top *La Parisienne* (FLC 2998)
p. 69 bottom left FLC – Sketchbook B8, no 488
p. 69 bottom right FLC – Sketchbook B8, no 515
p. 70 left Sketch for *Trois personnages* (FLC 1196)
p. 70 right FLC 3067
p. 71 FLC 3399
p. 72 FLC, Séquences 1 06924, 1 06926, 1 06621, 1 06754
p. 73 top, bottom left, bottom right FLC
p. 74 top left FLC 3466
p. 74 top right FLC
p. 74 bottom left *Totem* (FLC 236)
p. 74 bottom right *Nature morte Vézelay* (FLC 154)
p. 75 top left Tim Benton
p. 75 top right *Femme rouge et pelote verte* (FLC 103)
p. 75 bottom left FLC 4476
p. 75 bottom right *Nature morte au livre et au coquetier* (FLC 339)
p. 76 FLC/Lucien Hervé
p. 80 top left, bottom right FLC
p. 80 top right FLC, Séquence 13163
p. 80 bottom left *Composition avec figure et os* (FLC 4590)
p. 81, 82 Tim Benton
p. 83 FLC – Sketchbook B6, no 400
p. 84 *Spirales géometriques animées* (FLC 104)
p. 85 top FLC
p. 85 bottom FLC 4461
p. 87 top FLC E1(5)84-001
p. 87 bottom FLC
p. 89, 91, 94, 98, 100–101 Tim Benton
p. 97, 112 FLC
pp. 102–103, 104–105, 106–107, 108, 110, 111, 113 Manuel Bougot
p. 114 top *Le grand verre à côtes et l'écharpe rouge* (FLC 226)
p. 114 bottom *Taureau I* (FLC 158)
p. 115 top Tim Benton
p. 115 bottom Manuel Bougot
p. 116 From: Le Corbusier, 1948. *New World of Space,* New York, Reynal & Hitchcock, pp. 90–91, p. 99, pp. 100–101
p. 118 Tim Benton
p. 120 top, 120 bottom left and right, 121 top left and right, 121 bottom left, 122, 126 Manuel Bougot
p. 121 bottom right FLC/Lucien Hervé
pp. 124–125 FLC
pp. 128–129 Eileen Gray, ca 1910 (NMIEG, Berenice Abbott); Jean Badovici (NMIEG); Le Corbusier FLC L4(14)7 (detail)
pp. 130–131, 132–133 Tim Benton

ACKNOWLEDGEMENTS

The author would like to thank Robert and Magda Rebutato for their stimulus and support in the preparation of this book. Stéphanie Gregoire and Caroline Maniaque played key roles in the refinement of the original French text, as did Ria Stein for this English edition. Without the photographs of Manuel Bougot this book would have lost much of its impact. The Centre des monuments nationaux were helpful in providing permission to take photographs on the site. Jennifer Goff and the National Museum of Ireland were generous in their support. Michel Richard and Brigitte Bouvier, successive directors of the Fondation Le Corbusier, made the publication possible. Arnaud Dercelles and Isabelle Godinot, also from the Fondation Le Corbusier, provided quick and professional responses to requests for documents.

GRAPHIC DESIGN, LAYOUT AND TYPESETTING

e o t . Büro für Buchgestaltung/ Ausstellungsdesign

COPY EDITING AND PROJECT MANAGEMENT

Ria Stein

PRODUCTION

Anja Haering

PAPER

Magno Volume 135 g/m²

PRINTING

Grafisches Centrum Cuno GmbH & Co. KG, Calbe

This book is based on the French original edition *Le Corbusier Peintre à Cap-Martin* which was first published in 2015, with a second edition in 2021.

For the original edition:

The French original edition of this book was enabled by Cap Moderne Association, Fondation Le Corbusier, Centre des monuments nationaux, Conservatoire du littoral and Association culturelle Eileen Gray. Etoile de Mer. Le Corbusier.

Library of Congress Control Number: 2022951093

Bibliographic information published by the German National Library. The German National Library lists this publication in the Deutsche Nationalbibliografie; detailed bibliographic data is available on the Internet at http://dnb.dnb.de.

ISBN 978-3-0356-2653-7
e-ISBN (PDF) 978-3-0356-2657-5

This book is also available in a German language edition with the title *Le Corbusier – Der Maler. Eileen Grays Villa E1027 und Le Cabanon*, print-ISBN 978-3-0356-2654-4.

For the English and German edition:

P.O. Box 44, 4009 Basel, Switzerland

FONDATION LE CORBUSIER

ÉDITIONS DU PATRIMOINE
CENTRE DES MONUMENTS NATIONAUX

Conservatoire du littoral

Association culturelle Eileen Gray Etoile de Mer Le Corbusier